Effective Interviewing
Techniques and Analysis

Dorothy Molyneaux, Ph.D.
San Francisco State University

Vera W. Lane, Ph.D.
San Francisco State University

Allyn and Bacon, Inc.
Boston   London   Sydney   Toronto

To our parents, our husbands, our children—
three generations of satisfying experiences
in interpersonal communication

Library of Congress Cataloging in Publication Data

Molyneaux, Dorothy.
    Effective interviewing.

    Includes bibliographical references and index.
    1. Interpersonal relations.   2. Interviewing.
I. Lane, Vera W.   II. Title
HM132.M63   158′.3   81–10937
ISBN 0–205–07564–9   AACR2

Printed in the United States of America.

10 9 8 7 6 5 4 3 2   86 85 84 83 82

Contents

List of Tables

Preface

This book is intended as a practical resource and reference for both students in training and for experienced professionals working in fields where interviewing is an important activity. Interviews, which may be defined as "face-to-face conversations with a purpose," are commonplace occurrences in today's world. If your professional or business life is like that of most people, hardly a day goes by that you don't find yourself talking to someone in a fairly serious manner about something of consequence. Often, these purposeful, face-to-face conversations—or interviews—will have significant positive outcomes: a new staff member may be hired; an overworked colleague's resignation may be averted; a bright but bored highschooler may change to a more suitable and challenging course of study; a distraught mother may find a way of communicating her needs to members of her troubled family; the parents of a handicapped infant may progress beyond their initial dismay and confusion and make some decisions regarding a remedial program; an interpersonal problem that has been draining several people's energies may be satisfactorily resolved.

Sometimes an interview will have an unsatisfactory outcome or unpleasant repercussions. One or both of the participants may feel frustrated, depressed, confused, slightly "miffed," or downright angry when the interview ends. A problem may be intensified rather than alleviated. At such a time, conscientious interviewers are bound to ask themselves: "What happened? Was it my fault that things went wrong? What could I have done differently?"

Just what makes a person an effective interviewer is not always easy to identify, just as it is not always easy to determine why an interview is unsatisfactory to one or both participants. There are, however, certain basic interviewing techniques that have proved useful and generally productive over the course of time. There are also other interview occurrences that have proved to be generally counter-productive—practices that tend to hamper communication and thwart meaningful progress toward an effective goal.

This book is designed to help you become more aware of what goes on in an interview, with the principal aim of ultimately increasing your interviewing effectiveness. The book's organization is as follows. Chapter 1 discusses basic purposes of interviewing and distinguishing characteristics of interviews designed to achieve these purposes. Chapters 2, 3, and 4 delineate important aspects of human communication and motivation—the consideration of which may well influence your interviewing philosophy.

Chapters 5 through 8 are specifically concerned with preparing for and conducting an interview. Attention is focused in turn on the opening minutes, the main body, and closing period. Various techniques and interactions, as well as common problems that might occur, are described. Brief excerpts of transcribed interviews are included for purposes of illustration and clarification. Chapters 6, 7, and 8 contain what we have termed "aids to analysis," series of questions that can be used as a reminder to the interviewer of some of the suggestions included in the chapters.

A variety of techniques can be used to look at interviews and determine their effectiveness. Chapter 9 touches upon some methods of interview and interaction analysis. It is in this chapter that the Molyneaux/Lane Interview Analysis is introduced and described. Our analysis method is based upon a numerical system used to code and describe verbal utterances occurring in an interview. We have found the analysis method a workable and useful system adaptable to a wide variety of interpersonal verbal interactions. Chapters 10 and 11 are designed to teach you how to use the method.

Chapter 12 is intended to assist you in the personal application of ideas presented in the preceding chapters. You are encouraged to review your interviewing philosophy and analyze your interviewing style. Suggestions are provided for self-improvement techniques if you feel that change is desirable.

Our longstanding interest in interviewing and interpersonal relations has led us to draw upon many sources for ideas and information which we have shared with students and colleagues over a number of years. This book is our distillation of what we consider to be the most pertinent of this knowledge. We hope that it will prove beneficial to you in your interactions with others.

We express our appreciation to the authors and publishers who gave permission to include copyrighted work in this book. We express our appreciation to the parents and students who participated in the research described in Chapter 9. We gratefully acknowledge the technical assistance provided by Michael Kilkenny and G. A. Collado during their service as statistical consultants to the San Francisco State University Computer Center.

1

Basic Purposes of Interviewing

In any human interaction, the spoken word can serve a variety of functions. On the positive side, it permits two people to know something about each other, to establish a contact that permits at least a bit of sharing what goes on in each other's head. It serves to span interhuman space. Speech can serve as the medium by which needed information is exchanged about a particular topic, or about our feelings and desires. Speech can help us to control one another's behavior and to satisfy our basic needs. It can aid each of us in expressing and confirming our individuality and personality. It can be used to promote good will, relaxation, comradeship, and even intimacy.

On the negative side, however, speech can also serve to promote antagonism and ill-will. It can foster hostility, drive people apart, and increase anxiety and frustration. It can be used by one human being to deride, degrade, or deceive another, and thus to cause considerable heartache and unhappiness. In our daily functioning in human society, and in our attempts to satisfy our needs as human beings, speech can be both a powerful tool and a devastating weapon.

When we talk with others, our speech and theirs will be serving one or the other of the functions mentioned above. The functions being served give special characteristics and flavor to our everyday conversations, and to interviews as well. Interviews, however, are more than ordinary conversations; they have special aspects. In this chapter, we will discuss those aspects.

We have defined interviews as "conversations with a purpose," certainly a definition broad enough to encompass a wide variety of verbal interactions. We can now narrow our definition slightly. Elizabeth and Karl De Schweinitz (1962, p. 9) define an interview as verbal interaction that is both purposeful and *directed,* in which "one person takes responsibility for the development of the conversation." If we consider this added criterion— responsibility for direction—we can consider interviews on a continuum ranging from those in which we are barely able to designate one participant as the director of the conversation to interviews where we have absolutely no difficulty designating who is in charge.

Let us consider two examples. In one instance, a professional employed by a service agency may invite a colleague to come to his office. The purpose is to discuss the possibility of preparing an application to a philanthropic organization for funds to conduct an important research program. The person who initiated the meeting could thus be designated the "interviewer" and the other the "respondent" for purposes of interview analysis. Yet you would expect that at any point in the discussion, one person or the other might be taking the lead in the conversation—perhaps asking a series of pertinent questions for the other person to answer; perhaps sounding off about the utter impossibility of finding any free time to work on another project; perhaps suggesting a plan by which colleagues could be enticed into writing the application; or perhaps changing the subject to an upcoming social event with the hopes that the other person might forget about the original purpose of the meeting.

Contrast the above situation to what might occur several months later —providing, of course, that the application for funds was prepared and sent to the philanthropic organization. The chairman of the organization's Funds Allocation Committee has written a letter to our pair of professionals stating that she has set aside fifteen minutes on November 4, from 8:00 to 8:15 A.M., to interview one of the team members. It seems that the Committe has eliminated all but three applications for next year's research funds, and a fifteen minute interview with a representative from each of the three competing agencies will assist the chairman in casting the deciding vote. There should be no doubt in your mind who will be in charge of that interview.

In your business or professional contacts, you will often participate in purposeful conversations where the designation of one person as the inter- viewer and another as respondent is relatively arbitrary. At other times, though, you as the expert, or professional, or administrator will find yourself with the definite role of being the person designated or presumed to be in charge of a meeting with someone. This could be the case even though the other person may have originally requested the appointment with you. The De Schweinitzes (1962, p. 10) point this out in discussing interviews con- ducted under professional or institutional auspices:

> Here the interviewer operates within a special and defined setting and speaks from a background of organised experience and recognised com- petence. Interviewing in the social services is of this kind. So also is the interviewing of the lawyer, the newspaper reporter, the research investigator, the social worker, the personnel officer, the doctor. These interviews have

known and established purposes. The fact that the interviewer represents a profession or an institution or both, designed to provide a service or to obtain information, makes him primarily responsible for the direction of the conversation. His role has been predetermined. Before ever the interview starts he has been designated as the interviewer.

We should make one thing clear at this point. Counselors and psychotherapists employ interviewing as a major technique. Because people come to them for help with problems and depend on their professional training and skill, these counselors and therapists are responsible for directing the course of the helping sessions. This is true whether or not the counselors or therapists employ psychotherapeutic methods commonly called client-centered or even nondirective. Counselors are still in charge of the interviews, even though they may permit their clients to have considerable leeway in bringing up topics and/or feelings for examination and discussion. A nondirective counselor who does not maintain responsibility for the progress of a session is usually, if not always, a noneffective counselor as well.

You may consider yourself to be a professional or administrator who aims at all times to be democratic rather than authoritarian. You may feel strongly that the best type of interview is one in which an atmosphere of camaraderie and informal cooperation prevails. In fact, you may be downright uncomfortable in situations where you feel called upon to manipulate another's behavior or to tell others what to do. Yet, if you are to fulfill your role as an interviewer, you cannot disregard your responsibility for directing the interviewing session. Direction can assume many different forms, some that will suit your personality more than others. We will talk more about those forms in Chapter 6.

One more comment must be made regarding the responsibility for direction of the interview. Even though the person designated as the interviewer is in charge of the interview, we must never forget that what transpires in the interview itself—as well as the outcomes and relative effectiveness of the interview in relation to its purposes—is dependent upon both participants.

We have discussed the concept of direction in relation to interviewing. Let us return to the other characteristic specified in our definition: that of purpose. We have already mentioned basic functions that speech serves in everyday life. We will now consider some generally stated purposes that can influence and determine the direction of interviews.

Interviews are often described as fulfilling one or more of the following goals:

Information getting
Information giving
Expression and exploration of feelings
Problem solving
Planning for future action

Implicit in the successful accomplishment of most, if not all, of these interviewing purposes is that learning and/or observable behavioral change will take place in one or both participants as a result of the interview or series of interviews.

A professional interview is seldom limited strictly to a single one of the five purposes listed above. Often, an interview that is especially effective or satisfying to one or both participants turns out to have accomplished more than one of these goals. For purposes of discussion, however, we will consider each of the five general purposes in turn.

INFORMATION GETTING

Quite often, the goal of an interviewer is to acquire certain factual information from the respondent. Census-takers, workers on consumer surveys, and credit managers are some of the people who specialize in information-getting interviews. When we find ourselves cooperating with any of those people in the performance of their duties, we expect to have them ask us a variety of questions, and we expect to respond to those questions with a variety of information giving.

In a more specialized professional setting, the information-getting interview involves securing a case history from a client or patient. Such history-taking secures information on aspects of the respondent's background, life experiences, daily habits, and/or personality characteristics that will have a bearing on what our professional actions or recommendations will be.

There are several ways we can find out about a person. We can observe him or her in a variety of situations and circumstances, observing both verbal and nonverbal behavior. We can also examine a variety of documents relating to that person: existing documents (including diaries, medical records, and grade transcripts) and also elicited documents prepared or completed at our request (such as autobiographical essays, questionnaires, and rating scales). These documents may be prepared or completed by the individual or by others. In addition to observation and examination of documents, interviewing (of the person and of others who have had contact with him or her) is an important source of information.

Information-getting interviews are sometimes designated as either standardized or nonstandardized. In a standardized interview, certain predesignated items of information are sought. These are often items that the interviewer or his or her agency feel should be secured routinely from the respondents. A nonstandardized interview is more flexible; the interviewer is free to pursue topics without being bound to any particular line of investigation.

Standardized interviews can be further described as schedule or nonschedule. In the former, as well as the areas of questioning, the order of questioning and even the way in which the questions are asked are prescribed. In nonschedule standardized interviews, the areas of questioning are designated beforehand, but the order and wording of the questions are left up to the interviewer.

Polls and surveys are often conducted using standardized, schedule interviews, as are research projects where it is important to limit the number of variables. We should also remind ourselves that verbal intelligence tests and orally administered personality tests usually fall in the category of standardized, schedule interviews.

In order to evaluate whether or not the purpose of an information-getting interview was accomplished, we might well ask ourselves the following questions:

Did I secure the information I wanted?

Is the information pertinent?

Did the respondent appear to be cooperative and willing enough to try to provide me with honest, accurate information?

Is the information obtained from this one interview sufficient for my purposes, or should I validate or confirm it at other times and in other circumstances or with other means of information-getting at my disposal?

INFORMATION GIVING

On some occasions, your major purpose for an interview might be to give the person with whom you are meeting information that will prove helpful and worthwhile. Product demonstrators, librarians, and instructors in a variety of settings and fields of interest fall into this category of interviewer.

As a professional authority, you will often find yourself in interpersonal situations where the other person is expecting you to provide information. The requests for information may be framed in a variety of ways, for instance, as direct, straightforward questions or as hypothetical situations to which you are encouraged to respond. The person is basically asking for authoritative information from you. Perhaps an anxious mother is asking you what you have discovered after testing Susie for two hours on a variety of educational achievement tests. Perhaps an elderly hearing-impaired client wants you to tell him about the different types of hearing aids and what they can do to improve his ability to get along with his family and friends. Perhaps you have been asked to meet with a new member of your agency's staff to explain the agency's general philosophy as well as the paperwork and procedures required of all employees. In each of these instances, your effectiveness in the interview will certainly depend upon your ability to relate well to the respondent and to convey the required information in an appropriate and understandable manner. Your effectiveness, however, will depend most of all on your professional acumen and judgment and the depth of your understanding of your chosen field. In our experience, it is in this area of interviewing that inexperience or immaturity is most obvious. Beginning interviewers may do beautifully at asking questions and securing information in a pleasant, nonthreatening manner. They may also be able to present previously prepared instructional material with interest and clarity. Yet when it comes to responding intelligently to unexpected questions or to unusual requests for professional information, they may feel hopelessly inadequate. Role playing and spontaneity testing can help increase skills in this regard, but expertise in professional information giving is not easily achieved.

The following questions are some we might ask ourselves when evaluating the effectiveness of an information-giving interview:

Did I give the respondent the information that I planned and wanted to give?

Was I sensitive to the respondent's requests for additional information, even when those requests were framed in an indirect manner?

Did I pay attention to feedback from the respondent to determine whether or not I was presenting information in a nonthreatening and understandable way?

Did I furnish appropriate and professionally accurate information?

If I was unable to answer a professional question, did I acknowledge that inability in a straightforward manner? If appropriate and practicable, did I offer to try to secure the information for the respondent?

EXPRESSION AND EXPLORATION OF FEELINGS

In many interviews, the most important aspect of the interview may not be the getting or giving of factual information but rather the opportunity for one or both participants to make known their feelings about something or someone. The increased feeling of satisfaction and well-being that often comes with the full and free expression of pent-up emotions was known and encouraged even before Aristotle, in the fourth century B.C., extolled the virtues of drama and the emotional catharsis it engenders.

Many psychotherapists attempt to stimulate and encourage the expression of feelings—not only positive feelings but negative and ambivalent feelings as well—during interviews. The feelings that are revealed by the respondent during the course of the interview may be familiar ones to the person expressing them. Often, however, the feelings that emerge may be feelings that have been hitherto ignored, suppressed, or disavowed. The goal of the counselor or therapist during the interview, then, may be to increase the client's awareness and acceptance of those feelings. The general rationale behind many of these "insight therapies" is the conviction that until a person is fully aware and accepting of the underlying feelings that are motivating his or her behavior or triggering his or her defense mechanisms, that person will be unable to devote attention and psychic energy to the changing of behavior patterns or the reconstruction of his or her personality.

Many counselors are not aiming for a total reconstruction of a client's personality. Rather, they hope for an increase in the client's ability to solve problems and function more effectively in society with the personality he or she has. Many of these counselors also are convinced of the importance of providing an atmosphere in which respondents can express their innermost feelings with a minimum of defensive reactions. They feel that in such an atmosphere, the coping responses of respondents will be heightened and facilitated so that they will be able to choose more effective ways of behaving in their environment.

Carl Rogers has been one of the best-known and most influential therapists advocating the creation of a nonjudgmental, accepting atmosphere to facilitate expressions of feelings in an interview situation. Rogers (1961, p. 63) makes the following statement regarding a client's reaction as he experiences this nonjudgmental atmosphere:*

> . . . as he finds someone else listening acceptantly to his feelings, he little by little becomes able to listen to himself. He begins to receive the communications from within himself—to realize that he *is* angry, to recognize when he is frightened, even to realize when he is feeling courageous. As he becomes more open to what is going on within him he becomes able to listen to feelings which he has always denied and repressed. He can listen to feelings which have seemed to him so terrible, or so disorganizing, or so abnormal, or so shameful, that he has never been able to recognize their existence in himself.
>
> While he is learning to listen to himself he also becomes more acceptant of himself. As he expresses more and more of the hidden and awful aspects of himself, he finds the therapist showing a consistent and unconditional positive regard for him and his feelings. Slowly he moves toward taking the same attitude toward himself, accepting himself as he is, and therefore ready to move forward in the process of becoming.

Professionals in many different work settings are called upon to participate in interviews where the major portion or all of the time allotted to the interview is taken up with attention to the respondent's emotional reactions. Interviewers in crisis prevention or crisis intervention centers are well aware of the power of emotions and the intensity of effects they can

---

* Carl R. Rogers, *On Becoming a Person*. Boston: Houghton Mifflin, 1961, p. 63. Reprinted by permission.

engender. Workers in hospitals, emergency centers, and a variety of service agencies—as well as personnel in centers specializing in the diagnosis and care of severely handicapped and disabled children and adults—are familiar with mourning theory and the various stages of grief work that people must go through in recovering from severe loss and/or traumatic separation. Counselors working with people with problems know that often the first few of a series of appointments must deal entirely with feelings and attitudes before any actual steps of problem solving can be attempted.

Interviews that assist respondents to acknowledge, accept, and utilize the entire gamut of their emotions, and that increase their ability to cope with their environment and operate more effectively within it, are often known as "helping interviews." More will be said about helpful interviews in the pages to come, but the general philosophy underlying this type of interview is summarized in the following quotation from Alfred Benjamin (1974, p. 35):*

> I feel we can best help the interviewee to help himself through behavior which creates an atmosphere of trust, in which he feels wholly respected . . . We can best help him through behavior which demonstrates that we consider him responsible for himself, his actions, thoughts, and feelings, and that we believe in his capacity to use his own resources increasingly. In such an atmosphere he can confront himself and those thoughts and feelings which govern his behavior but which he hides, distorts, or denies to himself and to us.

Some questions interviewers might ask when evaluating their effectiveness in assisting respondents in the expression and exploration of feelings are:

Did I create an accepting, nonjudgmental atmosphere in which the respondent could express negative and ambivalent feelings as well as more socially acceptable or positive ones?

Was I alert to changes in facial expression, body movements, tone of voice, and other nonverbal cues that can indicate feelings not verbally expressed?

Did I try to make the respondent more aware and more accepting of his/her feelings by my acknowledging and verbalizing—in other words, reflecting—those feelings?

Did I stay with exploration of the respondent's feelings even though I felt uncomfortable at times in a situation much different from everyday conversation and socially acceptable small talk?

---

* Alfred Benjamin, *The Helping Interview*, 2d ed. Boston: Houghton Mifflin, 1974, p. 35. Reprinted by permission.

PROBLEM SOLVING

The general aim of most purposeful, directed conversations we call interviews is to help one or both participants operate more effectively in their environment. Sometimes, however, an interview will have this aim more specifically stated, in terms of some type of problem to be solved. One or both of the participants has a problem. The assumption is, of course, that when this problem is solved, the person's more effective functioning will engender greater happiness, contentment and/or self-satisfaction—in him- or herself, or perhaps in others as well.

At times, a person will come to you complaining of unhappiness or anxiety, or with a vague feeling that "there's got to be more to life than this." He may be aware of ineffective or unsatisfying functioning within his environment, but he has not been able to pinpoint any precise problem or whether or not circumstances can be changed. Your role as an interviewer might well be to assist him in clarifying the problem before helping him to explore possible solutions.

At other times, the aim of an interview may be to solve a specific problem that has already been identified and acknowledged—at least by one of the participants. The bulk of time in that type of interview may then be spent examining different ways of dealing with the situation causing the difficulties. The participants might then select what appears to be a workable behavioral alternative, or plan of action, given the current circumstances.

Lawrence Brammer (1979, p. 130) describes the evolution from problem awareness to goal setting in the following way:

> Helpees seldom come with neatly stated problems. They usually are expressed in vague feelings of confusion, dissatisfaction, or distress. Often complaints are focused on another person or institution. Thus, helpers begin, as in other styles of helping, with listening for understanding. They try to communicate this understanding, and often this is enough for the helpee to feel understood and comforted. But if the helper's listening reveals that the helpee needs to *act* differently, another strategy is needed. As the helpers listen they are gaining information about the specifics in helpees' lives—how they look at themselves and others, what they want, and what their environment is like. From these data about the helpee's initial complaints and feelings, the helper and helpee together *describe* how he *acts now* and how he would *like to act*. Thus, *goals* are formulated toward which he can work with some help from the helper in the form of suggested methods.

Dr. Thomas Gordon, in his workshops and publications on Parent Effectiveness Training, has done a great deal to promulgate and popularize the basic principles of problem solving. He advocates their use by family members or other associates in everyday relationships and situations. He feels that use of these principles can result in solutions that will be acceptable to all people involved in the problem situation. Gordon (1970, p. 237) summarizes the six steps of the "No-lose" method of conflict resolution as follows:

Step 1: Identifying and defining the conflict
Step 2: Generating possible alternative solutions
Step 3: Evaluating the alternative solutions
Step 4: Deciding on the best acceptable solution
Step 5: Working out ways of implementing the solution
Step 6: Following up to evaluate how it worked

Much has been said and written concerning the steps in problem solving. We will not discuss them at length here. However, there are two considerations we wish to mention. One of these involves the concept of ownership of a problem. A person "owns" a problem when his or her needs are being frustrated or not met, or when his or her behavior or circumstances are personally unsatisfying. When we admit ownership of a problem, we can become motivated to solve it by changing our behavior. Difficulties often arise when we want other people to change *their* behavior because it bothers *us*. Another person who will not admit ownership of a problem regarding that behavior will not be motivated to change. For example, in parent-child relationships, parents sometimes have difficulty admitting that a problem is theirs, not their child's; and at other times that a problem belongs to the child and can only be solved by him or her.

Another consideration related to problem solving involves not only defining the problem in specific terms, but also assigning some kind of priority rating when more than one problem exists. Sometimes, a person can be so overwhelmed by the number and complexity of the problems he or she owns that he or she is actually paralyzed into inactivity and thus prevented from taking any positive action. In that case, it is necessary for that person to select the most pressing problem and, at least temporarily, try to ignore the rest.

Roger Kroth, in discussing conferences between teachers and parents (1975, p. 110), makes the following suggestions:

. . . problem-solving is enhanced by being able to reduce global problems into entities that are measurable and observable. When behaviors have been defined in measurable terms then it helps place the problem in perspective, it takes away some of the subjectivity that surrounds the problem, and it is easier to determine when the problem has been solved. The teacher who serves as the catalyst in the problem solving conference will (1) reduce the problems to measurable terms, (2) restate the problem to verify her perception, (3) list the problems, (4) ask that the problems be prioritized, and (5) set up a procedure for measuring the behavior.

In evaluating the effectiveness of a problem-solving interview, we might ask ourselves the following questions:

> Was I, as the interviewer, alert to signs or expressions of anxiety, depression, or general frustration that could indicate the existence of some serious, unsolved problem?
>
> Did I help the respondent to reduce a general problem to more specific behavioral terms?
>
> Were we able to reach an accurate answer to the question, "Who owns the problem?"
>
> Did we establish priorities among the stated problems, so that neither of us was overwhelmed by the magnitude of the problem-solving task?
>
> Did I help the respondent develop and examine alternatives to his or her present behavior, and were the proposed alternatives possible and practical?
>
> As a result of our work together, has the respondent learned to use some of the basic principles of problem-solving so that he or she will be able to deal more efficiently and effectively with future problems?

PLANNING FOR FUTURE ACTION

On some occasions, a general plan of action or a future goal may have already been decided upon prior to an interview. In that case, interview time may be devoted to planning and scheduling specific activities designed to implement the chosen plan or achieve the chosen goal. We know that in order to decide on an appropriate direction for behavioral change, a person must first decide where the trouble lies and what possibilities there are for change in the troublesome circumstances. We also know that many factors come into play in determining what direction change will take: the person's physical and mental capacities, moral and ethical value systems, general level of understanding and experience, degree of insight into personal weaknesses and strengths, tolerance for risk-taking, and general flexibility and adaptability, to name a few.

The popularity of behaviorists and learning theorists has resulted in great emphasis today upon observable behavior as well as individual accountability and responsibility for behavioral change. Self-help books outline specific steps in problem solving and behavior changing, and the popularity of these books is evidence that people can—or at least want to—do it themselves. There is no doubt that many people do change their behavior to their benefit, often with a minimum of outside help.

Behavioral counselors caution against outlining goals for future action or change in terms of broad generalities. John D. Krumboltz (1966, p. 9) has stated that "in order to make such generalities useful they must be translated into specific kinds of behavior appropriate to each client's problems so that everyone concerned with the counseling relationship knows exactly what is to be accomplished."

Present and future behaviors—rather than past history or pure emotional catharsis—are emphasized by many of today's counselors. Elizabeth Webster (1977, p. 91) writes: "Basically, counselors serve four helpful functions for parents. They receive information from parents, give information to parents, help parents clarify their ideas, attitudes, and emotions, and help parents learn new behaviors."

Nathaniel Branden (1975, p. 150) also stresses the importance of behavioral change in the following statement: "The chief breakthrough in psychotherapy seems to occur when the client discovers, in terms personally meaningful to himself, that alternative, more satisfying ways of functioning are possible to him. In a sense, all techniques aim at this goal." He goes on to state that therapy moves along four major lines: providing information; leading the client to attain insight; releasing emotions; and encouraging the client to experiment with changes in his or her behavior.

Numerous colleagues in the educational field have been made more aware of the "planning for action" interview with the enactment of Public Law 93–380 (the Education Amendments Law) in 1974 and the enactment of Public Law 94–142 (the Education for All Handicapped Children Act) in 1975. Stuart Losen and Bert Diament (1978, pp. 257–262) discuss some of the provisions and ramifications of these two laws designed to provide full services for all handicapped children between the ages of three and twenty-one. They list the following significant features of PL (Public Law) 94–142:

1. PL 94–142 stipulated that *all* handicapped children should be provided with special education and related services—supporting the provision of full service for all special-education identified children.
2. The law provided for the use of federal monies for early (preschool) identification and screening programs.
3. PL 94–142 assured and required "complete due process" (appeal) procedures, including *regular parent or guardian* consultation.
4. The law assured that specific procedures should be developed to guarantee confidentiality of records or evaluation information, non-discriminatory testing, and the provision of an individualized program for all handicapped children.
5. PL 94–142 also required the development of a *written* educational program for each and every handicapped child, to be *designed initially in consultation with the child's parents or guardian* and to be reviewed at least annually.

These mandated provisions for active parental involvement in a child's educational program and process are an incentive for all educators to refine and extend their interviewing skills.

In evaluating how effectively an interview has met the "planning for action" goal, we might ask ourselves the following questions:

Is the planned behavior appropriate in light of the goal to be achieved?

Is the planned behavior appropriate for this particular respondent at this particular time and in these particular circumstances?

Have I involved the respondent in all stages of planning for future action, including the establishment of long-range goals, intermediate objectives, and the behaviors to be implemented?

Are the goals, objectives, and behaviors described in clear, precise, and verifiable terms?

How will we know when the planned behavior has been accomplished satisfactorily? What provisions are there for evaluation and feedback?

We have discussed several aspects of interviewing in this chapter, including the concept of interview direction and some general purposes or goals that interviews may serve. As we mentioned earlier, most effective interviews fulfill more than one of the functions discussed. An important criterion for effectiveness in an interview, then, is this: Did it accomplish the purpose or purposes for which it was conducted?

REFERENCES

Benjamin, Alfred. *The Helping Interview.* 2d ed. Boston: Houghton Mifflin, 1974.

Brammer, Lawrence M. *The Helping Relationship: Process and Skills.* 2d ed. Englewood Cliffs, N.J.: Prentice-Hall, 1979.

Branden, Nathaniel. "An Informal Discussion of Biocentric Therapy." In *Counseling and Psychotherapy: Classics on Theories and Issues,* edited by Ben N. Ard, Jr., pp. 135–152. Palo Alto, California: Science and Behavior Books, 1975.

De Schweinitz, Elizabeth, and De Schweinitz, Karl. *Interviewing in the Social Services.* London: The National Council of Social Service, 1962.

Gordon, Thomas. *Parent Effectiveness Training.* New York: Peter H. Wyden, 1970.

Kroth, Roger L. *Communicating with Parents of Exceptional Children: Improving Parent-Teacher Relationships.* Denver: Love Publishing, 1975.

Krumboltz, John D., ed. *Revolution in Counseling.* Boston: Houghton Mifflin, 1966.

Losen, Stuart M., and Diament, Bert. *Parent Conferences in the Schools: Procedures for Developing Effective Partnerships.* Boston: Allyn and Bacon, 1978.

Rogers, Carl R. *On Becoming A Person: A Therapist's View of Psychotherapy.* Boston: Houghton Mifflin, 1961.

Webster, Elizabeth J. *Counseling with Parents of Handicapped Children: Guidelines for Improving Communication.* New York: Grune and Stratten, 1977.

2

Aspects of
Communication

We have defined interviews as directed conversations with a purpose and have discussed some of the purposes interviews serve. Interviews are a special type of communication between two or more people. Each participant in an interview is an individual personality with a variety of behaviors and a variety of motives for those behaviors. Our thought processes and our ways of communicating are integral parts of our personality. Interpersonal communication, then, must be considered as the interacting of individual personalities.

In this and the next two chapters, we will focus attention on some aspects of the process of interpersonal communication. In this chapter, we will consider some characteristics of human communication and some of the basic forces operating to make people behave and interact as they do. These topics have been the inspiration for many books, articles, and lectures during the centuries of human history. Our choice of material for inclusion in these chapters must therefore be limited and subjective. We will present some concepts that have proved most personally useful in our interviewing experience. Hopefully, brief discussion of these concepts will whet your appetite to investigate these and other aspects further.

We feel strongly that some knowledge of the dynamics of communication and human behavior is absolutely essential to interviewing effectiveness. Sereno and Mortensen (1970, p. 3) put it this way:

Gaining an understanding of the dynamics involved in human interaction requires some insight into what happens when people communicate, a recognition of the forces which interact to produce complex communicative events, and an understanding of what is known about the effects of major variables as they influence specified communicative outcomes.

THE COMMUNICATION PROCESS

Communication can be defined very generally as a process by which information is transmitted from one to another. We can surely have a transmission of information by means other than words. We can have the transmission of information necessary to create an offspring from parents via the genetic code. We can have the natural emission of light waves, sound waves, or chemical emissions from something in the environment; these may be received by the sense receptors of a living organism and trigger a reflexive chain of elaborate behavior in response to the transmitted signal. Scientists who study nonhuman animal species have enlightened us with accounts of transfer of information among members of those species: the dance of the bee signaling the location of the pollen source to fellow hive members; the song of the male bird attracting a mate; the chest-beating and vocalizations of the chimpanzee leader in communicating his status to possible challengers —to mention just a few.

Human beings, befitting our status as the crowning glory of the animal kingdom, have communication systems unsurpassed in complexity and flexibility. By means of our highly developed sense receptors and our elaborate central nervous system, we are constantly taking in information from our environment. We integrate this information, attach significance to it, and respond to it with a variety of behaviors. At the same time, we are emitting a variety of information that is being received and acted upon by portions of our environment, including fellow human beings. It is, of course, this interpersonal communication we are interested in when we are considering improvement of our interviewing skills.

When two human beings are attempting to communicate with one another, they are each giving off messages to which the other can respond. Some of these messages may be consciously and voluntarily sent; others may be emitted without conscious awareness. Some of the messages may be framed in the actual words of our language; others may be conveyed through facial expressions, gestures, or vocal noises. The information conveyed through the messages being sent can concern the ideas, the feelings, or the general physical or emotional state of the sender. At any particular moment in the ongoing process of interpersonal communication, messages are being sent and received by each of the participants—even though at that particular moment, one person has the floor.

A COMMUNICATION MODEL

Many experts in the field of human communication have drawn or constructed models depicting the elements involved in human communication.

These vary from simple diagrams to elaborate three-dimensional structures, but certain elements are common to all of them. There is always a source or sender of messages, and there is always a receiver of messages. As a reminder that either participant in a human interaction can serve as both a sender and a receiver of information, both participants are often labeled as "source-receivers." In addition to the source-receivers, there must be a message being sent via some channel, or medium of transmission. Messages being transmitted can be described as verbal or nonverbal. A verbal message consists of words; a nonverbal message consists of behaviors other than words (for example, gestures, facial expressions, or vocal pitch changes) to which some type of meaning can be attached by the receiver. The most common way for messages to be received in human communication is for them to be heard or seen. Sound waves or light waves traveling through the air are the channel through which these messages are transmitted. People who are both deaf and blind learn to make use of other channels, such as a signal code tapped into their hand by a companion, as in the case of Helen Keller.

We have then the minimum essentials for a model of communication: a *sender*; a *message* or bit of information; and a *channel* via which the message travels so that it may be picked up by a *receiver*. From these minimum essentials, communication diagrams or models can be elaborated almost infinitely. At this point, we will mention only two other concepts often included in the models. One is the concept of continuous feedback. The message-sender, at the same time that he or she is emitting information, is receiving and processing arriving information related to that message or to the environment. For instance, as we speak, we hear and feel ourselves speak; and by means of that feedback we can tell if we are saying what we meant to say. At the same time, we are receiving information from our listener that gives us an idea if and how our message is being received. A smile, affirmative nod, muttered "mm-hm," or a wide-eyed look of interest on the part of the receiver of our message will encourage us to continue. A frown, look of puzzlement, or sound of disgust coming from our listener may well cause us to modify or reframe our message.

The other concept that complicates communication models is that messages are often multichannel. At any point in interpersonal communication, it is likely that several messages are being sent and received over one or more channels. These multichannel messages may enhance or augment each other; or they may interfere with one another, creating noise in the system. A number of factors will determine to which of these messages a receiver will attend and respond.

VERBAL COMMUNICATION

We have mentioned that human interpersonal communication can be divided into verbal and nonverbal forms. Verbal communication is accomplished by what we know as language. When we speak of language, we are referring to a particular kind of communication, one that employs arbitrary, agreed-upon symbols to convey a message from one person to another.

Students of language customarily refer to several distinct aspects of language. One aspect, termed phonology, is the assortment of individual sounds that make up the words of the language. For example, the word mat is made up of three sounds or phonemes—*m*, the short vowel *a*, and *t*. There can be slight variations in how any one of us says the three sounds. As long as enough similarity to other speakers exists, our listeners can recognize the three phonemes as mat.

Another aspect of language, syntax, concerns the arrangement of words into types of sentences. For example, we could use the word mat in a statement ("This is a mat."), in a question ("Where is the mat?"), or in a command ("Put the mat here!"). Each language has rules of syntax that enable us to produce an infinite variety of sentences and to understand the sentences of others.

Still another aspect of language, semantics, concerns the meaning of words, the connection between the arbitrary symbol and the thing for which it stands. For speakers of a language to communicate, a vocabulary must be used that both understand. If we are speaking of a mat, we must have some common definition of the word. We need to know if we are both talking about a mat for the floor or for the table; a mat finish on a photograph; or a mat of hair. How the word is used in a sentence (the context) will give us the necessary clues as to which meaning is intended, providing that we know these various meanings for the word mat.

Considerable interest in recent years involves a fourth aspect of verbal communication, known as pragmatics, which concerns how language is used in different environments and situations to serve the user's purposes. For example, when talking to a three-year-old, we would be unlikely to use the word mat in the sentence, "I like a mat finish on photographs more than a glossy finish." We might say, however, "Put your dish on the mat," or "Wipe your feet on the mat." The words we choose and how we use them are all included in pragmatics.

There can be difficulties or differences in any or all of these aspects. The sounds of one person's speech (phonemes) may be unfamiliar to the listener —either because he or she is speaking another language or a dialect of a common language, or because the speaker has some type of speech sound disorder. A speaker may use sentences (syntax) of such length and complexity that the listener is unable to process them appropriately. The speaker's vocabulary (semantics) may be such that his or her words do not call up in the mind of the listener what the speaker intended to convey.

We must keep in mind that words in themselves are merely arbitrary symbols. They have no one inherent meaning that will automatically be grasped by every user of the language. Two speakers of the same language may have various meanings for a particular word. It is necessary that at least a portion of that meaning be the same for two people or they will be unable to communicate at all. This portion of meaning that is held by both participants is the shared meaning.

As interviewers, we must be aware of the fact that—in addition to the shared meaning for any particular word—each participant in the conversation may also have private meanings for that word. These private meanings result from prior experience and learning and may not be shared by the other participant. If two people are talking about mother, for example, both will share the meaning of a female parent. However, one participant may be thinking of a graceful, silver-haired, gentle woman, while the other is thinking of a tired, overworked, nagging shrew. Shared meanings make conversation possible. Private meanings often account for some of the misunderstandings that occur in interviews.

A speaker may use language in a particular situation (the pragmatic aspect) that is inappropriate or unexpected. This may result in a breakdown in communication. For example, a flippant remark, "So join the crowd," made by an interviewer in response to a serious problem revealed by the other interview participant, may cut off any further discussion.

Most of us, in our day-to-day conversations, do not consciously pay special attention to the mechanics of language usage. When we experience breakdowns in communication, however, we may find attention to the phonologic, syntactic, semantic, and/or pragmatic aspects may provide clues as to the cause of the breakdown. We will be devoting considerable attention to pragmatics in future chapters as we discuss techniques used by interviewers in various interpersonal situations. For more detailed information regarding all four aspects of verbal communication, the interested reader may refer to the works of Winfred Lehmann (1972), Victoria Fromkin and Robert Rodman (1974), John Condon (1975), and Herbert and Eve Clark (1977)—to name a few of many informative sources.

NONVERBAL COMMUNICATION

Just as verbal communication has several aspects, so too does nonverbal communication, which can be defined as information that is transmitted by means other than words. It is important for interviewers to be aware of these aspects of nonverbal communication, because it is through nonverbal communication that information concerning the type of emotion and the intensity of the emotion is often conveyed. Some important functions that nonverbal communication serves are as follows:

Taking the place of verbal communication (when verbal communication is unnecessary or impossible)
Adding clarity to the meaning of verbal communication (by inflection, by stress, by tone of voice, by intensity, and so forth)

Revealing the general emotional state of the participants (for example, comfortable or tense, relaxed or fearful)

Revealing specific feelings regarding topics under discussion (not only the nature of the emotion but its relative intensity)

The various nonverbal aspects of communication are often classified into three general categories. The first, termed paralinguistics, includes all things that are done with the voice other than making words. Pitch changes, inflections, varying rate, pauses, and stress on different syllables or words are in this category. Another aspect, proxemics, involves the use and perception of an individual's personal space. The third major category, kinesics, involves facial expressions, gestures, and other bodily movements that accompany communication.

There are several other aspects of nonverbal communication that do not easily fit in these three categories but which can also influence the conduct and effectiveness of an interview. We have suggested the word chronemics to designate the utilization of time in interpersonal communication. Interviewers also need to be aware of another aspect of nonverbal communication: messages conveyed by a person's clothing and grooming, as well as the contents of the environmental setting. We have chosen to call this furnishings.

As George Gazda and his colleagues (1977, p. 88) have pointed out:

Facial expressions, the use of time, hand gestures, position a person takes in a room, eye contact, posture, style of dress, loudness of voice, touching, placement of furniture—each of these is a modality of nonverbal communication. There are many more. All of them are potentially important to a helping relationship because they can communicate underlying feelings and motives. . . .

Frequently, no single bit of nonverbal communication is meaningful. Still, the pieces add up, and for the perceptive helper nonverbal cues add color, richness, and depth to the understanding of the other person.

Paralinguistic Factors

A great deal of study, particularly in the last twenty or thirty years, has been done on the various nonverbal aspects of communication. Research on paralinguistic components of communication has revealed various information these components can convey. One type of information concerns the physical characteristics of the sender. Research indicates that, based on auditory cues, a speaker's age, sex, and physical condition can be fairly reliably estimated. We obtain the nonverbal cues from the tone of voice, the loudness and vigor of the voice, pitch changes or inflection patterns, and so forth. These same paralinguistic factors can also provide information regarding the speaker's emotional state. Vocal factors that accompany a speaker's words often give us a clue as to how the words are to be interpreted. The speaker may say, "It was *very* upsetting!" By the nature of stress and emphasis on the word very the listener can interpret the degree of "upsetness." The same utterance pronounced with rising inflection on the last word, on the other hand, will indicate to the listener that a question is being asked— "It was very upsetting?" Most children can easily interpret their mother's statement—"Will you wash the dishes, please?"—as a command and not a question.

Researchers have found that paralinguistic factors can also provide clues to personality characteristics, mental illness, group membership, status within a group, and occupation. There is wide variation in vocal characteristics considered normal in any culture. Normal, in this case, refers to characteristics that do not call undue attention to the voice. Noticeable or extreme variations may result not only from physical abnormalities but as concomitants of personality disturbances. Richard Luchsinger and Godfrey Arnold (1965, p. 303) remind us that *the state of the emotions exerts the greatest influence on the voice.* Barbara Hutchinson and her associates (1979, p. 209) describe certain emotional states that are reflected in the paralinguistic characteristics of the voice: "High pitch often reveals anxiety; hypernasality may indicate lethargy; harshness may reflect a desire to dominate; a weak voice may convey a weak ego, etc."

A youngster who has emotional problems adjusting to the deeper pitch of adolescent voice change may force the pitch of the voice to remain at the higher prepuberty range. Kenneth Wilson (1979, p. 44) alerts us to the fact that children who have voice problems without a physical reason may have the problem because of psychological factors:

> Psychological factors which may cause a functional voice disorder in children include personality differences, character defects, emotional disturbances, and disturbed parent-child relationships. . . .
> Psychological factors may result in a variety of vocal symptoms. . . . When a child is emotionally disturbed, either neurotic or psychotic, almost any type of voice problem may be present.

Proxemic Factors

Edward Hall has done considerable work in proxemics. He has defined (1966) four "distance zones," which characterize different types of human interaction. Hall reminds us that, depending on the distance between people in any kind of communicative interaction, there will be different characteristics of conversation and behavior. The distance noted for each zone is based on Hall's observations and interviews with middle-class white Americans; he and other researchers have found that the distances vary in different cultures. Hall's distance zones may be summarized as follows:

Intimate Distance

Close Phase: (up to 6 inches): used for very intimate contact such as lovemaking, wrestling, comforting, protecting
Far Phase: (6 to 18 inches): used for less intense but still intimate contact; not acceptable in public (in elevators, for example, defensive tactics are taken to neutralize the invasion of intimate space by strangers)

Personal Distance

Close Phase: (1½ to 2½ feet): used for discussing subjects of personal interest and involvement where it is possible to hold or grasp the other person
Far Phase: (2½ to 4 feet): for discussing subjects of personal interest and involvement and expressed as keeping someone at "arm's length"; extends from a point just outside easy touching distance by one person to a point where two people can touch fingers if they extend both arms—the limit of physical domination in a real sense

Social Distance

Close Phase: (4 to 7 feet): used for impersonal business, such as casual social gatherings or for people who work together
Far Phase: (7 to 12 feet): used for business and social discourse with more formal character, such as in offices or in homes where people can be uninvolved

Public Distance

Close Phase: (12 to 25 feet): used for formal conversation
Far Phase: (25 feet or more): used for communicating on public occasions; gestures must be exaggerated and voice amplified.

According to Hall (1966, p. 120), "The specific distance chosen depends on the transaction; the relationship of the interacting individuals, how they feel, and what they are doing." If two participants in an interview are discussing a tense family crisis, they may be within the close phase of the personal distance zone. As the conversation becomes more threatening, one of the participants may move a little away into the far phase personal distance zone. This moving away can be an indication that the course of the conversation is heading into an area that makes the person uncomfortable. Hall also pointed out that what one culture considers a personal distance may be an intimate distance for people in another culture. O. M. Watson and T. D. Graves (1966) found that Arabs stand closer, touch each other, are more likely to face head-on, use more eye contact, and speak louder than do people from the United States or England.

Hall (1974) has developed an elaborate coding system for coding nonverbal behaviors, which he has used in conjunction with his research on proxemics. Those who are interested in analyzing nonverbal aspects of their interviews may wish to use this system or at least obtain a copy of it for further inspection.

Kinesic Factors

Interest and research in kinesics has given us insight into how we convey information through body movements and facial expressions. One important kinesic factor is gaze, or eye contact. Michael Argyle (1972) noted that we indicate interest by looking; and that people look about twice as much while listening as while talking. In other research, Argyle and Dean (1965) found that the amount of looking is a signal for intimacy. Averting the eyes or looking away can signal lack of interest. Argyle has also noted that nodding plays an important role in communication—reinforcing what the speaker is saying, giving permission to continue speaking, or requesting permission to speak if the head nods rapidly.

Nonverbal behavior is a rich potential source of information about internal emotive states. Charles Darwin (1872) described facial expressions and body movements of persons suffering from excessive grief. Gary Schwartz and his colleagues (1976) studied facial expression in depressed subjects and found that electromyographic patterns of facial muscles could differentiate when the subjects were imagining happy versus sad scenes.

Paul Ekman and his associates (1972) have analyzed and summarized a number of research investigations dealing with recognition of emotional states by people representing a variety of cultures. Ekman and his associates (1972, p. 179) conclude that:

> There is one fundamental aspect of the relationship between facial behavior and emotion which is universal for man: the association between the movements of specific facial muscles and specific emotions. This has been found true for the facial appearance associated with anger, sadness, happiness, and disgust, and perhaps also for surprise and fear.

It should be noted that the universality of expressions of emotion refers to the immediate reaction evidenced in emotion-arousing situations. How the person acts once the immediate emotion has been triggered varies considerably among individuals and among cultures. Ekman and his associates (1972, p. 179) hypothesize that "there are culture-specific display rules, which dictate how facial behavior is to be managed in particular social settings, by intensifying, deintensifying, neutralizing, or masking facial behavior associated with emotion." Interviewers, then, must be aware that a particular person's way of expressing feelings is likely to be a combined product of cultural tradition and personal conditioning.

Ray Birdwhistell, considered by many to be a pioneer in the field of kinesics, has developed a notation system (1970) for describing facial and other body movements. Birdwhistell feels that the kinelogical analysis of nonverbal communication is comparable to phonological analysis of speech. He states (1970, p. 99) that there are regional variations in the body movements of people that can be likened to regional speech dialects:

> In America, there exist body motion areas with locally special variations of movement as distinctive as the variations to be heard in the varied speech communities. . . . Tentative and preliminary research upon French, German, and English movers suggest that the body motion languages vary comparably to the range of difference heard between these in their spoken language. However, this remains suggestive rather than definitive. Only when full kinesic analyses exist from each of these cultural communities can we speak of national kinesic systems with any confidence.

Chronemic Factors

Just as we use space to communicate nonverbally so, too, can we use time—chronemics—to signal information to our receiver. We communicate to others how much time we are willing to invest in an interaction. We are expected to provide greater or lesser amounts of time to others in various situations. Some people's time is considered more valuable than that of others. In certain situations, one person is expected to wait—to use more of his or her own time—to conserve the other person's time. For example, appointments with professionals are designed to be the most efficient for the expert. The amount of time spent by the person seeking the professional's attention and skills is not often taken into consideration. Thus, most people expect to wait for the doctor, the dentist, or the therapist. As one elderly woman said while waiting in her physician's office, "I know why we are called patients—that's because we have to have so much of it." Some people are also willing to wait for celebrities. The autograph-seeker is willing to wait for hours for a glimpse of his or her idol in the hope that a few moments will be available for a signature on a piece of paper. Many parents are resigned to frequent interruptions in their own activities (no matter how personally important or culturally significant) by family members requesting attention.

Nancy Henley (1977) suggests that the amounts of time we use in various interactions are analogous to Hall's four distance zones but with a direct rather than an inverse relationship. In other words, length of time spent with another is directly related to the degree of intimacy—the more intimacy, the more time. With distance zones, the less the distance the more intimate the situation. Henley designates the "time zones" as follows:

Public Time (few seconds to few minutes): used for anonymous and/or uninvolved interactions, such as asking directions or checking out library books

Social Time (few minutes to 15 minutes): used for impersonal business such as making purchases or asking about services

Personal Time (15 minutes to 30 minutes): used for ordinary "spacing" of interactions such as appointments with doctor or dentist or job interview

Intimate Time (more than 30 minutes): used for more intensive interactions such as a fifty-minute therapy session or time spent with family members and intimates

Given some degree of freedom in scheduling, and barring emergency situations where gravely important matters must be resolved in a few moments, the amount of time we devote to an interaction is often an indication of the importance we attach to it and/or to the other participant. As interviewers, our allocation or manipulation of time will be noticed and interpreted by the respondent. For example, imagine the contrasting impressions a client would form in the following two instances:

1. An interviewer arrives twenty-five minutes late for a scheduled half-hour appointment, saying there was a ball game on television he didn't want to miss; but that he must still leave in five minutes for an *important* appointment.

2. As an interview nears its scheduled time for completion, the interviewer says she will make arrangements to delay her next appointment to allow more time to continue this important discussion.

Furnishings

Our furnishings—the clothes we wear and the settings in which we place ourselves—also convey various nonverbal messages. We do not have as much control over our facial features, skin color, and height as we do over our hair style, grooming, and clothing. However, our total appearance reveals information about ourselves often termed "self-presentation." Our physical settings—decor, furniture, even the colors we choose—convey information to the observer. Rooms are described as homey, lived-in, comfortable, masculine, feminine, formal, cold, sterile, and so forth. We must acknowledge, however, that in these times of mass media, the furnishings (both dress and setting) representing varieties of socio-economic levels, occupations, and subcultures are familiar to many. These furnishings, therefore, can be readily assumed or adopted. An observer can thus be misled regarding the actual characteristics or group membership of the pretender.

INTERPRETING COMMUNICATION

Congruent and Incongruent Messages

Human communication is a complex process. At any moment in that process there are many variables that are contributing to the interaction. We've talked about the verbal aspects—the actual words being said—and the nonverbal aspects—everything except the actual words. In most conversations, the nonverbal behaviors we use tend to supplement and augment what is being said by the words. When the verbal and nonverbal messages are conveying the same general meanings we speak of *congruence,* or agreement between the verbal and nonverbal aspects of communication. Sometimes, though, the verbal and nonverbal aspects do not seem to agree, and the participant in the conversation is forced either consciously or unconsciously to decide which is most important. When what a person is saying does not seem to coincide with what we are hearing in his or her tone of voice or seeing or receiving through some other sense receptor, we often say the person is sending a double message, or is incongruent.

The nonverbal aspects of our behavior are less under our conscious control than the verbal aspects; we are not as aware of the messages we are sending nonverbally. Sometimes a person tries very hard to send a congruent message to deceive but there may be some type of giveaway. The betrayal can occur in either the tone of voice, some facial expression, or bodily movement. This is often referred to as leakage. An astute observer can be sensitive to instances of leakage and made more alert to possible deceptive behavior.

Sigmund Freud described slips of verbal behavior that permit true feelings to slip past our verbal censors. The Freudian slips, however, occur rarely compared to nonverbal leakage. Paul Ekman and Wallace Friesen studied nonverbal leakage in body movements and facial expressions. These researchers caution (1969, p. 103) that some people are exceptions to leakage clues because they do not "leak" very much: "they are professional, convincing non-verbal liars—for example, the professional dancer or actor, the skilled courtroom lawyer, the shrewd diplomat or negotiator, and the successful (sometimes psychopathically so) used-car salesman." We might add that the successful "confidence man" is a master at feigning congruence.

Several additional cautions are in order in interpreting nonverbal communication. As Gordon Wiseman and Larry Barker (1967, p. 230) point out:

> Interpreting nonverbal messages involves inference and subjective evaluation. Verbal communication also involves inferences in interpretation, of course, but nonverbal messages can be even more ambiguous than verbal ones. The interviewer must recognize that his observations are subjective.

He must further realize that his interpretations of these observations involve only degrees of probability. The degree of probability that the interviewer's inferences are correct is dependent upon his life orientation, his knowledge of the interviewee, other nonverbal cues, and the interviewee's spoken message. The more messages he receives from the interviewee through verbal and nonverbal channels, the greater the probability that the inferences will be accurate.

We have noted that nonverbal communication varies from culture to culture. Because of these cultural variations interviewers must take care in interpretation. When an interviewer is interacting with a person whose cultural background is different from his or her own, it is important to be aware that either participant may misinterpret nonverbal cues. We know very quickly when we cannot speak other people's verbal language; but we are less aware of our ignorance regarding their country's or culture's equally important paralinguistic, proxemic, chronemic, or kinesic customs and traditions.

Status and Power Messages

The relative status and power of participants in an interaction are conveyed by verbal and nonverbal means. A variety of interesting research has been concerned with the nonverbal aspects. Nancy Henley (1977) devotes considerable attention to the nonverbal manifestations of power that she terms "body politics." She describes how power and status, dominance and superiority are evidenced nonverbally in interpersonal relationships. She also describes how sex differences, class differences, and race differences in behavior can often be traced to differences in power.

Henley cites numerous examples of the effects of power. She contrasts the amount of space available to the rich while the poor are crowded. She notes that poor people must spend a great deal of time waiting for services— usually time taken from working hours, thus losing pay—while the rich are not expected to wait and do not lose pay. Henley discusses the constriction and invasion of women's time and space. She also describes the demeanor of the less powerful when in the presence of the more powerful.

When discussing the politics of touch, Henley (1977, p. 95) describes the following exercise:

> Think of interactions between these pairs of persons of differing status and picture who would be more likely to touch the other—put an arm around the shoulder, a hand on the back, tap the chest, hold the wrist, and so on; teacher/student; master/servant; police officer/accused person; doctor/patient; minister/parishioner; adviser/advisee; foreman/worker; businessman/secretary. If you have had the usual enculturation, I think you will find the typical picture to be that of the superior-status person touching the inferior-status one.

Erving Goffman (1966) studied body "tightness and looseness" and the variations of body positions we assume in different social and public gatherings. Goffman noted that there are symmetrical and asymmetrical rules in demeanor and that there is more symmetry between equals and more asymmetry between unequals. Individuals in higher positions are allowed more latitude in behavior.

Interviewers' awareness of their use of time, space, and touch helps to insure that they send accurate messages regarding their perceptions of their own status and perceptions of their respondents' status. The interviewer may observe clues in the respondent's behavior that indicate misinterpretations of status. The respondent may treat the interviewer as an awesome authority figure, for example, when the interviewer wishes to be treated as an equal. The interviewer may then wish to modify his nonverbal communication which could be reinforcing such misinterpretations.

The important thing for us to remember as interviewers regarding verbal and nonverbal communication is that an individual in a communicative situation is sending many messages simultaneously. These messages are in complementary and sometimes competing channels. Shirley Weitz (1979, p. 347) describes multichannel communication as "the natural mode of our reception of interactional messages—through all channels at once." As interviewers, we send information through many channels and the receiver of our communication responds (in varying degrees) to these simultaneous messages. An interviewer may be concentrating attention on selecting the right words while a respondent might be focusing on one particular nonverbal aspect. We all differ in our sensitivity to these communicative aspects.

Various writers and researchers have concentrated on one or another aspect of communication. Their focus on a particular aspect has certainly added to our knowledge. They remind us that we must be alert to these aspects of communication in order to understand what the other person is trying to tell us and what we may be telling them. However, we must always keep in mind that communication is an imperfect but dynamic, ongoing, reciprocal process, and is much more than the sum of its parts.

REFERENCES

Argyle, Michael. "Non-Verbal Communication in Human Social Interaction," in *Non-Verbal Communication* edited by Robert A. Hinde, pp. 243–269. Cambridge: Cambridge University Press, 1972.

Argyle, Michael, and Dean, J. "Eye-contact, Distance and Affiliation." *Sociometry* 28 (1965): 32–49.

Birdwhistell, Ray L. *Kinesics and Context*. Philadelphia: University of Pennsylvania Press, 1970.

Clark, Herbert H., and Clark, Eve V. *Psychology and Language: An Introduction to Psycholinguistics*. New York: Harcourt Brace Jovanovich, 1977.

Condon, John C., Jr. *Semantics and Communication*. 2d ed. New York: Macmillan Publishing Co., 1975

Darwin, Charles. *The Expression of Emotions in Man and Animals*. Chicago: University of Chicago Press, 1965 (originally published 1872).

Ekman, Paul, and Friesen, Wallace. "Non-Verbal Leakage and Clues to Deception." *Psychiatry* 32 (1969): 88–105.

Ekman, Paul; Friesen, Wallace V.; and Ellsworth, Phoebe. *Emotion in the Human Face: Guidelines for Research and an Integration of Findings*. New York: Pergamon Press, 1972.

Fromkin, Victoria, and Rodman, Robert. *An Introduction to Language*. New York: Holt, Rinehart and Winston, 1974.

Gazda, George M.; Asbury, Frank R.; Balzer, Fred J.; Childers, William C.; and Walters, Richard P. *Human Relations Development: A Manual for Educators*. 2d ed. Boston: Allyn and Bacon, 1977.

Goffman, Erving. *Behavior in Public Places: Notes on the Social Organization of Gatherings*. 2d ed. New York: Free Press, 1966.

Hall, Edward T. *The Hidden Dimension*. Garden City, N.Y. Doubleday and Co., 1966.

Hall, Edward T. *Handbook for Proxemic Research*. Washington, D.C.: Society for the Anthropology of Visual Communication, 1974.

Henley, Nancy M. *Body Politics*. Englewood Cliffs: Prentice-Hall, 1977.

Hutchinson, Barbara B.; Hanson, Marvin P.; and Mecham, Merlin J. *Diagnostic Handbook of Speech Pathology*. Baltimore: The Williams and Wilkins Co., 1979.

Lehmann, Winfred P. *Descriptive Linguistics: An Introduction*. New York: Random House, 1972.

Luchsinger, Richard, and Arnold, Godfrey E. *Voice-Speech-Language*. Belmont, Calif.: Wadsworth Publishing Co., 1965.

Schwartz, Gary; Fair, Paul L.; Salt, Patricia; Mandel, Michael R.; and Klerman, Gerald L. "Facial Expression and Imagery in Depression: An Electromyographic Study." *Psychosomatic Medicine* 38 (1976): 337–347.

Sereno, Kenneth K., and Mortensen, C. David, eds. *Foundations of Communication Theory*. New York: Harper & Row, 1970.

Watson, O. Michael, and Graves, T. D. "Quantitative Research in Proxemic Behavior." *American Anthropologist* 68 (1966): 971–985.

Weitz, Shirley, ed. *Nonverbal Communication*. 2d ed. New York: Oxford Press, 1979.

Wilson, D. Kenneth. *Voice Problems of Children*. 2d ed. Baltimore: The Williams and Wilkins Co., 1979.

Wiseman, Gordon, and Barker, Larry. *Speech—Interpersonal Communication*. San Francisco: Chandler Publishing Co., 1967.

3

Principles of
Human Motivation

We have discussed the communication process and some of its significant aspects because an interview is, above all, interpersonal communication. An effective interviewer is aware of and sensitive to the various ways information is conveyed from one person to another. An interviewer tries to understand the person with whom he or she is communicating, and to provide information, feedback, or assistance to that person. To do this, the interviewer is alert to verbal and nonverbal messages and to their congruence or incongruence, both on the respondent's part and on his or her own.

An interviewer's goal is to facilitate, not impede, communication. He or she therefore encourages the free, easy flow of messages from one sender-receiver to the other. In terms often used in communication models, we attempt to minimize the noise in the system—any factors that impede informational exchange. Attention to *how* we communicate is therefore an important consideration in evaluating and improving our interviewing effectiveness.

Not only is our manner of communicating important. *What* we communicate is equally significant. In our dealings with others, what we communicate depends partly on the general purpose of the encounter. It also depends on our own personality characteristics and on our philosophy of human behavior and interpersonal relationships. When we communicate with others, we are almost always trying to influence them or their behavior in some way. This influence may be limited to having them listen and absorb factual information we are trying to impart; it may be to have them provide us with information we desire. We may be trying to encourage release of pent-up feelings, or problem-solving, or carrying out an ambitious plan of action. If we are going to do an effective job of influencing people to communicate cooperatively with us and even to change their behavior, it behooves us to have some idea of what makes people behave as they do.

In some communicative interactions, we may be content with influencing our partner's behavior for just a few moments—as in the securing of momentary cooperation in poll-taking or a brief sales transaction. In other interactions, we may be interested in having people change long-standing, habitual behavior. Psychotherapists and counselors are often working with people who have asked for assistance in changing their entire way of life.

From the vast accumulation of published theories and research findings, of old wives' tales and new-fangled notions, what few comments might be most relevant for interviewers? As in the discussion of aspects of communication, we take the prerogative of a personal selection of some basic principles we have found most useful in our interviewing experience. We shall discuss the concepts of homeostasis, the "fight-or-flight" response, basic human needs, developmental stages and tasks, and coping versus defense mechanisms.

HOMEOSTASIS

The human body is a fascinating and complex organism that requires certain fundamental conditions for its physical survival. The cells of our bodies must have a special internal milieu or environment in order to function. For fully effective functioning, the various organs within the body must perform their tasks so that life functions can be carried out. Edward Murray (1964, p. 21) described the necessary internal environment as follows:

> The basic life processes—the production of energy, bodily growth, and the repair of damaged tissue—depend on a delicate set of chemical conditions in the individual cells of any organism. In man, temperature must not vary more than a few degrees from the optimal 98.6 degrees Fahrenheit for any length of time, the water level of the blood and lymph must be more or less constant, chemical constituents of the blood—oxygen, sugar, salts, and so on—must not vary beyond safe limits, and the blood must not become too acid or alkaline. Failure to maintain these conditions leads to a disruption of general functioning and, eventually, death.

In the latter half of the nineteenth century, Charles Darwin (1859) and his contemporary Claude Bernard, a physiologist, investigated phenomena of animal environmental adaptation. Bernard (1865) described physiological mechanisms that operate to assist an organism in maintaining the relatively constant internal state that is necessary for physical survival. In the 1930s Walter Cannon, another physiologist, popularized the concept of "homeostasis." He (1939) pointed out that when homeostasis is upset or thrown into "disequilibrium," the body initiates certain reactions to remedy the situation. If insufficient oxygen is available, breathing will speed up; if body temperature is rising beyond the safe limits, perspiration occurs in an attempt to cool the body; and so on.

Cannon also pointed out that this internal stability of the body must be maintained despite a variety of external circumstances. Every living being exists in an environment, a small portion of the universe in which we must survive at any particular moment. Continued existence depends on coming to terms with our external environment. Air, food, and water must somehow be obtained. Waste products must be eliminated. A variety of substances must be provided for bodily utilization. The energy and behavior initiated by the organism in order to meet these bodily needs and thus regain physiological equilibrium is known in psychological parlance as a "drive."

Cannon's concept of homeostasis has had several significant effects upon psychological theory. For one thing, it has encouraged students of human behavior to think in terms of certain needs that must be satisfied in order for a person to maintain internal balance or equilibrium. The concept of human behavior occurring to obtain satisfaction or pleasure was not new. The homeostasis theory provided a more scientific basis for those hypotheses. The individual's attempts to meet various needs by drives or expenditures of energy came to be regarded as the motivation for behavior. Today, a variety of needs theories exist to explain human motivation and behavior. An exhaustive history of the development of those theories and a listing of all of those currently promulgated are beyond the scope of this book. We will mention a few favorites shortly.

Cannon's homeostasis theory had another significant effect upon the field of psychology—particularly the areas of psychotherapy and counseling. The term homeostasis originally referred solely to basic physiologic adaptation. The term now has been broadened to describe an individual's maintenance of effective, satisfying behavior in whatever environment that individual finds him- or herself. For example, the concept of homeostasis or striving to maintain balance might be used to explain abnormal behavior on the part of a child in a family environment. The hypothesis might be that one of the child's basic needs is being frustrated within that environment. The problem behavior represents her attempt somehow to meet that need through the only means she senses are at her disposal.

The concept of homeostasis is also occasionally used on an even broader level; we hear mention of family homeostasis. The implication is that the family unit, in order to keep functioning as a family, must have each of its members fulfilling his or her particular family role and functions. The departure of any one member from the expected role or functions may throw the family unit into disequilibrium. It may then require much expenditure of energy and behavior to recover the family balance.

THE FIGHT-OR-FLIGHT RESPONSE

Another important concept—also verified and elaborated by Cannon—is that of the "fight-or-flight" response. The response is initiated in many animals, including humans, when physical survival is in jeopardy. Any information perceived by our sense organs that signals a possible threat to survival will trigger a response in our central nervous system. The response gears our body up for immediate action and heightened physical activity. Our heart rate increases; more blood is pumped to the peripheral muscles and less to our digestive tract. Our attention to the impending danger is heightened and our body stands ready to do battle with the intruder or carry us away from the scene as quickly as possible.

The fight-or-flight response (also known as the "general adaptation response" or "stress response") has been studied extensively by Hans Selye. Selye (1974) has made us aware that this automatic bodily response to a sensed threat to homeostasis and survival can be triggered by a wide range of incoming stimuli in the modern human being. The response, with its accompanying emotions of fear and excitement, can be triggered not only by a ferocious animal or menacing fellow human coming towards us, or by being trapped in a tunnel with insufficient oxygen; it can also, through conditioning processes, be triggered by the sound of a dentist's drill, or a frown on father's face, or the score on an examination paper, or even the approach of a mild-mannered interview client.

Fighting or fleeing is necessary in some situations as a short-term emergency adaptive response. Our modern society, with its many anxiety- and fear-producing possibilities, may arouse our body's defenses over long periods of time. This frequent and long-lasting arousal of adaptive responses can lead to physical ailments and emotional disturbances. The fight-or-flight response is a universal one, then; but some of the sensory messages that trigger it vary greatly among humans because of prior experience and conditioning.

BASIC HUMAN NEEDS

Another important concept in the study of human motivation is that of basic human needs. This involves the view that human functioning consists of primary organismic needs that must be met in order to insure continuation in one's environment. Behavior is prompted by frustration of one or more of these needs and attempts to satisfy them. Clark Hull (1943) felt that all human behavior is motivated by internal drives aroused by deprivation of basic physiological needs or by secondary drives that have developed as an outgrowth of those primary drives. To many authorities, the definition of happiness is "the emotion which accompanies satisfaction of a need."

Motivation theorists generally agree that deprivation of the primary biological needs of air, food, water, sex, and sensory stimulation motivates behavior. However, theorists have also proposed additional needs that they consider universal. They feel that these needs must be met if an individual is going to function fully and effectively as a human being.

One of the most popular lists of basic human needs is that proposed by Abraham Maslow (1956). Maslow has made an influential contribution to our understanding of human behavior. Many of the earlier needs theories —or so-called tension-reduction theories—were developed by researchers who worked almost exclusively with animal species other than human. Their applications to human behavior tended, therefore, to emphasize needs and frustrations common to human and other animal species. Maslow's work was concerned more directly with humans as social creatures who manifest some distinctly human developmental characteristics and behaviors in addition to their more primitive, biological ones.

Maslow arranged his list of basic human needs in a hierarchical form. Even though all of the needs must be met in order for a human to function at his highest level of effectiveness and capability, Maslow felt that the needs gradually emerge developmentally. The most basic level of the hierarchy contains needs that are prepotent to all others as far as actual physical survival.

Maslow (1956, pp. 243–244) summarizes his Hierarchy of Basic Human Needs as follows:

1. Most basic of all are the animal needs, those which we share with most of the other higher animals, the needs for food, for water, for sleep, for rest, for sex, for warmth, and so on.
2. Then comes the necessity for safety and for security, for the absence of danger and threat, for being cared for when necessary, being able to be dependent and helpless and weak without feeling endangered.
3. To belong to a group of some sort, and more specifically to be able to love and to be loved, these also are needs in the sense that their fulfillment makes further and higher growth possible. . . .
4. We need to respect ourselves, to be strong, to have a good sound self-esteem. Generally this good self-esteem rests on three foundations; first, respect and approval from other people; second, on actual capacity, achievement and success and third, on the acceptance of and acting upon our own inner nature.
5. In addition to these needs we also have the so-called cognitive needs and the aesthetic needs . . .

The growth of knowledge, of understanding, and the development of a philosophy of values therefore seem to be necessities rather than luxuries.

Maslow designated this fifth group of needs as self-actualization needs, which he (1968, p. 25) defined as:

... ongoing actualization of potentials, capacities and talents, as fulfillment of mission (or call, fate, destiny, or vocation), as a fuller knowledge of, and acceptance of, the person's own intrinsic nature, as an unceasing trend toward unity, integration or synergy within the person.

We can summarize Maslow's Hierarchy of Basic Human Needs as follows:

Level I.   Biological needs
Level II.   Safety needs
Level III.   Love and affection or "belonging" needs
Level IV.   Esteem needs (including self-esteem)
Level V.   Self-actualization needs

Although it is obvious that a person could survive physically with frustration of needs on levels III, IV, and V, that person would do so only with what Maslow (1971, p. 34) termed "diminutions of humanness." It is interesting to note that Maslow proposed that as the child is developing, he must have his needs at one level met quite consistently before he can meet his needs on each successive level. In a mature adult, frustration of any level of the needs will motivate behavioral attempts to meet those needs and will tend to occupy our energies. Some adults can stand extreme deprivation of a lower level need in order to satisfy a need at a higher level For example, an artist may forego regular meals to buy a canvas for her masterpiece. A researcher may neglect his love life to conduct a large number of interviews needed for data collection.

Understanding of these basic human needs can be helpful in understanding human behavior. Although the needs are universal, the ways in which people endeavor to meet those needs (their goal selection) are highly varied, and may be vastly different from our own preferred ways. Three men may be hungry. One may attempt to satisfy his hunger by a handful of seaweed and some grains of rice. Another may sit down to a meal of herring and boiled potatoes. The third may relish his hot dog and French fries. Three women may be frustrated in their need for esteem and respect from others. One may invite her friends to an elegant party. Another may enroll in an assertiveness-training course. The third may devote three years of nights and weekends to writing a book.

According to the homeostatic theory, a psychological drive—with its subsequent resulting activity aimed toward meeting a frustrated need— stems from a personal, internal disequilibrium. In organisms as complex as humans, a variety of needs can be aroused at any one time; goal selection and the organization of behavior to meet those goals, therefore, can be a very intricate process.

Another thought-provoking formulation of basic needs common to humans has been presented by Snell and Gail Putney (1966). In common with other theorists, they include basic physical needs: for example, oxygen, water, sleep, food, and bearable temperatures. They also list needs that are not absolutely essential to physical survival but which they feel also have an innate biological basis, such as the needs for muscular, mental, and sexual activity. They mention the tremendous inter- and intracultural variations in the ways people try to meet these needs, and discuss the extent to which various cultures make it easy or difficult to attain necessary satisfactions. A major contribution the Putneys make to the understanding of human needs as they motivate behavior lies in their description of what they term the "self needs". They feel that certain needs common to all humans are the result of the basic process of socialization rather than our actual physical structure. They point out that all over the world, young children learn how to be social beings, and in the process, they develop consciousness of themselves as separate, distinct beings. The Putneys (1966, p. 27) develop this thesis as follows:

> Having become conscious of self, the child loses the unreflective simplicity of the animal. He is irrevocably altered. Barring brain damage or permanent coma, he cannot escape self-awareness once it has developed. And *along with this awareness of self there emerge certain self needs, needs which will hereafter claim an important part of the individual's time and energy.* The development of these needs, common to all socialized men, is as irreversible as the consciousness of self.
>
> The needs of the self are closely interrelated, but for analytic clarity we shall separate them into three major aspects: (1) *the need for an accurate and acceptable self-image;* (2) *the need to verify this self-image and expand the self through association;* (3) *the need to verify the self-image and expand the self through action.* Along with the physical needs previously discussed, these self needs constitute the basic needs of man, the driving force behind human behavior.

The Putneys, in common with many other psychologists, believe that the experiencing of tension or unhappiness results from frustration of a basic need. They point out that a person is often aware of tension, but does not recognize the frustrated need that is provoking the tension. Misinterpretation of needs and misdirected energies in attempting to meet needs or reduce tension cause much human unhappiness.

In relation to faulty interpretation of human need, the Putneys describe the concept of "particularization," the constriction of a person's recognition of ways of meeting a need to only one or a very few alternatives. For instance, a man may be convinced that only a glass of ice-cold, pure spring water will assuage his thirst. In that case, he is likely to endure much more discomfort than if he is willing to accept the available unrefrigerated canned juice or some leftover soup. A young woman may be absolutely convinced that a master's degree in administration from San Francisco State University's School of Business is her one and only guarantee of successful entrance into the competitive world of corporate business. If that is the case, she is likely to be devastated by the school's denial of her admission application. If she has particularized her goal selection to an inordinately high degree, she will continue to be inconsolably devastated even with the arrival of a scholarship offer from Harvard University.

The Putneys (1966, p. 165) summarize the concept of particularization in this way:

> Human needs are broad and can be satisfied in a variety of ways. But the person who is blinded by habit and by the conventional assumptions of his culture perceives not his need but only his customary and highly particular means of satisfying it. . . .
>
> The person caught up in particularization may be deprived simply for want of the capacity to perceive—or to accept—alternatives. He may be aware that other people find other ways to satisfy their needs, yet feel that only the familiar ones will satisfy *him*.

Eric Berne is well known for his system of personality theory, known as transactional analysis. He has also postulated his version of basic human needs, particularly as they are reflected in an individual's day-to-day behavior. Berne (1961) points out that our time can be spent in any one of a number of ways. The ways we do spend our time represent our attempts to satisfy three drives or "hungers": stimulus or sensation hunger; recognition hunger; and structure hunger.

Stimulus or sensation hunger reflects the human organism's need for constant communication with its environment. This communication is necessary to maintain relative homeostasis and effective functioning. Our highly developed sense organs require a minimum amount of varied stimuli to process. Without sufficient stimuli, we become lethargic or bored on the one hand, or—in case of more extreme sensory deprivation—become highly disturbed and even begin to hallucinate.

A person, as a social animal, also requires at least some acknowledgment and acceptance by other living beings. Berne feels that this "recognition hunger" is an outgrowth or derivation of the particular forms of sensory stimulation provided early in life. These include social handling and being physically cared for by another. As the infant grows, and as conditioning processes occur, the child learns to make do with less actual physical mothering, settling for more subtle and even symbolic forms of recognition—a brief pat on the head, a smile, or a wave of greeting from across the playground, for example.

As we mature, our need for recognition by another continues to influence our behavior. Berne (1961, pp. 84–85) describes ways in which society tries to meet some of its recognition needs:

The *stimulus-hunger,* with its first order sublimation into *recognition-hunger,* is so pervasive that the symbols of recognition become highly prized and are expected to be exchanged at every meeting between people. Deliberately withholding them constitutes a form of misbehavior called *rudeness,* and repeated rudeness is considered a justification for imposing social or even physical sanctions. The spontaneous forms of recognition, such as the glad smile, are most gratefully received. Other gestures, like the hiss, the obeisance, and the handshake, tend to become ritualized. In this country there is a succession of verbal gestures, each step implying more and more recognition and giving more and more gratification. This ritual may be typically summarized as follows: (a) "Hello!" (b) "How are you?" (c) "Warm enough for you?" (d) "What's new?" (e) "What else is new?" The implications are: (a) Someone is there; (b) Someone with feelings is there; (c) Someone with feelings and sensations is there; (d) Someone with feelings, sensations, and a personality is there; (e) Someone with feelings, sensations, a personality, and in whom I have more than a passing interest, is there.

The third type of hunger which Berne postulates—structure hunger—seems to reflect what many investigators feel is a universal human need to make sense of the world around us. We need to impose some organization or order upon the multitude of stimuli that bombards our central nervous system. This need for some type of organization extends to filling our waking hours with an assortment of behaviors, some of which hopefully help us to meet our other basic needs. Berne (1961, 1963, 1964) has described this need to structure our time. He has described in detail our various time-filling behaviors: pastimes, rituals, games, activities, and intimacy. Berne (1972) also describes ways in which our habitual and preferred behaviors assist us in fulfilling our various needs—particularly the overriding need to be recognized in some fashion by others.

DEVELOPMENTAL STAGES AND TASKS

Thus far, in our discussion of the motivation of human behavior, we have mentioned the concept of homeostasis, the availability of the fight-or flight response, and the concept of a common or universal core of basic human needs. Another useful approach in considering varieties of human behavior is that of developmental tasks or crises.

Sigmund Freud revolutionized twentieth-century thinking with his conception and description of psychosexual stages through which humans progress (if they are fortunate and do not remain fixated at an early level) on their way to adulthood and social maturity. Freud (1927) conceived of infant behavior as motivated by the pleasure principle. He postulated that available energy—or libido—is directed in ways that will reduce tension and provide satisfaction to the infant. As the infant grows, activities providing new satisfactions are centered upon various body zones and their particular functions.

Freud's psychosexual stages have been summarized by Ernest Hilgard and Richard Atkinson (1967, p. 73), as follows:

> Freud considered the childhood stages as having to do with deriving pleasure from different zones of the body at different ages, leading up to the gratifications of adult sexuality. By using a very broad definition of sexuality, these stages came to be known as *psychosexual* stages, of which the chief ones were *oral* (gratification through stimulation of the lips and mouth region, as in nursing or thumbsucking), *anal* (gratification through withholding and expelling feces), *phallic* (gratification through fondling the sex organs), *Oedipal* (a sexual desire for the parent that is said to be concurrent with the phallic phase, the name deriving from Oedipus who, in the Greek tragedy, fell in love with his mother and was punished for it), *latency* (in which sexual interests are no longer active, so that the child of elementary school age turns his interests to the environment), and, finally, *genital*, at which point normal heterosexual interests arise.

Freud acknowledged a striving for balance similar to what we have described as homeostasis. He stated that imbalance engenders unpleasant feelings and that restoration of balance results in feelings of pleasure. He postulated that athough behavior is governed by the pleasure principle during infancy, it is gradually modified by the reality principle. The individual learns to delay or modify gratification of pleasure to conform more closely to the demands of society.

Erik Erikson, in the 1960s, followed the psychoanalytic tradition. He postulated that eight stages of what he termed psychosocial development could be traced in the developing human. At each stage, certain psychosocial crises must be resolved for the child as his or her range of significant social contacts broadens, and new personal and interpersonal problems arise. Table 3–1 depicts Erikson's stages of psychosocial development and the personal qualities that emerge as the successive stages are successfully completed.

Another investigator/educator, Robert Havighurst, developed another theory of life stages. He characterized the stages by particular problems or life crises that the individual has to meet in order to mature. Havighurst published a pamphlet in 1948 introducing his concept of developmental tasks. He listed what he considered the major tasks confronting humans in the United States from infancy to old age. The list was revised on several occasions. The following excerpts from the 1972 edition (1972, pp. 5, 6) summarize Havighurst's viewpoint on developmental tasks in human behavior:*

* Robert J. Havighurst, *Developmental Tasks and Education*. 3rd ed. New York: Longman, 1972, pp. 5, 6. Reprinted by permission of Longman, New York, and the author

TABLE 3–1   Erikson's Eight Ages of Ego Development

Success Brings	*Failure Brings*

1st Age
Early Infancy
(birth to about one year)
(corollary to Freudian oral sensory stage)

Basic Trust	*vs.*	Mistrust
Result of affection and gratification of needs, mutual recognition.		Result of consistent abuse, neglect, deprivation of love; too early or harsh weaning, autistic isolation.

2nd Age
Later Infancy
(about ages one to three years)
(corollary to Freudian muscular anal stage)

Autonomy	*vs.*	Shame and Doubt
Child views self as person in his own right apart from parents but still dependent.		Feels inadequate, doubts self, curtails learning basic skills like walking, talking, wants to "hide" inadequacies.

3rd Age
Early Childhood
(about ages four to five years)
(corollary to Freudian genital locomotor stage)

Initiative	*vs.*	Guilt
Lively imagination, vigorous reality testing, imitates adults, anticipates roles.		Lacks spontaneity, infantile jealousy, "castration complex," suspicious, evasive, role inhibition.

4th Age
Middle Childhood
(about ages six to eleven years)
(corollary to Freudian latency stage)

Industry	*vs.*	Inferiority
Has sense of duty and accomplishment, develops scholastic and social competencies, undertakes real tasks, puts fantasy and play in better perspective, learns world of tools, task identification.		Poor work habits, avoids strong competition, feels doomed to mediocrity; lull before the storms of puberty, may conform as slavish behavior, sense of futility.

5th Age
Puberty and Adolescence
(about ages twelve to twenty years)

Ego Identity	*vs.*	Role Confusion
Temporal perspective		Time confusion
Self-certain		Self-conscious
Role experimenter		Role fixation
Apprenticeship		Work paralysis

TABLE 3-1 (Continued)

Success Brings	Failure Brings
Sexual polarization	Bisexual confusion
Leader-followership	Authority confusion
Ideological commitment.	Value confusion.

6th Age
Early Adulthood

Intimacy	vs.	Isolation

Capacity to commit self to others, "true genitability" now possible, *Lieben und Arbeiten*—"to love and to work"; "mutuality of genital orgasm."		Avoids intimacy, "character problems," promiscuous behavior; repudiates, isolates, destroys seemingly dangerous forces.

7th Age
Middle Adulthood

Generativity	vs.	Stagnation

Productive and creative for self and others, parental pride and pleasure, mature, enriches life, establishes and guides next generation.		Egocentric, nonproductive, early invalidism, excessive self-love, personal impoverishment, self-indulgence.

8th Age
Late Adulthood

Integrity	vs.	Despair

Appreciates continuity of past, present, and future, acceptance of life cycle and life style, has learned to cooperate with inevitabilities of life, "state or quality of being complete, undivided, or unbroken; entirety" (Webster's Dictionary); "death loses its sting."		Time is too short; finds no meaning in human existence, has lost faith in self and others, wants second chance at life cycle with more advantages, no feeling of world order or spiritual sense, "fear of death."

"Erikson's Eight Ages of Man's Ego Development" (pp. 578–580) from INTERPRETING PERSONALITY THEORY, 2nd edition by Ledford J. Bischof. Copyright © 1964, 1970 by Ledford S. Bischof. Reprinted by permission of Harper & Row Publishers, Inc.

The tasks the individual must learn—the *developmental tasks of life*—are those things that constitute healthy and satisfactory growth in our society. They are the things a person must learn if he is to be judged and to judge himself to be a reasonably happy and successful person. *A developmental task is a task which arises at or about a certain period in the life of the individual, successful achievement of which leads to his happiness and to success with later tasks, while failure leads to unhappiness in the individual, disapproval by the society, and difficulty with later tasks . . .*

Some tasks arise mainly from physical maturation, such as learning to walk, learning to behave acceptably to the opposite sex in adolescence, and (for women) adjusting to the menopause in middle life. Other tasks, arising primarily from the cultural pressure of society, are learning to read, and learning to participate as a socially responsible citizen in society.

There is a third source of developmental tasks—namely, the personal values and aspirations of the individual, which are part of his personality, or self. The personality, or self, emerges from the interaction of organic and environmental forces. As the self evolves, it becomes increasingly a force in its own right in the subsequent development of the individual. Already by the age of three or four the individual's self is effective in the defining and accomplishing of his developmental tasks.

Examples of tasks arising primarily from the personal motives and values of the individual are: choosing and preparing for an occupation, and achieving a scale of values and a philosophy of life.

Thus developmental tasks may arise from physical maturation, from the pressure of cultural processes upon the individual, from the desires, aspirations, and values of the emerging personality, and they arise in most cases from combinations of these factors acting together.

Following is a list of the developmental tasks of the six age periods differentiated by Havighurst and described by him in his 1972 publication. The listing also serves as a delineation of common life problems facing people in the twentieth century in many parts of the world. The average age for a particular task's emergence and the relative importance attached to specific tasks varies considerably from culture to culture.*

Developmental Tasks of Infancy and Early Childhood
(birth to approximately six years of age)

1. Learning to walk
2. Learning to take solid foods
3. Learning to talk
4. Learning to control the elimination of body wastes
5. Learning sex differences and sexual modesty
6. Forming concepts and learning language to describe social and physical reality
7. Getting ready to read
8. Learning to distinguish right and wrong and beginning to develop a conscience

Developmental Tasks of Middle Childhood
(approximately six to twelve years of age)

1. Learning physical skills necessary for ordinary games
2. Building wholesome attitudes toward oneself as a growing organism

---

* Robert J. Havighurst, *Developmental Tasks and Education*. 3rd ed. New York: Longman, 1972. Reprinted by permission of Longman, New York, and the author.

3. Learning to get along with age-mates
4. Learning an appropriate masculine or feminine social role
5. Developing fundamental skills in reading, writing, and calculating
6. Developing concepts necessary for everyday living
7. Developing conscience, morality, and a scale of values
8. Achieving personal independence
9. Developing attitudes toward social groups and institutions

Developmental Tasks of Adolescence
(approximately twelve to eighteen years of age)

1. Achieving new and more mature relations with age-mates of both sexes
2. Achieving a masculine or feminine social role
3. Accepting one's physique and using the body effectively
4. Achieving emotional independence of parents and other adults
5. Preparing for marriage and family life
6. Preparing for an economic career
7. Acquiring a set of values and an ethical system as a guide to behavior—developing an ideology
8. Desiring and achieving socially responsible behavior

Developmental Tasks of Early Adulthood
(approximately eighteen to thirty years of age)

1. Selecting a mate
2. Learning to live with a marriage partner
3. Starting a family
4. Rearing children
5. Managing a home
6. Getting started in an occupation
7. Taking on civic responsibility
8. Finding a congenial social group

Developmental Tasks of Middle Age
(approximately thirty to sixty years of age)

1. Assisting teen-age children to become responsible and happy adults
2. Achieving adult, social and civic responsibility
3. Reaching and maintaining satisfactory performance in one's occupational career
4. Developing adult leisure-time activities
5. Relating oneself to one's spouse as a person
6. To accept and adjust to the physiological changes of middle age
7. Adjusting to aging parents

Developmental Tasks of Later Maturity

1. Adjusting to decreasing physical strength and health
2. Adjusting to retirement and reduced income
3. Adjusting to death of spouse
4. Establishing an explicit affiliation with one's age group
5. Adopting and adapting social roles in a flexible way
6. Establishing satisfactory physical living arrangements

Havighurst's investigation of human motivation, goal selection, and value clarification led him to conclude that there are six ways by which a person may come to desire a particular object or state of affairs:

1. Through satisfaction of physiological drives
2. Through satisfactory emotional experience
3. Through concrete reward and punishment
4. Through association of something with the love or approval of persons whose love and approval are desired
5. Through inculcation by someone in authority
6. Through reasoning or reflective thinking

The particular developmental problems and crises facing adult humans —including the elderly—have been given considerable further attention in recent years. The work of Robert Havighurst and other educators; the popularization of adult passages, critical life crises or turning points, by Gail Sheehy (1976); and the studies of Roger Gould (1972), Daniel Levinson (1978), and George Vaillant and Charles McArthur (1972) have made important information available. Many researchers feel that disruption of a person's satisfactory progression from one life stage to the next can be the cause of much unhappiness and many personality problems. Familiarity with materials available on life stages and transition events can help interviewers understand what problems their respondents may be facing. Such information may also shed light on the interviewer's personal current concerns.

COPING VERSUS DEFENSE MECHANISMS

The last topic to be included in this chapter concerns another important motivation for human behavior: how we deal with unpleasant situations. When we think about differences in people, we realize that people deal with frustration, fear, and conflict in a variety of ways. Each of us has likely ways of dealing with unpleasant events. These habitual reaction patterns often constitute personality characteristics which our friends and acquaintances recognize in us.

Take, for example, the contrasting behavior of five artists out of 200 who entered paintings in a competition at the civic art museum. We shall assume that each of these five contestants is serious about painting, devoted long hours to the completion of the entry, and felt that the painting represented his or her best work and merited professional recognition. When the contest winners are announced, none of our five entrants is awarded a prize or honorable mention. The five unsuccessful entrants respond to the news with the following behaviors. One takes the painting home and burns it. One seeks out a member of the panel of three judges and requests an objective critique of the painting and its strengths and weaknesses. A third contestant writes a scathing letter to the community newspaper, denouncing the judges as incompetent and lacking in true dedication to artistic principles and the fostering of creative talent. The fourth contestant seems totally unaffected by the decision. In fact, his wife marvels at how unemotional and matter-of-fact he is when he tells her the name of the winners. She knows the news must be disappointing, especially when he had worked so long and enthusiastically and was so hopeful that he would win the contest. The fifth unsuccessful contestant, who is already eighty-five pounds overweight, stops at the local ice cream shop on the way home from the contest and wolfs down a jumbo banana split. People who know these five contestants well would not be surprised at their behavior; the friends would recognize the response pattern and consider it typical.

Varieties of reaction patterns to frustration and disappointment carry over into life experiences both less and more personally significant than failing to win an art contest. Suppose, for instance, the most significant, cherished person in your life—your wife, husband, housemate, child, or parent—developed a disabling physical condition. The condition would be such that this person could no longer function independently. He or she could no longer communicate well. He or she could no longer help you to satisfy some of your most basic needs. Can you predict your reactions and your behavior over a period of time in that situation?

Professional counselors and therapists who work with many people in situations such as the one described can attest that people cope with the problem in varying ways. Some find out what can be done realistically for the patient. They try to make the most satisfactory arrangements to meet the patient's needs without completely sacrificing themselves or giving up in total despair. Others react by escaping from the situation. The escape may be through actual physical desertion of the patient or through excessive use of alcohol, tranquilizers, or other drugs. Others so repress the facts of reality that they deny the severity of the problem or completely block out any show of emotions regarding it. Others may blame doctors or hospitals for the presence or continuance of the patient's medical difficulties. They may take the patient from one doctor or faith healer to another seeking some miraculous cure. Often in interviews, particularly in helping interviews, you will be working with people such as those described. These people will exhibit a variety of responses to serious disruptions of their life patterns and homeostasis and to their failure to regain effective functioning.

We have already mentioned some of Sigmund Freud's contributions to our theories and knowledge of human motivation and behavior. Freud (1949) also contributed the concept of defense mechanisms to personality theory. Some of the behaviors described in the preceding paragraphs are examples of defense mechanisms in operation. Freud felt that human behavior consists of the interacting of driving forces and restraining forces. The driving forces, known as cathexes, are represented in his concept of the Id. The restraining forces, known as anticathexes, are represented in the concept of the Superego. To Freud, the Id represents the source of energy necessary for human functioning; undischarged energy can build to an uncomfortable level, referred to as tension. The Id then seeks to reduce painful tension and obtain pleasure or satisfaction by discharging excess energy. Freud proposed the existence of the Ego as that portion of the personality that directs our energies into behavioral interactions with the environment in order to reduce excess tension and meet basic needs.

According to Freud, there are certain constraints on our behavior because of values and moral standards that we have internalized from our parents and other caretakers. That portion of our personality that acts as this restraint or conscience was designated by Freud as our Superego. We see then that in Freud's personality theory, the Ego acts as an executive directing our energies into behaviors that will be satisfying to the Id but also acceptable to our Superego. When this is possible, we function relatively effectively and in a manner satisfying to us.

In most lives, there are times when the Ego is unable to fulfill its demanding task of reconciling the demands of the Id with the restraints of the Superego. According to Freud, anxiety is the result. Vernon Nordby and Calvin Hall (1974, pp. 48, 49) describe the Freudian concept of anxiety and resulting defense mechanisms:

> In Freudian terms, anxiety is produced by excessive stimulation which the ego is unable to control. There are three types of anxiety: *reality anxiety*, *neurotic anxiety*, and *moral anxiety*.
>
>> *Reality anxiety* is caused by real threats and dangers from the environment.
>> *Neurotic anxiety* is the fear that the instincts in the id will break loose (overcome the anticathexes) and cause the person to do something for which he will be punished.
>> *Moral anxiety* is fear of the conscience. A person with a well-developed superego feels guilty when he does something or even thinks of doing something that is contrary to his moral code . . .
>
> Under the pressure of excessive anxiety, the ego is forced to take extreme measures to relieve the pressure. These measures are called defense mechanisms, because they defend the ego against anxiety.

Definitions of anxiety vary with different personality theorists. However, the concept of defense mechanisms as explanation for some of our behaviors is widely accepted. Sometimes we can alleviate anxiety by direct action known as coping behavior, through which the situation causing the anxiety will be changed in a less overwhelming or ego-threatening direction. When we cannot alleviate anxiety through direct action, we tend to employ defense mechanisms to reduce the anxiety. It should be noted that defense mechanisms *do* accomplish a purpose; they tend to reduce anxiety, at least temporarily. The unfortunate aspect is that the use of defense mechanisms necessitates distortion or denial of the realities of a situation. It avoids facing the facts of the situation which is causing us such concern. In that sense, defense mechanisms are self-defeating and energy-consuming without getting to the heart of the problem. They deter us from realistic identifications and appraisal of the anxiety-producing situation. They prevent us from directing our energies into effective coping behavior.

Table 3–2 describes some common defense mechanisms and cites an example of each. As an interviewer, you will occasionally meet with examples of defensive behavior on the part of your respondent. In some individuals particular defense mechanisms operate so consistently that they are present in most of that individual's interpersonal contacts. With other respondents, your comments or nonverbal communication during the interview may actually prove anxiety-producing. Defense mechanisms may be triggered in the respondent as a direct result of your behavior.

You—as a human being as well as an interviewer—can also fall prey to overwhelming anxiety and its possible consequences. If this happens, it is helpful to become consciously aware of specific anxiety-producing situations, or existing conflicts between your beliefs and your behaviors. It is helpful to bring your energies to bear directly on the anxiety-producing situations rather than to deny or distort their existence. And it is hoped you will be able—either with or without professional assistance—to explore your needs and new ways of meeting them. These new ways of behaving will be more effective and more compatible with your self-confirmed beliefs and values, and therefore less anxiety-provoking.

As we have mentioned, defense mechanisms are ways of avoiding painful realizations. We can combat this escape or avoidance by attention and awareness of our feelings and behaviors in the here and now—even if the here and now is painful or uncomfortable. In the words of Fritz Perls (1969, p. 46):

> An absolutely healthy person is completely in touch with himself and with reality. The crazy person, the psychotic, is more or less completely *out* of touch with both, but mostly with *either* himself *or* the world. We are in between being psychotic and being healthy.

In most interviews, this is true of both the interviewer and the respondent.

TABLE 3–2 Common Ego Defense Mechanisms

REPRESSION—excluding unacceptable impulses, ideas, or feelings from consciousness. For example, in repression, feelings of hatred or lust toward one's parents are blocked from awareness.

REGRESSION—returning to a less mature level of adaptation, especially under extreme frustration or stress. For example, regression may be seen in the fired executive who begins to act in an extremely dependent and helpless fashion, requiring relatives to attend to his or her every need.

PROJECTION — attributing unacceptable ideas or impulses to others rather than acknowledging them as one's own. For example, unconscious homosexual impulses may be projected upon others, so that now the person is troubled by the homosexual behavior of other people and not by his or her own desires.

RATIONALIZATION—justifying an act or idea that is unacceptable because it is unreasonable, illogical, or inconsistent. For example, the individual who fails to achieve a much-desired and hard-fought-for goal then decides that failure really was "for the best" or "a blessing in disguise."

REACTION FORMATION—transforming dangerous or painful urges into their opposite forms, though the original urges persist unconsciously. The transformed urges often are felt or expressed in excessive and exaggerated ways, for example, a mother's hatred of her child is transformed into maternal oversolicitousness.

DENIAL — rejecting or distorting those aspects of reality which consciously are unacceptable. For example, the person maintains that the death of a loved one "just did not happen."

SUBLIMATION — modifying unacceptable impulses into socially acceptable activities. For example, sexual impulses may be channeled into painting or sculpturing nudes, while aggressive tendencies may be discharged by choosing to become a movie critic.

DISPLACEMENT — shifting impulses and feelings about one person or object toward a safer or less dangerous person or object. For example, aggressive feelings toward the boss are totally inhibited, but expressed later toward family members, pets, or furniture.

INTELLECTUALIZATION — removing or isolating feeling from a thought so that the thought can remain conscious without the associated affective charge. Thinking about impulses to murder someone without getting upset or anxious, or talking in a detached way about a recent divorce or personal failure without feeling the disappointment and hurt are common examples.

IDENTIFICATION — incorporating the thoughts, feelings, and actions of another to increase one's sense of worth or to reduce threat from powerful others. The child acquires parental standards and values partly through identification with its parents.

The above defense mechanisms are a sample of those typically employed in everyday life. Their moderate use may help protect the individual from disturbing negative emotions like anxiety, guilt, and shame, though excessive use may impair adjustment. These mechanisms are believed to operate unconsciously. Most defense mechanisms, especially repression, are used in conjunction with other defenses and, hence, are seen only rarely in their "pure" forms.

From Lazarus/Monat, PERSONALITY, 3/e, © 1979, pp. 163. Reprinted by permission of Prentice-Hall, Inc., Englewood Cliffs, New Jersey.

Awareness and understanding of the principles of human motivation discussed in this chapter can be helpful in your work as an interviewer. For one thing, it can help you to understand other people's behavior—including that of your respondent—and what may be motivating it. It can also help you to understand your own behavior and motivations. The proponents of many schools of psychotherapy have promoted various theories to explain human behavior. Table 3–3 summarizes some of these basic philosophies.

TABLE 3–3   Basic Philosophies of Eight Therapy Approaches

Psychoanalytic Therapy	Human beings are basically determined by psychic energy and by early experiences. Unconscious motives and conflicts are central in present behavior. Irrational forces are strong; the person is driven by sexual and aggressive impulses. Early development is of critical importance, for later personality problems have roots in repressed childhood conflicts.
Existential-Humanistic Therapy	The central focus is on the nature of the human condition, which includes capacity for self-awareness, freedom of choice to decide one's fate, responsibility and freedom, anxiety as a basic element, the search for a unique meaning in a meaningless world, being alone and being in relation with others, finiteness and death, and a self-actualization tendency.
Client-Centered Therapy	The view of humans is positive; humans have an inclination toward becoming fully functioning. In the context of the therapeutic relationship the client experiences feelings that were previously denied to awareness. The client actualizes potential and moves toward increased awareness, spontaneity, trust in self, and inner directedness.
Gestalt Therapy	The person strives for wholeness and integration of thinking, feeling, and behaving. The view is antideterministic, in that the person is seen to have the capacity to recognize how earlier influences are related to present difficulties.
Transactional Analysis (TA)	The person has potential for choice. What was once decided can be redecided. Although the person may be a victim of early decisions and past scripting, self-defeating aspects can be changed with awareness.
Behavior Therapy	Humans are shaped and determined by sociocultural conditioning. The view is basically deterministic, in that behavior is seen as the product of learning and conditioning.
Rational-Emotive Therapy (RET)	Humans are born with potentials for rational thinking but with tendencies toward crooked thinking. They tend to fall victim to irrational beliefs and to reindoctrinate themselves

TABLE 3-3 (Continued)

	with these beliefs. Therapy is cognitive/behavior/action oriented and stresses thinking, judging, analyzing, doing, and redeciding. This model is didactic-directive. Therapy is a process of reeducation.
Reality Therapy	The person has a need for identity and can develop either a "success identity" or a "failure identity." The approach is based on growth motivation and is antideterministic.

Every human being seeks homeostasis and fulfillment of basic human needs. Our awareness of this can result in more effective interviews, as we assist fulfillment rather than thwart it. We can use information regarding developmental tasks to respond more appropriately to individuals in various life stages. Awareness of the mechanism of the stress (fight-or-flight) response may assist us in dealing with fear or anxiety. And, finally, our awareness of the distinction between coping and defensive behavior may enable us to promote the former rather than the latter.

REFERENCES

Bernard, Claude. *An Introduction to the Study of Experimental Medicine.* New York: Macmillan, 1927 (originally published 1865).

Berne, Eric. *Transactional Analysis in Psychotherapy.* New York: Grove Press, 1961.

Berne, Eric. *The Structure and Dynamics of Organizations and Groups.* New York: J. B. Lippincott Co., 1963.

Berne, Eric. *Games People Play.* New York: Grove Press, 1964.

Berne, Eric. *What Do You Say After You Say Hello?* New York: Grove Press, 1972.

Bischof, Ledford J. *Interpreting Personality Theory.* 2d ed. New York: Harper & Row, Publishers, 1970.

Cannon, Walter B. *The Wisdom of the Body.* rev. New York: Norton, 1939.

Corey, Gerald. *Theory and Practice of Counseling and Psychotherapy.* Monterey, California: Brooks/Cole Publishing Co., 1977.

Darwin, Charles. *The Origin of Species.* London: John Murray, 1859.

Erikson, Erik H. *Childhood and Society.* 2d ed. New York: W. W. Norton & Co., Inc., 1963.

Freud, Sigmund. *The Ego and the Id.* London: Hogarth Press, 1927.

Freud Sigmund. *An Outline of Psychoanalysis.* New York: Norton, 1949 (originally published in German, 1930).

Gould, Roger. "The Phases of Adult Life: A Study in Developmental Psychology," *American Journal of Psychiatry,* 129 (1972), 521–531.

Havighurst, Robert. *Developmental Tasks and Education,* 3rd ed. New York: Longman, 1972.

Hilgard, Ernest, and Atkinson, Richard. *Introduction to Psychology.* 4th ed. New York: Harcourt, Brace & World, 1967.

Hull, Clark. *Principles of Behavior.* New York: Appleton-Century-Crofts, 1943.

Lazarus, Richard S., and Monat, Alan. *Personality.* 3rd ed. Englewood Cliffs, N.J.: Prentice-Hall, 1979.

Levinson, Daniel L. *The Seasons of a Man's Life.* New York: Knopf, 1978.

Maslow, Abraham. "Personality Problems and Personality Growth." In *The Self: Explorations in Personal Growth,* edited by Clark E. Moustakas, pp. 232–246. New York: Harper & Brothers Publishers, 1956.

Maslow, Abraham. *Toward a Psychology of Being.* 2nd ed. New York: Van Nostrand Reinhold Co., 1968.

Maslow, Abraham. *The Farther Reaches of Human Nature.* New York: The Viking Press, 1971.

Murray, Edward. *Motivation and Emotion.* Englewood Cliffs, N.J. Prentice-Hall, 1964.

Nordby, Vernon J., and Hall, Calvin S. *A Guide to Psychologists and Their Concepts.* San Francisco: W. H. Freeman and Co., 1974.

Perls, Frederick S. *Gestalt Therapy Verbatim.* Lafayette, Calif.: Real People Press, 1969.

Putney, Snell, and Putney, Gail. *The Adjusted American: Normal Neuroses in the Individual and Society.* New York: Harper & Row, 1966.

Selye, Hans. *Stress Without Distress.* New York: J. B. Lippincott Co., 1974.

Sheehy, Gail. *Passages: Predictable Crises of Adult Life.* New York: E. P. Dutton & Co., 1976.

Vaillant, George, and McArthur, Charles C. "Natural History of Male Psychologic Health. I. The Adult Life Cycle From 18–50," *Seminars in Psychiatry,* 4 (1972), 415–427.

4

Dynamics of Human Interaction

In Chapter 2, we discussed some of the basic aspects of the communication process. In Chapter 3, we focused attention on possible motivations for human behavior. We come now to examining more directly what happens when two people come together in a communicative interaction.

We know that people and communicative situations come in infinite variety, and the progress and outcome of any particular situation will be influenced by a number of factors. The nature of the communicative setting, the circumstances under which the interaction takes place, and the reasons for it certainly affect the interaction. The personality and characteristics of each individual and his or her effects upon the other participant are also crucial determinants of the quality of the interaction and its outcome. In this chapter, we will discuss what each person brings to an interaction and how each person has developed his or her style of interaction with others. We shall also discuss some identifiable characteristics of interaction style. The chapter concludes with a brief discussion of the dynamics of group interaction.

S-O-R VARIABLES

One way of describing each individual in a particular setting is to consider what are often termed the "S-O-R variables" involved. The S, O, and R variables refer to the variations that can occur in the "stimulus," within the "organism," or in the "response."

Stimulus Variables

In our efforts to survive in our environment, we are constantly taking in information from the environment, processing it, and responding to that information in some way. What is available to be responded to will be different from situation to situation; in any one situation, what *will* be responded to differs from individual to individual.

The actual objects and events—the stimuli—in the environment at any one moment, as well as the richness or paucity of stimuli, will differ. We have already discussed various verbal and nonverbal possibilities within an interview that can serve as stimuli to affect the behavior of the interview participants. Various internal happenings—including unmet basic needs—can also serve as stimuli to which the individual will attend. These internal happenings could be a sudden increase in our heartbeat or our perspiration; a severe abdominal, chest, or head pain; "grumblings" of our stomach as mealtime is past due; or fantasies or day-dreams that are more appealing than external realities. These and many other internal stimuli can capture our attention as well as noises or sights or smells or other sensations coming to us from the outside. The variety of these messages that can be picked up by our sense receptors and transmitted to our central nervous system for processing are often termed stimulus (or S) variables.

We distinguish between actual and potential stimuli. Actual stimuli are those taken into and processed by the nervous system. Potential stimuli are all the happenings or disturbances in the individual's environment to which his or her sense receptors are capable of responding, even though he or she may not do so. For instance, your increasing skill as an interviewer may include becoming aware of nonverbal behavior you would not have noticed earlier in your career. This information can provide clues to help you recognize your respondent's feelings. In other words, what would have been only potential stimuli in the environment for a less experienced or astute interviewer have become actual stimuli processed by you.

Response Variables

At any particular time, many stimuli available in our external environment, as well as within our bodies, may evoke responses from us. These responses may take many different forms. These, then, can be termed the response (or R) variables in the situation. At any one time, there are likely to be many stimuli impinging on our sense receptors. We respond to some and disregard others; and those to which we do respond are processed at a variety of levels within our nervous system. We respond to some at a level of the nervous system below that which triggers conscious awareness of the information. For instance, minor variations in respiration rate, body temperature, or postural adjustments go unnoticed by us even though they take place in our bodies to maintain physiological homeostasis.

Other reflexive responses occur of which we are aware because messages are sent to our cerebral cortex at the same time the response occurs involuntarily at another part of our body. We realize, for example, that we have blinked our eye to avoid an insect that has flown near our eyelid; but the defensive maneuver took place without our conscious direction. Emotional responses are often of this nature. Sometimes, for example, we are first aware that we are fearful of something when we feel our heart beating faster or our mouth getting dry.

Still other responses are voluntarily accomplished by us after processing, interpreting, and integrating various stimuli at a completely conscious level. An interviewer may decide deliberately to move closer to his respondent in an interview, for example, when he senses that the distance between their chairs seems too stiff and formal for the confidential material being discussed. Or an interviewer may decide to rephrase and repeat a question she has asked when she hears how vague or confused it sounds the first time.

Responses to stimuli can be one-cell simple or extraordinarily complex. They can be completely reflexive and involuntary or intricately calculated and voluntary. And they can be all stages in between. From a wide variety of potential stimuli, we selectively perceive only a small portion of those that will then determine our responses. This selectivity of perception is vital in enabling us to concentrate our attention. However, this selective perception is also often the cause of stereotyped responses, in which a limited set of visual, auditory, tactile, or even olfactory stimuli automatically evokes a particular behavior or emotional response. The sight of food particles on a man's beard may automatically evoke a frown, for example; a command received over an intercom from a voice of authority may evoke an automatic "Yes, sir"; and the smell of freshly made coffee may pull us from our desks no matter how high the work is stacked or how near the deadline.

In each of the above examples, a person is exhibiting an habitual, ready-made response to a limited set of perceived stimuli. As we mentioned earlier, people often form judgments of others in just such a stereotyped manner. They note a limited set of stimuli, those indicating male or female, young or old, white or black, and the like. They quickly classify the observed person into a general category on the basis of that limited set. They then react with an habitual, automatic response to that general category. As can be expected, such a limited response repertoire on the part of an interviewer can interfere markedly with relating to a respondent on the basis of his or her individual attributes and needs.

In addition to voluntary, involuntary, and stereotyped responses, another set of terms used to describe responses is the covert/overt classification. If a response to a stimulus or combination of stimuli can be observed by another person, we term it an overt response. If it is unobservable by another, it is called a covert response. Both types of responses are taking place in both participants throughout an interview. In the discussion of nonverbal communication, we noted that there can be leakage of clues that can provide an attentive observer with some information regarding basically covert responses in the interview participants. However, there are still many reactions going on inside the head of each participant. These are unknown to the other participant unless there is later voluntary sharing of previously undisclosed information.

In any human interaction, the response—or R—variables can be remarkably numerous. The variety of voluntary responses available to humans is a result of the extensive development of our cerebral cortex. This potential for varied response is a vital factor in our supremacy in the animal hierarchy. As an aside, however, we must note that having the potential for a variety of appropriate responses does us little good if our actual response repertoire is limited to a few habitual, stereotyped behaviors.

In the realms of psychology and learning theory, the stimulus/response paradigm has been described, researched, and manipulated for centuries. Within the past century, behaviorists have become more and more influential in the precise manipulation of human behavior through the selective reinforcement of certain behavioral responses. Ivan Pavlov (1927) and B. F. Skinner (1938, 1953) are two of the best known of these investigators. Pavlov demonstrated the existence of what is now known as classical or Pavlovian conditioning. In classical conditioning, behavioral responses that occur automatically or reflexively in the presence of a certain stimulus can be evoked eventually by a previously neutral stimulus. This occurs if both stimuli are presented simultaneously or with the neutral stimulus slightly preceding the natural one during the training period. The classical example of this type of conditioning is a dog salivating to the sound of a bell. The dog salivates even in the absence of the food that naturally calls forth the response and that was originally presented as the bell was rung.

Discussion of classical conditioning can be found in most general psychology books. We will not go into details of the phenomenon here. We should remind ourselves, however, that the responses being aroused by the natural and then by the conditioned stimuli are automatic, involuntary, reflexive responses. Examples of these responses include bodily adaptations, the fight-or-flight response, and the arousal of emotions. When the sight, sound, smell, or feel of something in our environment automatically brings forth an emotional response (which may or may not be similar to the response of other people in the same situation), we may well be demonstrating the results of classical conditioning that occurred at an earlier point in our life.

In contrast to Pavlovian conditioning, which involves the substitution of one stimulus for another in calling up a particular response, the early work of B. F. Skinner concentrated primarily on what is often termed operant conditioning. This involves the strengthening or increased recurrence of a particular response out of a variety of possible ones, and is accomplished through positive reinforcement of the desired response. Today, the principles of behavior modification based on selective reinforcement of various behaviors are widely known and employed. They will not be discussed further at this point. Suffice to say that in any situation, our selection of any particular behavioral response (out of the variety of possible behaviors) is due in large part to the fact that, in the past, that particular behavior has paid off for us in some way. The payoff may have been relief of tension, satisfaction of a basic need, or approval by someone whom we respected or admired. Or perhaps our behavior merited a mark on a progress chart, ten of which earned a gold star or other tangible treat.

One other point to be made regarding behavior modification as it applies directly to behavior in the interview situation: either interview participant may be engaged in modifying the other's behavior during the interview itself. This is done by selectively rewarding (positively reinforcing) certain types of verbal responses or other behavior. It is also done by ignoring other responses or actually punishing them by disapproval or other unpleasantness. In Chapter 7, we will talk more about the use of approval and disapproval and other potential behavior modifiers during the interview.

Organismic Variables

Thus far, we have been concerned with S (stimulus) and R (response) variables. The particular nature of S and R variables can be noted and described in any behavioral situation or human interaction. In contrast to the traditional behaviorists' emphasis upon these S and R variables, other investigators have focused their major attention on what have been termed the organismic (or O) variables in human behavior. The O variables go on *inside* the individual to determine the perception, processing, and integration of stimulus information and the selection, formulation, and execution of a behavioral response. Each participant in a communicative interaction will come to that interaction as a unique personality with a set of personal characteristics that will greatly affect perception and processing of available information and the responses made to it. Regarding this, Robert Carson (1969, pp. 87–88) makes the following statement:

> Consider the situation of a person about to undergo his initial encounter with another person. What he brings to that situation is an enormously complex system of "knowledge" and cognitive apparatus for processing new information, a variety of potential emotional reactions which might be cued off by particular events, a set of "values" that represent his immediate and long-range objectives, and a rich store of behavioral Plans that constitute his established strategies and tactics for maximizing his hedonic outcomes.

Carson's attention to the organismic variables that each individual brings to an interaction is representative of theorists who are known by a variety of designations: perceptual theorists, cognitive theorists, Gestaltists, field theorists, personality theorists, phenomenologists, and humanists, to name a few. The major interests of these theorists lie in the current interaction of the unique individual human with his or her immediate environment and the people in it. These theorists have described many internal factors that will affect an individual's perception of stimulus variables and that will influence the responses he or she makes. Some of these organismic variables that each interview participant will bring to the encounter include:

Age, sex, skin color, physical build, and other physical characteristics

The capacity and functioning of the sense receptors, other bodily systems, and the central nervous system

Perceptual experience and the concepts acquired to organize and make sense of perceptions

Personality characteristics—habitual ways of reacting to stimuli and of maintaining homeostasis

Previously learned responses and memories of past events

The basic need structure, including the degree to which those needs were met in the past and the extent to which any of the needs are currently frustrated or satisfied

The pattern of motivation and goal selection—habitual ways of striving to satisfy the basic needs

Beliefs and attitudes—the emotional component of the individual's conceptual structure

Injunctions and constraints imposed by the individual's culture

The value system under which the individual operates

The individual's self-concept and his or her concept of the "ideal self," and the degree of congruence between the two

The individual's degree of self-awareness and self-acceptance

The individual's defense system—the particular ways he or she escapes conflict by forms of temporary adjustment known as defense mechanisms

The relative strength and availability of effective coping behaviors, as opposed to a system of defense mechanisms

The role repertoire demanded in the individual's life and his or her effectiveness in those roles

The individual's perception of the roles of both participants in the interview and his or her specific expectations about the encounter

The individual's awareness of the communication process and his or her sensitivity to verbal and nonverbal behaviors; his or her ability and willingness to engage in turn-taking behaviors necessary in interpersonal communication

The individual's interpersonal behavioral and communication style and his or her basic life position in regard to others

The nature and extent of the individual's stereotyped responses

The individual's experience with and willingness to engage in self-disclosure

Each participant in an interview will arrive with his or her own unique mixture of these organismic variables. This amalgam will affect each individual's selection and perception of stimuli in the particular situation. It will also determine the individual's responses to the interview situation and the other interview participant. In other words, these organismic variables determine our ways of relating to others—our interpersonal style.

DEVELOPMENT OF INTERPERSONAL STYLE

Numerous child psychologists have contributed to our knowledge of how a young child develops ideas about who he or she is, what the world is like, and about other people. A child must be cared for to survive. Early in life, the child depends upon just a few people for food, protection, and that mixture of care and cuddling we designate as love. A child, then, must learn very quickly how to get along with those important people in his or her life.

The child develops ways of responding in certain life situations through processes of classical and operant conditioning. Behavior that gets basic needs satisfied will tend to recur. Behavior that keeps the caretakers coming around to take care will also tend to recur. Thus, behaviors that promote *satisfaction* and *security* tend to be incorporated in the child's interpersonal style.

The growing child continues to learn how to behave around different people in order to achieve satisfaction and/or security. In order to make life pleasant at home, it's nice to please mommy and daddy. In order to have a playmate keep playing rather than run home crying or pouting or bored, there are certain ways she must be treated. There are some things you just don't say to a neighborhood bully unless you're a physical match for him. And when you are interacting with baby brother or sister or a neighbor's young child, there are certain rules of gentleness and carefulness to obey if you don't want to get into trouble. Children, then, grow up in a variety of environments and with a variety of behaviors that have proved satisfying and serviceable.

Harold Mosak (1979, p. 56) describes the child's development of this interpersonal style as follows:*

> Growing up in the social environment of the family, the child attempts mastery of his environment. In so doing, he learns about his strengths, abilities, deficiencies, and his place in the scheme of things. To learn, he must size up his environment. Although the child ordinarily is an excellent observer, he is often a poor evaluator and interpreter . . .

* Reprinted by permission of the publisher, F. E. Peacock Publishers, Inc., Itasca, Illinois. From Raymond J. Corsini and Contributors, *Current Psychotherapies*, second edition, 1979, p. 56.

Parents, siblings, peers, institutions, and the culture exert influences in their efforts to socialize him. Until he learns what is expected of him, he is relatively helpless, incompetent, inferior. So he observes his environment, makes evaluations, and arrives progressively at various conclusions about himself, his worth, and his environment, what it demands of him, and how he can acquire "citizenship in the new world." Through observation, exploration, trial and error, and by getting feedback from his environment, he learns what gains approval and disapproval and how he can achieve significance. Aside from his perceptions and evaluations, the child is not a passive receptor of family influences. He actively and creatively is busy modifying his environment, training his siblings, and "raising" his parents . . . He wants to belong, to be a part of, to count . . .

Whether this need to belong is biological or learned, every child searches for significance. He jockeys for position within his family constellation looking for a "place in the sun." One sibling becomes the "best" child, another the "worst" one. Being favored, being one of the favored sex within the family, adopting the family values, identifying or allying oneself with a parent or sibling may provide the grounds for the feeling of having a place. Handicaps, organ inferiorities, or being an orphan are other "position makers" for some children.

In the words of John Milton (*Paradise Regained*), "The childhood shows the man, As morning shows the day." As adults, we come to interpersonal relationships with a variety of behaviors that have enabled us to meet our needs in the past without being killed off or banished by fellow human beings—especially bigger or more powerful ones. We tend to seek and sustain relationships that will afford us some degree of satisfaction and security. And when we find ourselves in interpersonal situations, we tend to behave in ways that have proved serviceable in the past.

Virginia Satir (1972), in her work as a family therapist, has identified four ways that people typically respond when they feel insecure in an interpersonal situation. She feels that these ways of communicating develop from childhood as the child tries to meet stressful situations. Satir notes that stressful situations often carry with them the threat of rejection. The child needs security, but also needs to protect his or her self-esteem; so in stressful situations with important people, the child tries to conceal weakness by responding in one of four ways: placating, blaming, computing, or distracting. Adult communicators often use the same response patterns in stressful interpersonal situations.

Satir (1972, pp. 64, 66, 68, 70) describes the four types of communicators in the following way:*

The *placator* always talks in an ingratiating way, trying to please, apologizing, never disagreeing, no matter what. He's a "yes man." He talks as

* Virginia Satir, *Peoplemaking*. Palo Alto, Calif.: Science and Behavior Books, 1972, pp. 64, 66, 68, 70. Reprinted by permission.

though he could do nothing for himself; he must always get someone to approve of him . . .

The *blamer* is a fault-finder, a dictator, a boss. He acts superior, and he seems to be saying, "If it weren't for you, everything would be all right." . .

The *computer* is very correct, very reasonable with no semblance of any feeling showing. He is calm, cool, and collected. He could be compared to an actual computer or a dictionary . . .

Whatever the *distracter* does or says is irrelevant to what anyone else is saying or doing. He never makes a response to the point . . .

Do any of these communicators sound familiar? Some of the descriptions may hit close to home. Satir describes the tones of voice and body postures accompanying each of the communication types. She suggests that each of us can benefit by practicing each type. We can assume the characteristic postures and gestures and the vocal and speech characteristics, and make typical comments. This type of role playing can help us to understand some of the feelings that may accompany them. Sometimes, we communicate in one manner with certain people and much differently with others. Some differences are dictated by the situations and the patterns of behavior considered appropriate for our respective roles. But some differences cannot be explained on this basis. We are all familiar with portrayals of the shy, retiring, placating office clerk who is a tyrannical, blaming despot with his wife and children. And occasionally an office party can be considerably enlivened by a usually tense-jawed, tight-lipped, inhibited junior executive whose computer casing is dissolved in holiday punch.

Virginia Satir points out that these ways of communicating are often learned early in life. She also points out that—in contrast to the four types mentioned—there is another, more personally healthful way of communicating in interpersonal situations. She (1972, p. 72, 73, 74) calls this leveling and describes it as follows:*

> In this response all parts of the message are going in the same direction— the voice says the words that match the facial expression, the body position, and the voice tone. Relationships are easy, free and honest, and there are few threats to self-esteem. With this response there is no need to blame, retreat into a computer, or to be in perpetual motion . . .
>
> The leveling response is real for whatever it is. If a leveler says, "I like you," his voice is warm and he looks at you. If his words are, "I am mad as hell at you," his voice is harsh, and his face is tight. The message is single and straight.
>
> Another aspect of the leveling response is that it represents a truth of the person at a moment in time. This is in contrast, for example, to a blaming response where the person is feeling helpless, but is acting angry— or is hurting, but is acting brave.

* Virginia Satir, *Peoplemaking*. Palo Alto, Calif.: Science and Behavior Books, 1972, pp. 72, 73, 74. Reprinted by permission.

A third aspect of the leveling response is that it is whole, not partial. The body, sense, thoughts, and feelings all are shown, in contrast to computing, for example, where nothing moves but the mouth and that only slightly.

There is an integration, a flowing, an aliveness, an openness and what I call a *juiciness* about a person who is leveling. You trust him, you know where you stand with him, and you feel good in his presence. The position is one of wholeness and free movement. This response is the only one that makes it possible to live in an alive way, rather than a dead way.

In your interviews, you will undoubtedly want your respondent to engage in leveling behavior rather than the other forms of communication Virginia Satir describes. Leveling is especially important when we try to understand some of the organismic variables operating within the interview participants. Often, the only way we can know what is going on inside a person's head is through that person's voluntary self-disclosure. However, our discussion of defense mechanisms has reminded us that people are not always consciously aware of what is going on inside their heads, much less being able and willing to put it into words. One way of visualizing the problem is through the Johari Awareness Model.

THE JOHARI AWARENESS MODEL

The Johari Awareness Model—or Johari Window, as it is sometimes called —is a model of interpersonal behavior developed by *Joseph* Luft and *Harry* Ingham. Figure 4–1 is a reproduction of the basic Johari Window. The plan

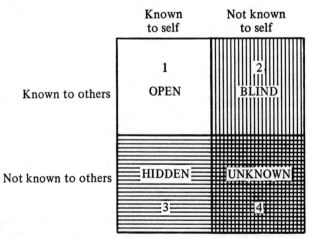

From Of Human Interaction *by Joseph Luft by permission of*
Mayfield Publishing Company. Copyright © 1969
by the National Press.

FIGURE 4–1   *Quadrants of the Johari Awareness Model*

of the Awareness Model is described by Joseph Luft (1969, p. 13) as follows:*

> The four quadrants represent the total person in relation to other persons. The basis for division into quadrants is awareness of behavior, feelings, and motivation. Sometimes awareness is shared, sometimes not. An act, a feeling, or a motive is assigned to a particular quadrant based on who knows about it. As awareness changes, the quadrant to which the psychological state is assigned changes . . . Each quadrant is defined:
>
> 1. Quadrant 1, the open quadrant, refers to behavior, feelings, and motivation known to self and to others.
> 2. Quadrant 2, the blind quadrant, refers to behavior, feelings, and motivation known to others but not to self.
> 3. Quadrant 3, the hidden quadrant, refers to behavior, feelings, and motivation known to self but not to others.
> 4. Quadrant 4, the unknown quadrant, refers to behavior, feelings, and motivation known neither to self nor to others.

The Johari Model represented in Figure 4–1 has all four quadrants of the same size. Each person's representative awareness model would have different relative proportions of the four quadrants. Some people, for instance, are willing to make a large portion of their behavior, feelings, and motivation known to others. Their quadrant 1—or open quadrant—would be portrayed as relatively larger in size than quadrant 3, the hidden quadrant.

Other people are very reluctant to share their private feelings and attitudes with others. In most of their interpersonal relationships, their awareness model would be portrayed as having a larger quadrant 3 (the hidden quadrant) as contrasted with quadrant 1. It is conceivable, however, that a relatively shy, retiring, close-mouthed person might have one or two people with whom she was considerably more open. With those few, her Johari Model would assume different proportions.

In Chapter 3, we discussed the Freudian concept of defense mechanisms, through which certain undesired aspects of a person's behavior are suppressed from consciousness. A person riddled with numerous defense mechanisms would have relatively larger second and fourth quadrants than you would normally expect to find. However, a Johari Model representing his interaction with his psychiatrist would probably contain a second quadrant relatively larger than the other portrayals.

The Johari Model is an interesting way of depicting what ordinarily happens in an interview relationship. In any interview, some information concerning one of the interview participants will be shared openly and voluntarily with the other participant. Other information—either factual or concerning feelings, beliefs, and attitudes—will be kept covert or secret

---

* From *Of Human Interaction* by Joseph Luft by permission of Mayfield Publishing Company. Copyright © 1969 by the National Press.

from the other. One interview participant may be particularly alert to visual information supplying nonverbal clues to the other participant's internal state. In certain types of interview situations, the interviewer reveals very little of him- or herself, while the respondent is expected to be very frank in expressing innermost thoughts and feelings. In other relationships, intimacy grows as, little by little, each participant shares an increasing amount of previously hidden material with the other.

Luft (1969, p. 14) lists eleven principles of change as they are related to the Awareness Model. Nine of these are particularly pertinent to the interviewing process.*

1. A change in any one quadrant will affect all other quadrants.
2. It takes energy to hide, deny, or be blind to behavior which is involved in interaction.
3. Threat tends to decrease awareness; mutual trust tends to increase awareness.
4. Forced awareness (exposure) is undesirable and usually ineffective.
5. Interpersonal learning means a change has taken place so that quadrant 1 is larger, and one or more of the other quadrants has grown smaller.
6. Working with others is facilitated by a large enough area of free activity. It means more of the resources and skills of the persons involved can be applied to the task at hand.
7. The smaller the first quadrant, the poorer the communication.
8. There is universal curiosity about the unknown area, but this is held in check by custom, social training, and diverse fears.
9. Sensitivity means appreciating the covert aspects of behavior, in quadrants 2, 3, and 4, and respecting the desire of others to keep them so.

Increase in our self-awareness and awareness of others, as well as our willingness to communicate with others, can often come about through our own efforts. Sometimes, though, we can benefit immensely from some assistance. Abraham Maslow (1971, p. 52) states:

> What the good clinical therapist does is to help his particular client to unfold, to break through the defenses against his own self-knowledge, to recover himself, and to get to know himself . . .
>
> It is a Freudian principle that unconscious aspects of the self are repressed and that the finding of the true self requires the uncovering of these unconscious aspects. Implicit is a belief that truth heals much. Learning to break through one's repressions, to know one's self, to hear the impulse voices, to uncover the triumphant nature, to reach knowledge, insight, and the truth—these are the requirements.

* From *Of Human Interaction* by Joseph Luft by permission of Mayfield Publishing Company. Copyright © 1969 by the National Press.

DIMENSIONS OF INTERACTION

A number of research studies have been conducted to identify dimensions on which interpersonal behavior can be described or measured. Robert Carson (1969, pp. 102, 112) summarizes the findings of the various research studies:

> On the whole, the conclusion seems justified that major portions of the domain of interpersonal behavior can profitably and reasonably accurately be conceived as involving variations on two independent, bipolar dimensions. One of these may be called a *dominance-submission* dimension; it includes dominant, assertive, ascendant, leading, controlling (etc.) behaviors on the one hand, and submissive, retiring, obsequious, unassertive, following (etc.) behaviors on the other. The poles of the second principal dimension are perhaps best approximated by the terms *hate* versus *love*; the former includes hateful, aggressive, rejecting, punishing, attacking, disaffiliative (etc.) behaviors, while the latter includes accepting, loving, affectionate, affiliative, friendly (etc.) social actions . . . Generally speaking, complementarity occurs on the basis of reciprocity in respect to the dominance-submission axis (dominance tends to induce submission, and vice versa), and on the basis of correspondence in respect to the hate-love axis (hate induces hate, and love induces love).

Several investigators have constructed models of human interaction using these dimensions of dominance-submission and hate-love. One of the most interesting and elaborate of these models was published by Timothy Leary in 1955. The Leary Model (sometimes designated as the Leary Circumplex) is reproduced in Figure 4–2, along with a descriptive paragraph by its author.

The investigations of Leary and other researchers have shown that certain types of behavior on the part of one person tend to elicit particular types of behavior on the part of the other person in the interaction. Leary termed these reciprocal types of interactional behavior "interpersonal reflexes." An examination of Figure 4–2 will make these interpersonal behaviors more clear. Leary mentions that people vary considerably in their repertoire of interpersonal behaviors. They also vary in the range of interpersonal behaviors they employ in day-to-day interactions, and in the ease with which they can adapt to another person's behavior to make the interaction proceed smoothly and in a satisfying manner for one or both partners.

Leary also noted the characteristics of neurotic and psychotic patients in regard to the dimensions of their personal interactions. One of the interesting characteristics he notes is the constriction of behavior to a very limited segment of ordinary interpersonal behaviors (1955, pp. 156–157):*

CLASSIFICATION OF INTERPERSONAL BEHAVIOR INTO 16 MECHANISMS OR REFLEXES†

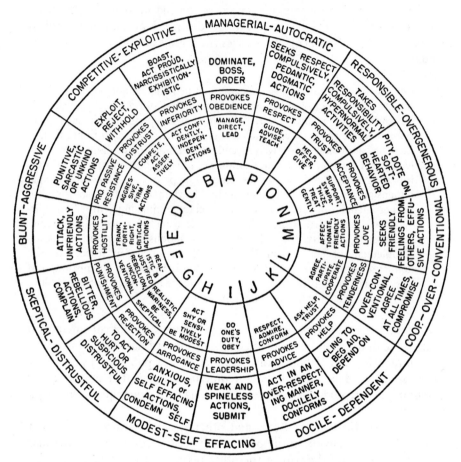

† Each of the 16 interpersonal variables is illustrated by sample behaviors. The inner circle names adaptive reflexes, such as *manage*. Proceeding outward, the next ring indicates the type of behavior that this interpersonal reflex tends to 'pull' from the other one; thus the person who uses the reflex A tends to call up in others *obedience*. These findings involve two-way interpersonal phenomena—what the subject does and what the other does in return—and are therefore less reliable than the other interpersonal categories presented in the inner and outer rings. The next circle illustrates extreme or rigid reflexes, such as *dominates*. The perimeter of the circle is divided into eight general categories employed in interpersonal diagnosis. Each of these general categories has a moderate (adaptive) and an extreme (pathological) intensity, such as *managerial-autocratic*.

From Timothy Leary, "The Theory and Measurement Methodology of Interpersonal Communication," Psychiatry 18 (1955): Copyright © 1955 by the William Alanson/White Psychiatric Foundation.

FIGURE 4–2   *The Leary Circumplex*

Each person shows a consistent preference for certain interpersonal reflexes. Other reflexes are very difficult to elicit or are absent entirely. It is possible to predict in probability terms the preferred reflexes for most persons in a specific situation. A small percentage of persons get others to react to them in the widest range of possible behaviors and can utilize a wide range of appropriate reactions. But most persons tend to train others to react to them within a narrower range of behaviors, and in turn show a restricted set of favored reflexes. Some persons show a very limited repertoire of two or three reflexes and reciprocally receive an increasingly narrow set of responses from others . . .

I have tried to stress the surprising ease with which human beings can get others to respond in a uniform and repetitive way. Interpersonal reflexes operate with involuntary routine and amazing power and speed. Many subjects with maladaptive interpersonal patterns can provoke the expected response from a complete stranger in a matter of minutes. The defiant chip-on-the-shoulder attitude; the docile, fawning passivity; the timid, anxious withdrawal—these are some of the interpersonal techniques which can produce the reciprocal reaction from the other person with unfailing regularity. Severe neurotics—defined at this level as persons with limited ranges of reflexes—are incredibly and creatively skilled in drawing rejection, nurturance, and so on, from the people with whom they deal. In many cases the "sicker" the patient is, the more likely he is to have abandoned all interpersonal techniques except one, which he can handle with magnificent finesse.

The concept of interpersonal reflexes and complementary interpersonal behaviors is helpful in understanding why we behave as we do with some people. It also can help us to understand why people often react to us in certain fashions. Carson, Leary, and other investigators believe that complementary relationships develop because they provide security and satisfaction for the participants. Investigators also point out that much of our interpersonal behavior is prescribed by the life-roles we are called on to play, or deliberately choose to play. Mothers are supposed to exhibit certain behaviors with young children, for example. College students feel obligated to behave in certain ways with their professors or supervisors. The chairman of the board can expect certain treatment from the organization's employees. The participants in an interview will often have ideas as to appropriate behaviors in the interview setting.

Eric Berne is another investigator of human interaction. He has taught us that we often seek out people with whom we can interact in our favorite manner. His system of Transactional Analysis provides a way of describing how we structure our time to engage in interactions which will help satisfy our stimulus and recognition hunger. His best-selling book on *Games People Play* (1964) describes in detail the way people structure their interpersonal relationships and encounters to achieve familiar and somehow rewarding payoffs. Berne also reminds us that our early relatively superficial contacts with new acquaintances ("rituals" and "pastimes") provide us with opportunity to size up these new acquaintances. These early contacts help us to determine whether satisfying interpersonal transactions will be possible.

Eric Berne and the transactional analysts delineate three ego states that comprise our personality. One of these ego states is the "Parent"—the state of mind of a parent figure. The Parent can be either prejudiced or nurturing, as a real-life parent can be. Another ego state is that termed the "Adult." This aspect of the personality is concerned with objective processing of environmental data and computing probabilities. The "Child" ego state functions in an archaic way with behavior typical of childhood. The Child can be either "natural"—that is, behaving as a child not under parental influence—or "adapted"—behaving as the child learned to behave in order to interact successfully with his or her caretakers.

According to the theory of transactional analysis, all social interactions (transactions) originate from one of the ego states of the initiator of the transaction (known as the agent). They are addressed to one of the three ego states of the recipient of the communication (known as the respondent). "Transactional stimulus" designates the verbal or nonverbal behavior exhibited by an individual hoping to elicit a response. "Transactional response" designates the behavior of the individual who is reacting to the transactional stimulus.

Using these transactional terms, we can then refer to interactions as complementary or crossed transactions. Glen Holland (1973, p. 375–376) describes these as follows:

> In complementary transactions, the same ego states are involved in both the transactional stimulus and the transactional response. In crossed transactions, the ego state addressed in the social stimulus is not the ego state from which the social response is forthcoming. Thus a social stimulus from Agent's Adult and addressed to Respondent's Adult would be complemented by a response from Respondent's Adult to Agent's Adult. However, a response from Respondent's Parent to Agent's Child would cross the vector of the stimulus and produce a crossed transaction.

Figure 4–3 depicts transactional diagrams for a complementary transaction and a crossed transaction. The arrows indicating the origin, direction, and destination of the behaviors are known as vectors.

Familiarity with the concepts and principles of transactional analysis can be very helpful to interviewers. Transactional diagrams of some of our particularly challenging interview experiences might indicate a possible reason why the relationship was such a stormy or unsatisfying one. Transactional analysis might also indicate why another interview was satisfying but not particularly productive. As interviewers, we can have our interpersonal reflexes triggered without realizing what has happened. We can be hooked into a respondent's games without realizing that we are perpetuating that respondent's undesirable behavior.

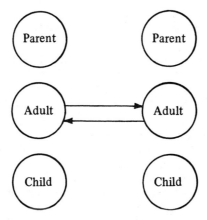

Depiction of "complementary" transaction. The "transactional stimulus" originates from Adult of Agent and is addressed to Adult of Respondent. It is complemented by a response from Respondent's Adult to Agent's Adult.

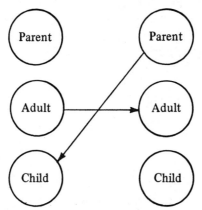

Depiction of "crossed transaction. The "transactional stimulus" originates from Adult of Agent and is addressed to Respondent's Adult. It is "crossed" by a response from Respondent's Parent addressed to Agent's Child.

FIGURE 4-3 *Depiction of Complementary and Crossed Transactions*

Complementary transactions encourage communication, while crossed transactions can cause the interaction to be frustrating and even terminated. Sometimes we may want to cross a transaction because a complementary response might be detrimental to our respondent or ourselves. For example, it can be pleasant and even satisfying to play Parent to your respondent's Child. However, an Adult to Adult transaction might be more appropriate to the purpose of the interview and the task at hand.

In commenting on this particular problem as it relates to psychotherapy, Holland (1973, p. 376) makes the following observation:

In the relationship between patient and therapist, complementary trans-actions serve to enhance rapport and positive regard. However, this com-plementarity, when nurtured and maintained by the therapist, enhances rapport at the expense of development or change in the patient, who has no motive to change or even to consider his own responses so long as the therapist maintains complementarity in their interaction. Therefore, at a certain point in the therapeutic relationship, the therapist may deliberately cross transactions as a means of stimulating the patient to become more aware of the nature of his own responses. The timing of this maneuver is determined by the time required to develop a state of rapport sufficiently strong so that the disruptive impact of the deliberately crossed transaction does not threaten the continuance of the relationship. The correct calcu-lation of the psychological forces involved is undoubtedly a skill acquired primarily through experience and may constitute an essential element in the "art" of psychotherapy.

Thomas Harris popularized many of the tenets of transactional analy-sis in his best-selling book *I'm OK—You're OK* (1969). The title of the book calls attention to another important concept: that of the "life posi-tion." The transactional analysts teach that each of us operates under the influence of the basic attitudes we hold regarding our own worth and com-petence and that of others. There are four possible life positions:

1. I'm not ok—you're ok
2. I'm not ok—you're not ok
3. I'm ok—you're not ok
4. I'm ok—you're ok

Harris states that by the third year of life, a child has decided on one of the first three positions. The experiences of the first year of life tend to lead the child to the "I'm not ok—you're ok" decision. By the beginning of the third year of life, the child has either settled into that position firmly or has changed to position 2 or 3. From then on, the child holds to the chosen position and is governed by it. Harris says that the child will main-tain that position for the rest of his or her life, unless he or she later con-sciously and voluntarily changes it to the "I'm ok—you're ok" position. Trying to figure out your own current life position, as well as the basic life positions of some of the people with whom you interact, can be a challeng-ing and interesting process.

We see that transactional analysis has much to suggest regarding the dynamics of human interaction. Understanding of the terms and concepts used can broaden our perspective concerning our relationships with others. We don't need any specialized vocabulary, though, to understand this com-ment by Eric Berne (1961, p. 133) regarding differences among human relationships:

Qualitatively, there are at least four possibilities in "a relationship": some people get along "well" together; some enjoy fighting or arguing with each other; some cannot stand each other; and some just have nothing to say to each other. These alternatives may be characterized respectively as *sympathy, antagonism, antipathy*, and *indifference*.

We have noted that several investigators of dimensions of human interaction have agreed upon the dominance-submission and hate-love dimensions. One other study will be mentioned in this regard. Myron Wish (1979) reports research done by him and fellow investigators in which five dimensions of interpersonal communication were revealed. The dimensions were obtained through multidimensional scaling analyses data obtained from subjects who rated communication episodes. The five dimensions are as follows:

Dimension 1: Cooperative vs. Competitive
Dimension 2: Intense vs. Superficial
Dimension 3: Task vs. Nontask Oriented
Dimension 4: Dominance vs. Equality
Dimension 5: Impersonal and Formal vs. Personal and Informal

There are certainly elements of dominance-submission and hate-love (unfriendliness-friendliness) dichotomies in these dimensions. However, they also provide additional ways of viewing interactions.

Any student of human interaction and interpersonal communication is likely to be astounded at the subtleties and intricacies involved. Before we conclude this section, we must remind ourselves once more that both verbal and nonverbal behavior provide clues and signals that are used to facilitate interaction. They are used to maintain some type of balance or homeostasis in our interpersonal relationships. Michael Argyle (1972, p. 261) talks about these equilibrium processes:*

There is more to interaction than individuals responding to one another— those present must behave in a highly coordinated way for there to be any interaction at all. There must be coordination over (1) the content of interaction, i.e. the nature of the activity, (2) the role-relations e.g. whether a candidate is being interviewed for a job or whether he is assessing the firm, (3) how intimate the encounter is (warm-cold), (4) the dominance relations (inferior-superior), (5) the emotional tone (anxious, serious, happy, etc.), (6) the proper sequence of acts (questions should lead to answers, gestures should be responded to), and (7) the timing and amounts of speech (who shall talk most, and when). To work out a pattern of

* Michael Argyle, "Non-Verbal Communication in Human Social Interaction," in *Non-Verbal Communication*, ed. by Robert A. Hinde. New York: Cambridge University Press, 1972, p. 261. Reprinted by permission.

interaction between two or more people where such synchronising occurs requires some rapid group problem-solving; this problem-solving is carried out mainly by the use of minor NV [nonverbal] cues. Small attempts may be made at intimacy or dominance, with careful study of how the other reacts, so that these can be withdrawn if his reaction is too negative. To sustain the interaction a sufficient supply of rewards must be delivered to the other in order to keep him in the situation. Encounters often begin with a period of informal chat, the purpose of which is probably to enable some degree of synchronising to be established. Little information is exchanged during this period, but the interactors are able to emit signals conveying interpersonal attitudes and other NVC [nonverbal communication] and to begin building up an equilibrium.

We can summarize the requisites of effective face-to-face communicative interaction as follows:

Both people have to be present.
Each person has to attend to the other person.
Each person has to be able to impart information in some fashion.
Each person must be able to receive and attach some meaning to the transmission of the other.
Each person has to be willing to prolong or continue the interaction.
Each person has to be willing to talk and willing to listen—and willing to share at least a portion of him- or herself.
Each person must be willing to communicate what he or she expects from the interaction.
Each person must be willing to adapt his expectations to what the other person expects.
Each person has to be willing to cooperate in achieving any agreed-upon purpose of the interaction.

And still, at any moment, the interaction may be disrupted or destroyed because of the behavior of one or both of the participants.

UTILIZING BASIC INTERVIEWING PRINCIPLES
IN GROUP INTERACTIONS

Our discussion up to this point has focused on the interaction between two people—a dyadic relationship. We may often find ourselves in interview situations that involve more than one other person. Let us consider briefly another setting for interpersonal communication: the small group. The basic principles we have discussed thus far for working with individuals are also applicable to working with groups.

The principles we have learned about *organismic variables* in individuals will be useful in understanding the members of groups. Groups are, after all, composed of individuals. The physical and emotional states and needs of each person in the group—their life positions, defense mechanisms, coping strategies, and so on—will affect the behavior and thus the atmosphere of the group and the direction in which the group may go. According to Joseph Luft (1969, p. 81–82):*

> Groups can be arranged in terms of values, goals, or functions or whatever it is that binds members to each other. There is no limit to the kinds of properties or classifications by which groups may be described . . .
>
> In some ways, groups behave like individuals, e.g., talkative families or disorganized communities or biased clubs. Just about any quality ascribed to an individual may be ascribed to a group . . .
>
> Groups develop lives of their own and ways of their own. An important group quality is the extent to which the members are aware of the behavior and feelings of the group as a whole.

Some of the factors we find in one-to-one interviews are similar for groups as well. Both group and individual interactions have a beginning, a middle, and an end. Both group and individual interviews can serve any of the five purposes of interviewing: information getting, information giving, expression and exploration of feelings, problem solving, or planning for future action.

Many of the verbal interactions in a group are dyadic or one-to-one interchanges between two participants; however, the particular combination of participants may vary from moment to moment. Alfred Benjamin (1978) describes the major emphasis in a dyadic helping relationship as *intrapersonal*, whereas in a group more emphasis is placed on *interpersonal* relationships (1978, p. 8–9):

> The group tends to emphasize *social*, while the dyad emphasizes *personal*, competence. It must not be overlooked, however, that when the group leader and a member interact in a helper/helpee relationship within the group, a dyadic situation has been created for the moment that may benefit not only that particular member but, vicariously, the entire group.

Whether we are communicating in a dyadic relationship or in a group, we still have messages being sent through channels. However, instead of one sender/receiver, there are many sender/receivers. This does present a more difficult situation for the group leader because the reactions of *all* the members must be observed. The group leader must be alert to verbal and nonverbal cues from all the group members and must be able to make rapid decisions regarding how to respond to these observed cues. The size of the group is an important variable in this regard: the larger the

* From *Of Human Interaction* by Joseph Luft by permission of Mayfield Publishing Company. Copyright © 1969 by the National Press.

group the more cues, or potential stimuli. For example, proxemic cues can provide important information. The members of a group may find themselves—or choose to be—at varying distances from one another and from the group leader.

Benjamin (1978) provides some suggestions that may be helpful when making decisions about the size and composition of a group, assuming there is a choice in the matter. He points out that the smaller the group, the more active the leader will have to be. He suggests that the beginner work with groups of ten or more. When the focus of attention is on the group members, the group should be smaller than when the focus is on persons external to the group. According to Benjamin, it is best not to ask total strangers to meet with people who are well known to each other. He feels that such a practice immediately establishes two subgroups. He also suggests that it is helpful to include a few talkers in the group to cut down on long periods of silence. However, he recommends that the number of aggressive members be limited.

It is important to realize that as the size of the group increases, each additional member increases the complexity of interactions. This multiplies the possible subunits into which the participants may combine. Interactions within the group may be on verbal and/or nonverbal levels. The larger the group, the more possibilities there are for game playing. There are also more triggers of interpersonal reflexes, and more possibilities for splits, alignments, scapegoating, and power struggles. Some group members may require more individual attention because of the special or singular nature of their problem. Some people may actually be unable to function in a group.

A. C. Filley (1970, p. 432) describes some of the factors that may affect individual group members:

> Variables related to changes in group size include the individual's capacity to "attend" to differing numbers of objects, the effect of group size on interpersonal relations and communication, its impact on problem-solving functions, and the "feelings" that group members have about proper group size and the nature of group performance. To be sure, the effects of these variables are interrelated . . .
>
> Each member in a committee attends both to the group as a whole and to each individual as a member of the group. There seem to be limits on a person's ability to perform both of these processes—limits which vary with the size of the group and the time available.

The interviewer who has had considerable experience with individuals will find this experience invaluable when working with groups. However, success with individuals does not guarantee success in groups. Benjamin (1978) suggests that the neophyte professional first become familiar with and secure in dyadic relationships, as this will ease the transition to working with groups.

Particular styles of interviewing used with individuals may lead to different results in group settings and therefore may require modification.

We may find a nondirective approach very successful in working with individuals. When we apply this approach to a group, however, we may find we are not providing the leadership needed to prevent the group from floundering. On the other hand, a leader with a strong, directive style may inadvertantly suppress responses of group members that could be helpful and meaningful. Harold Zelko (1973, p. 424) discusses the activities of a group leader:

> *Leadership* involves the major functions of guiding, stimulating, and controlling the discussion. To accomplish these, a leader should have certain essential qualities including an attitude of open-mindedness and group-centeredness rather than being dogmatic and self-centered. He must be pleasant and animated in his manner, tactful in handling comments of members, a good listener, and a good speaker. These do add up to a big order.

R. Wayne Pace and Robert Boren (1973, pp. 328–329) provide a more extensive outline of leadership-role behavior:*

> Although by no means exhaustive, an outline of major leadership-role behaviors might appear as follows:
>
> 1. Structures initial communication patterns by focusing the attention of the group on the individual members rather than on the leader; avoids moving into a central or pivotal position in the network and tries to minimize power discrepancies.
> 2. Facilitates an open, permissive, communicative mood by exhibiting high trust and willingness to respond nondefensively to comments from all group members.
> 3. Encourages independence of group members by refusing to accept responsibility for their decisions; firmly places decision-making responsibility on group members.
> 4. Calls attention to issues over which group members seem to be disagreeing and which need to be resolved, without centralizing responsibility for reducing anxiety or tension.
> 5. Enacts specific functional task-roles, such as initiator, information-and-opinion seeker, coordinator, energizer, and procedural technician; but avoids trying to influence others to play any particular role.
> 6. Takes on a variety of maintenance roles, such as encourager, harmonizer, gatekeeper, and follower—all of which foster cohesiveness; accepts disagreements and conflict as problems to be confronted and analyzed.
> 7. Participates in decision-making processes to achieve consensus, but approaches quickly attained unanimity with some suspicion because the strength of decision making stems from unity born out of diversity.

---

* From *The Human Transaction* by R. Wayne Pace and Robert R. Boren. Copyright © 1973 by Scott, Foresman and Company. Reprinted by permission.

8. Encourages a systematic and creative analysis of problems and solutions in both accomplishing the task and keeping the group functioning, realizing fully that no single problem-solving format works best for every group.

There are, of course, often advantages to group interactions as compared to dyadic interactions. The group leader, for example, can work with more than one person at a time; this can be an efficient use of both time and energy. A topic may be brought up by one member of the group that is pertinent to—but unspoken by—other members. A potential wealth of information and possible solutions to problems is available within a group's membership. A skillful group leader can assist in tapping this valuable source.

When we are able to choose between individual interviews or group meetings, it is helpful to keep in mind the goals to be accomplished, the characteristics and needs of the people involved, and our own particular needs and capabilities. In the following chapters, the focus of our discussion will be on one-to-one relationships. However, you will be able to apply many of the techniques and suggestions in group interactions as well.

REFERENCES

Argyle, Michael. "Non-Verbal Communication in Human Social Interaction." In *Non-Verbal Communication*, edited by Robert A. Hinde, pp. 243–269. Cambridge: Cambridge University Press, 1972.

Benjamin, Alfred. *Behavior in Small Groups*. Boston: Houghton Mifflin Co., 1978.

Berne, Eric. *Transactional Analysis in Psychotherapy*. New York: Grove Press, 1961.

Berne, Eric. *Games People Play*. New York: Grove Press, 1964.

Carson, Robert. *Interaction Concepts of Personality*. Chicago: Aldine Publishing Co., 1969.

Filley, A. C. "Committee Management: Guidelines from Social Science Research." In *Readings in Interpersonal & Organizational Communication*, 2d ed., edited by Richard C. Huseman, Cal M. Logue, and Dwight L. Freshley, pp. 430–446. Boston: Holbrook Press, 1973.

Harris, Thomas. *I'm OK—You're OK*. New York: Harper & Row Publishers, 1969.

Holland, Glen. "Transactional Analysis." In *Current Psychotherapies*, edited by Raymond Corsini, pp. 353–399. Itasca, Illinois: F. E. Peacock Publishers, 1973.

Leary, Timothy. "The Theory and Measurement Methodology of Interpersonal Communication," *Psychiatry*, 18 (1955), 147–161.

Luft, Joseph. *Of Human Interaction*. Palo Alto, California: National Press Books, 1969.

Maslow, Abraham H. *The Farther Reaches of Human Nature*. New York: The Viking Press, 1971.

Milton, John. "Paradise Regained." In *The Poems of John Milton*, edited by John Carey and Alastair Fowler, pp. 1063–1167. London: Longmans, Green and Co., 1968.

Mosak, Harold H., and Dreikurs, Rudolf. "Adlerian Psychotherapy." In *Current Psychotherapies*, 2d ed., edited by Raymond Corsini, pp. 44–94. Itasca, Illinois: F. E. Peacock Publishers, 1979.

Pace, R. Wayne, and Boren, Robert. *The Human Transaction*. Glenview, Illinois: Scott, Foresman and Co., 1973.

Pavlov, Ivan P. *Conditioned Reflexes: An Investigation of the Physiological Activity of the Cerebral Cortex*. Translated and edited by G. V. Anrep. Oxford University Press: Humphrey Milford, 1927.

Satir, Virginia. *Peoplemaking*. Palo Alto, Calif.: Science and Behavior Books, 1972.

Skinner, B. F. *The Behavior of Organisms: An Experimental Analysis*. New York: Appleton-Century-Crofts, 1938.

Skinner, B. F. *Science and Human Behavior*. New York: The Macmillan Co., 1953.

Wish, Myron. "Dimensions of Dyadic Communication." In *Nonverbal Communication*, edited by Shirley Weitz, pp. 371–378. New York: Oxford University Press, 1979.

Zelko, Harold P. "When You Are 'In Conference'." In *Readings in Interpersonal & Organizational Communication*, 2d ed., edited by Richard C. Huseman, Cal M. Logue, and Dwight L. Freshley, pp. 421–429. Boston: Holbrook Press, 1973.

Preparing for the Interview

LONG-TERM PREPARATION FOR INTERVIEWING

We have seen in the preceding chapters how each participant in a relationship or interaction comes to that particular event as a unique blend of physical characteristics, habitual reaction patterns, emotional tendencies, beliefs, and value systems. Each of us differs in regard to past experiences, the nature and extent of our education, and in our specialized training. We differ from others also in the availability and efficiency of our coping behavior and in the nature and arousal of our defense mechanisms. Patterns of need frustration and preferred methods of meeting those needs vary. All of these factors influence our readiness and performance in any current situation. In a very real sense then, we have been preparing all our lifetime for the encounters of the present. However, in terms of ongoing processes that contribute more specifically to our effectiveness as interviewers, several activities come to mind.

First of all, there are the formal requirements to prepare for a particular field or profession. These can include undergraduate and graduate study, practical field experiences, and perhaps an apprenticeship or internship under the supervision of a fully qualified member of the profession. Nowadays, continuing education is encouraged and even mandated in many professions. The information explosion has made it difficult for any professional to keep abreast of all the current findings. To insure that professionals maintain up-to-date information, continuing education units are required in many fields in order to maintain licensure or certification.

Continuing education courses, conferences, and workshops are relatively formal, structured activities that enable us to learn about different theories and techniques of interviewing and counseling and to observe distinguished professionals applying and using these techniques. Classes often provide opportunities for interviewing practice or role playing and for valuable feedback through review of our performance via video- and/or audiotape. Learning even one new approach or technique that can be used in our own professional or day-by-day activities can make a continuing education experience worthwhile.

Our ongoing preparation for interviewing can also involve relatively unstructured activities, such as reading professional publications and contemporary journals, as well as current magazines that highlight problems facing people of all ages and all cultures. The whole realm of observing and relating to people in all walks of life is an important one. The more we become familiar with lifestyles and cultures different from our own, the more likely we are to understand the various people with whom we interact. Observation and contact with a variety of people can have many positive outcomes, for there are many nonprofessionals who are naturally effective leaders or interviewers. We can learn a great deal from watching someone who gets along well with people or with whom we ourselves feel comfortable and at ease. We can also learn from situations in which we feel uncomfortable, rebuffed, or humiliated, if we are willing to try to analyze them with objectivity after they occur.

A final important consideration in our ongoing preparation for interviewing involves our willingness to examine our own interviews closely in order to learn from them. It is not necessary to be enrolled in a formal course or workshop to analyze our interviews. It can be helpful to have someone serve as a supervisor, to listen in on interviews and jot down comments or suggestions. However, we can accomplish a lot on our own by taping an interview, listening to it afterward, and evaluating it in light of the purpose and whether or not that purpose was fulfilled. We can analyze the extent to which we used techniques that we consider desirable. We can become aware of certain things we did during the interview that seemed to work for us. We can note other things that seemed to hamper forward movement or arouse the respondent's defenses. Additional ways of evaluating interviews will be discussed in coming chapters, but a word of caution is in order. Looking more closely at our performance and effectiveness in interviews involves the risk of being disappointed or threatened by some of what we learn. We may find ourselves forced to consider change that can involve additional risk, as well as time and energy. Hopefully, the rewards that come with increased effectiveness will justify the effort.

SHORT-TERM PREPARATION FOR
SPECIFIC INTERVIEWS

We come now to what we might call short-term preparation—things that need to be done immediately prior to conducting an interview. One of the first things to consider is scheduling the interview. We know that we have to allow adequate time for a satisfactory interview, but we also know that that isn't always easy to do. The type of contact and the general purpose of the interview is going to affect the time we allow for it. It also makes a difference whether the interview must be a one-time-only meeting or whether additional meetings can be scheduled if required.

In some work settings, the time segments for interviews are predetermined and relatively fixed. The psychiatrist's "fifty-minute hour" is notoriously inflexible. In some agencies, a half-hour allowance for certain types of intake interviews is routine. Classroom teachers may allow just fifteen minutes per parent at the school's twice-yearly open house. People vary considerably in regard to their specifications and their strictness of scheduling. It might be very appropriate in some circumstances to ask someone to "drop by between twelve and twelve-thirty on the twenty-third," or to "come over next Monday and we'll hash this out; I'll be in my office all afternoon." At other times and in other circumstances a definite appointment met exactly to the minute may be a necessity.

Even though our appointment scheduling can be relatively flexible, a problem sometimes arises when a person has requested an interview with us but has given no indication of the reason for the request. Then it is difficult to know if we've allowed sufficient time for it. We just have to make the best of that. Sometimes when a person requests an appointment time, we can get some idea if the time we have allotted is appropriate. Perhaps a student will say: "Oh, it will just take a few minutes. I have the program for that conference I'm attending next month and I'd like to get your opinion on which of the workshops I should register for." Or perhaps a troubled parent may hesitate and say: "Well, I don't know. How much time do you have? This could take me quite a while to explain the situation thoroughly." The time allotment is still our responsibility, but at least we have some idea regarding the nature of the appointment.

It is important that both participants be aware of any time limitations on the interview. It can be unfortunate to give a client or colleague the impression that there is a limitless amount of time and then have to say —just as he or she begins to discuss the heart of the matter—"I'm sorry, I have another appointment scheduled in two minutes." Mentioning the time allotted for the interview can occur at the time of scheduling or early in the actual meeting. Such comment is particularly important if the time available is limited and the limits are inflexible. One last remark about scheduling appointments: be sure to give yourself an occasional breather between appointments if at all possible. This is especially important if you do a lot of interviewing in the course of a day. It is often necessary to make a few notes regarding the interview just completed, or to make a phone call, or just to clear your mind a bit before moving to another new and no doubt challenging interaction.

Another area of preparation to consider is the interview setting. The setting can be considered as furnishings—an aspect of nonverbal communication discussed in Chapter 2. Anyone who has ever been forced to conduct an important conversation with someone while various people traipsed in and out of the room and phones rang or buzzers sounded, recognizes the need for privacy. If this need is not met, the interview will suffer. The same seems to be true regarding the physical comfort of the interview setting. People vary in their sensitivity to physical settings. Some find themselves distracted or actually upset if the interview room is either excessively cluttered or inordinately barren. Others don't seem to be affected by physical setting, provided that there is a place for both participants to sit, that the air is relatively pleasant and fresh, and that it is possible to hear each other without acute discomfort or strain. Nowadays, the issue of smoking versus nonsmoking comes up occasionally. We know that a smoker can be very uncomfortable in a setting where smoking is not permitted. On the other hand, if one person smokes and the other is a nonsmoker, this can also cause discomfort. Each of us has to handle this issue in our own way.

Settings certainly vary. Sometimes settings are actually stage set to emphasize the relative importance of one of the participants or to symbolize the roles which the two participants play. Some offices of corporation executives resemble a throne room in which the head of state receives a lowly subject. The office may contain a massive desk and regal chair for the executive, contrasted with small straight chairs available for people who come in for an audience, usually on command. There is no doubt that an office such as this sets the scene for inequality of participation. There are other people (census or poll takers, for example) who find themselves interviewing people in many different settings and circumstances—perhaps in a kitchen, or by a swimming pool, or in the corridor of a tenement, or in a barnyard. An unusual or humble setting does not necessarily make for an inferior interview, providing both participants can still devote the necessary time and attention to the interaction.

Each of us probably has our own conception of what constitutes a range of acceptable interview settings. Some interviewers feel strongly that an office must be completely uncluttered and neatly arranged to insure an effective conference or interaction. It has been our experience that, first and foremost, an interviewer has to be comfortable in his or her own office. It is probably best to keep our office pleasantly neat but not so unnatural that we don't recognize it as our own. Yet, we cannot be oblivious to the fact that others' impressions of us are derived, at least in part, from our apparent efficiency, organization and neatness. As we have said, some people seem to be particularly oblivious to settings; others are particularly sensitive to them. We are never quite sure where our respondent will fall in those categories.

Roger Kroth and Richard Simpson (1977, pp. 74–75) discuss office settings in relation to the conduct of parent conferences. They feel that:

> professionalism implies an atmosphere where those items in clear view of the parents are related to the task at hand. Thus it is imperative that you

screen the room before the conference begins so that non-task-related items can be discarded or moved out of easy view. Items such as lunch remains, crossword puzzles, controversial posters or hangings, and other materials that may take away from the professional atmosphere or which could potentially impede the conferencing process should not be in easy view of parents.

The authors go on to say that sometimes there are items in the immediate environment that may be professionally appropriate but that may also be distracting or anxiety-provoking for the parents. In this regard, they cite the following example (1977, p. 75):

> . . . the mother of a hyperactive child who was being evaluated for a research project became extremely upset over a book entitled *Nine Rotten Lousy Kids* (Grossman, 1972) that was lying on the desk. The book title was quite upsetting for this parent, and was the apparent stimulus for a reaction which did not aid in the establishing of rapport. Probably if the book had been on the bookshelf with other materials, the mother would not have responded as she did. However, since that particular book was off the shelf, even though it had nothing to do with the parent or the child, the mother assumed that it was pertinent to her son's condition.

In summarizing our minimum requisites for an interview setting, we might list a pleasant, quiet room; chairs of relatively equal dimensions to foster equality of participation; and perhaps a desk or table nearby in case notetaking or tape recording is desired. Basically, most of us are concerned with the setting only insofar as it does not interfere with the interview and is consistent with our personality and work style.

We might remind ourselves that a pleasant interview setting includes some minimum personal requisites of neatness and hygiene. Beyond the essentials of bodily cleanliness and nonoffensive breath, lies the whole realm of personal grooming and "dressing for success," which is the subject of many recent publications. We might also remind ourselves that certain styles of dress—our particular furnishings—may lead to our being stereotyped by the respondent. We may thus arouse some of his or her attitudes and feelings customarily directed to that stereotype. For instance, we may think that wearing a white laboratory coat enhances our professional image whereas the respondent may have negative reactions to such a potent reminder of medical crises. A woman executive in an ultra feminine dress may give a party impression rather than the business-like impression she desires.

Another aspect of preparation for an interview is the consideration of the interview participants and any special needs they present. For instance, it may be necessary to provide a wheelchair or other assistance to an aged or physically handicapped person. We may even find it necessary to shift our actual interview setting if the planned meeting room is inaccessible to our respondent.

Not only must we consider physical needs; we must also consider possible communicative barriers. If, for example, we know that the person communicates minimally or not at all in our language, we must arrange for an interpreter, either accompanying the person or provided by us. This applies as well to respondents who communicate via manual communication such as American Sign Language. Sometimes, we overlook the fact that there can be a language barrier even when both participants ostensibly speak the same language. We are referring to use of vocabulary and sentence structure that is inappropriate to the communication level of the respondent—either too complex or too simple—and to the inordinate use of professional or trade jargon.

In addition to possible language barriers, we must consider possible barriers related to cultural differences. This is where our knowledge of other cultures can serve us in good stead. Much of our discussion of nonverbal communication in Chapter 2 applies here. For example, maintaining eye contact is considered desirable in many cultures and yet can be insulting in others. Researchers in the fields of kinesics (the study of facial expressions and body movements) and proxemics (the study of space usage and territoriality) have explained how an individual from one culture can unwittingly offend someone from another culture. For example, we may find ourselves backing off from another person who continues to move closer as both of us try to establish what we feel is a socially appropriate and comfortable conversational position.

There are no doubt times when an interviewer is thought of as being cold, and a respondent is thought of as being forward, merely because of cultural communicative stances. Nan Lin (1973, p. 76) summarizes some of the research findings in this area:

> In each culture, then, there is a set of defined distances, each of which identifies the proper stance for a particular situation and a particular participant. An erroneous use of the distance either leads to the bewilderment and embarrassment of the participants (Garfinkel, 1964) or induces immediate disengagement from the exchange and discourages future exchange (Felipe and Sommer, 1966).

Another consideration in planning for the interview is the inclusion or exclusion of potential interview participants. In some circumstances, the presence of others may be legally required or professionally prudent. For instance, in the educational setting, planning a handicapped child's special program requires the presence of a number of school personnel as well as the child's parent. In a judicial setting, many an accused person refuses to answer possibly incriminating questions without the presence of his or her attorney. On the other hand, there are times when we may wish deliberately to exclude a person from the interview. A youngster may feel much freer to discuss a troubling situation privately with his physician or pastor rather than in the presence of one or both parents. A relatively new university instructor may be much more comfortable hearing the results of student evaluations of her first semester's teaching in a private interview with one diplomatic member of the departmental Hiring, Retention, and Tenure Committee rather than in the presence of the entire group.

Short-term preparation can also include collection of information prior to the interview. One of our considerations concerns data regarding the respondent that we may wish to know before we meet for the first time. People vary in their philosophy regarding this. For instance, in interviewing a job applicant some employers feel it is wise to review the applicant's employment history and references before the appointment. Other employers place a heavy emphasis upon first impressions and do not wish to be influenced unduly by what psychologists refer to as "selective perception." In selective perception, our preconceived notions regarding somebody actually affect the way we view that person for the first time.

There are times when we must go into an interview with information that the respondent will expect us to have. If a parent has asked for an appointment to discuss a child's current academic problems, we certainly would want to have some idea of the child's last report card and the teacher's evaluation. If we have the unpleasant task of firing someone, especially in these days of legal ramifications, we would be wise to collect precise evidence to substantiate our claim that the employee's work record has not been satisfactory. Sometimes, the information that we bring to an interview may reflect circumstances that could influence the interview outcome and that we feel should be shared with the respondent. It may be important to know, for example, that for approximately one hundred people seeking acceptance to a company's management training program, there is only one opening available.

In addition to the prior securing of information, the preparation or collection of actual materials or equipment to be used during the interview may be helpful in certain circumstances: color swatches for an interior decorator; brochures and calculator for a tax annuity consultant; x-rays for the physician who is going to describe needed surgery to a patient; a bible and appropriate devotional materials for a minister who is going to visit a hospitalized parishioner; a bag of dirt for the door-to-door vacuum cleaner sales representative. Pen and paper for note taking is standard equipment for most interviewers; and for many interviewers interested in analyzing the interview or their interviewing techniques, a well-functioning tape recorder falls into the same category.

METHODS OF RECORDING INTERVIEW INFORMATION

Many times, it will be necessary to remind ourselves and perhaps others of what transpired in an interview. Some important information may be obtained from our respondent that must be included in a file or report. Some crucial beliefs, attitudes, or behaviors may be mentioned that will be significant areas to consider in problem solving or planning for action or in further discussion. Plans may be made or decisions reached that we do not trust ourselves to remember in detail without a written reminder. Topics that evoke emotional responses, particularly negative or ambivalent feelings, may be highly significant in determining the direction and development of a helping interview.

Personal note taking is often the method of choice for recording interview information. Note taking is so much a part of business and professional life these days that it is readily accepted by the vast majority of interview participants. The procedure ordinarily does not affect the progress of the interview unless the interviewer becomes so involved in the process that it interferes with attending to and communicating with the respondent.

We have to face the fact that, even with a personal shorthand system of note taking, we can record only the barest essentials of what transpired in the interview. When it comes to analyzing in detail the dynamics of the interview or our personal performance in it, it is preferable to rely on a more objective, extensive method of recording. Some of these methods, which admittedly vary in objectivity, include: a secretary taking minutes, an observer with a behavioral checklist, a court reporter, an audiotape recorder, a videotape recorder, and a movie camera.

With any of these recording methods just listed, the interview participants may feel more self-conscious, apprehensive, or uncomfortable than with occasional note taking. In most interviews, however, the participants tend to relax and pay less attention to the recorder as they become more engrossed in actual conversation and interaction. It has been our experience that the interviewer plays an important role in bringing this about. His or her attitude toward the recording procedure influences the respondent's attitude and consequently the degree to which these procedures impinge upon the interview. The more unobtrusive a recording procedure, the easier it is to ignore. Ethical considerations dictate that the respondent's permission be obtained prior to initiating the recording. This permission does not automatically erase feelings of uneasiness and apprehension, however. Apropos of this point, Alfred Benjamin (1974, p. 62) makes the following statement:*

> But how about the interviewee? How will he react to being taped? I am firmly convinced that after the first few minutes he will not react to it at all for he will no longer notice it. It is my belief that, as a matter of ethics, the fact the interview is being taped should not be concealed. If I tell him that it is my custom to record interviews to learn from them afterwards and

---

* Alfred Benjamin, *The Helping Interview*, 2d ed. Boston: Houghton Mifflin, 1974, p. 62. Reprinted by permission.

that the tape will be kept confidential, he will usually not object. He will not be uneasy unless he feels that I am.

Our comments to the respondent regarding the interview recording system should be straightforward and brief. One approach might be: "If it's all right with you, I'm going to tape record this session so I can go over it and make notes regarding it. I find that much more satisfactory than trying to take many notes while we're talking. Of course, the tape is for my use only." If our intention is to share the record of the interview with anyone else, this should be made clear to the respondent. Gerald Corey (1977, p. 221) develops this point with particular reference to counseling and psychotherapy:*

> . . . information obtained from therapeutic relationships should be discussed with others for professional purposes only and with persons who are clearly related to the case. In my opinion, it is good practice to inform the client early in the relationship that you may be discussing certain details of the relationship with a supervisor or colleague. This practice can also apply to the use of a tape recording. There are times when a therapist may want to share a tape recording of a particular session with a colleague simply because the therapist wants to confirm his or her perspective by obtaining another viewpoint of the dynamics of the therapeutic relationship. The possibility of consultation should be discussed with the client so that the client knows that it may occur.

Our discussion thus far has focused on the value of various recording procedures from the interviewer's standpoint. Alfred Benjamin (1974, p. 62) points out that respondents can also profit from a recording of the interview.**

> I am very impressed with the benefit interviewees can derive from listening to their own tapes. . . The interview is a serious, purposeful conversation carried on between two people. By listening to his own interview, the interviewee often acquires a deeper appreciation of its seriousness, clarifies for himself his purpose in it, and obtains much significant insight. As far as I know, we tend to use taped interviews solely to promote our own learning. They can, I am suggesting, promote learning on the part of the interviewee as well.

Many interviewers rely to a large extent on audiotape recording of interviews because of the economy, availability, and portability of the necessary equipment. However, we should not overlook the tremendous ben-

* From *Theory and Practice of Counseling and Psychotherapy*, by G. Corey. Copyright © 1977 by Wadsworth, Inc. Reprinted by permission of the publisher, Brooks/Cole Publishing Company, Monterey, California.
** Alfred Benjamin, *The Helping Interview*, 2d ed. Boston: Houghton Mifflin, 1974, p. 62. Reprinted by permission.

efit that we can derive from at least an occasional videotape recording of one of our interviews. The opportunity to scrutinize and analyze both verbal and nonverbal behavior provides us with a wealth of information for insight and personal growth.

PLANNING FOR INTERVIEW ANALYSIS

Your first experience in listening to an audiotape recording of one of your interviews can be an eye-opening (and possibly ego-deflating) experience. The stumblings and stammerings, the "ers," the "you-knows" and incomplete sentences, not to mention the times you rudely interrupt your respondent in the middle of a sentence, can be discouraging. And, of course, if you have never even heard a recording of your *voice*, that in itself can be traumatic. Once you have become reconciled to the characteristics of normal conversation, your attention can be directed to the content and dynamics of the interview, as well as to analysis of your performance. For analysis purposes, you may prefer to prepare—or have prepared—a typed verbatim transcription of one of your interviews.

There are numerous ways of reviewing an interview tape or transcription to learn from it and to benefit from it. You may want to review the session in the light of its primary purpose or objective and whether or not that purpose was accomplished. You might ask yourself some of the questions proposed in Chapter 1 as pertinent to your goals or your respondent's goals for the interview. You might want to review the interview in the light of various aspects of communication (discussed in Chapter 2), forces motivating human behavior (discussed in Chapter 3), and dimensions of interaction (discussed in Chapter 4).

Another way of analyzing an interview involves focusing attention on various portions of the interview: the beginning (or opening), the main portion (or body) of the interview, and the closing portion (denouement or wrap-up) of the session. In Chapters 6, 7, and 8, we will talk more about these various aspects of an interview and offer some suggestions for your consideration and possible adaptation. The possible importance of every minute of an interview cannot be overlooked or underestimated.

REFERENCES

Benjamin, Alfred. *The Helping Interview.* 2d ed. Boston: Houghton Mifflin Company, 1974.

Corey, Gerald. *Theory and Practice of Counseling and Psychotherapy.* Monterey, California: Brooks/Cole Publishing Company, 1977.

Felipe, N. J., and Sommer, R. "Invasions of Personal Space," *Social Problems,* 14 (1966), 206–214.

Garfinkel, H. "Studies of the Routine Grounds of Everyday Activities," *Social Problems,* 11 (1964), 225–250.

Grossman, H. *Nine Rotten Lousy Kids.* New York: Holt, Rinehart and Winston, 1972.

Kroth, Roger L., and Simpson, Richard L. *Parent Conferences as a Teaching Strategy.* Denver: Love Publishing Company, 1977.

Lin, Nan. *The Study of Human Communication.* New York: The Bobbs-Merrill Company, 1973.

6

The First Minutes of the Interview

The importance of the first impressions in any encounter is generally acknowledged. It has been said that "you never get a second chance to make a first impression." In an interview, the first few minutes can be crucial because they set the tone for the remainder of the interaction.

Certain interviewer objectives are appropriate for the opening portion of an interview. These include:

Making the respondent comfortable and at ease

Obtaining preliminary perceptions that may influence the conduct of the interview

Obtaining permission to tape record the session or to permit observation of the session

Alerting the respondent to any time limitations or procedural restrictions of which he or she may not be aware

Establishing a working relationship with the respondent

Creating an atmosphere that will facilitate the type of interview you wish to conduct

Each participant will quickly form perceptions that will influence the role each plays in the interview. These perceptions will also influence the direction of the interview. Certain stereotypes may be activated on the part of either participant in response to visual clues before any words are spoken. In fact, stereotypes triggered visually may actually influence the first words. As words are then exchanged, each participant may confirm, expand, reject, or modify the possible stereotypes, and additional impressions are formed.

Any prior information either participant has about the other may also affect the first minutes of the interview. In his discussion of possible elements that can influence one person's acceptance of another, Aristotle noted the importance of *ethos*—the positive effects of a fine reputation upon the perceptions humans have of one another.

During the first minutes of the interview, you may become aware of circumstances that will influence the way you are going to conduct the interview. The person may be obviously affected by alcohol or other drugs; he or she may appear ill or seriously upset; some visual or hearing or language difficulties may become apparent; the interviewee may be accompanied by another person who insists on being included in the interview; or the person you expected to interview may be replaced by someone else. It is even possible that under some circumstances you may feel continuation of the interview is unwise.

The respondent may also be in for a surprise during the first few minutes of the interview. Your sex, your age, your face, even your furnishings, may be much different from what your respondent had envisioned or hoped for. The respondent's reaction may not be apparent to you, or it may be communicated by verbal or nonverbal means. You have the option of responding to or ignoring the reactions that are conveyed to you. Basically, the intensity of the reaction will most likely influence your choice.

SOCIAL AMENITIES—SMALL TALK

The first exchange in an interview usually consists of social amenities—greetings, welcome, and what is generally considered to be small talk. This can be a relatively neutral period in which both participants have the opportunity to size up the other. The small talk in which you or your respondent engage can reveal information regarding your philosophy of interviewing and your role as an interviewer. These amenities, for example, can be directive or nondirective, or they can encourage prolongation of nonpertinent small talk. Contrast the following three interviewer remarks, all referring to the client's coat:

> "You're too hot in that heavy coat! Take it off and I'll put it over here for you."
> "Would you care to take your coat off? Perhaps you'd be more comfortable."
> "Oh yes, you can put your coat there. What an unusual coat! I saw one like it when I was in Hong Kong last year. Did you buy it there?"

You may recall that in previous chapters we discussed verbal and nonverbal behaviors that can indicate perceptions of status and power relationships and can involve dimensions of dominance or submission as well as of friendliness or hostility. An interviewer will want to be aware of possible consequences of his or her behavior in the first few minutes of the interview. The interviewer may wish to make the first few minutes a relatively neutral period so that nervousness or anxiety may be allayed.

Some interviewers, on the other hand, feel that the anxiety the client experiences can be used to move from nonpertinent discussion to the basic purpose of the interview. Gerald Corey (1977, p. 47) states that "anxiety is a basic human characteristic. It is not necessarily pathological, for it can be a strong motivational force toward growth." Corey (1977, pp. 47–48) notes the counseling implications of anxiety:*

> Many clients enter a counseling office with the expectation that the counselor will remove their suffering or at least provide some formula for the reduction of their anxiety. The existentially oriented counselor is not, however, devoted to mere removal of symptoms or to anxiety reduction per se. In fact, the existential counselor does not view anxiety as undesirable. He or she might work in such a way that the client might experience increased levels of anxiety for a time.
>   ... If clients experienced no anxiety, their motivation for change would be low. Anxiety can be transformed into the needed energy for enduring the risks of experimenting with new behavior.

An interviewer may be unwilling to leave the safety of small talk, and spend an unusual amount of time in irrelevant discussion. It goes without saying that prolonging small talk makes less time available for the actual work of the interview. The prolongation of small talk may be an indication of nervousness on the part of either or both interview participants.

Nervousness or anxiety in the interview situation may be caused by any of the following:

Fear of an unknown, strange situation
Fear of self-disclosure
Fear of being overwhelmed by aroused emotions
Fear of being judged evil or inadequate
Knowledge of personal or communicative inadequacies

A small amount of nervousness at the beginning of an interview is natural and to be expected. Often it can best be handled by ignoring it or by acknowledging it with a brief comment or two.

* From *Theory and Practice of Counseling and Psychotherapy,* by G. Corey. Copyright © 1977 by Wadsworth, Inc. Reprinted by permission of the publisher, Brooks/Cole Publishing Company, Monterey, California.

STRUCTURING

An unnatural degree of nervousness or anxiety may have to be dealt with more directly by the interviewer. The interviewer may choose to prolong small talk in an effort to relax the respondent; the interviewer may verbalize his or her observations and encourage the respondent to discuss any fears or anxieties he or she may have regarding the interview; or the interviewer can, without verbal reference to the respondent's nervousness, attempt to allay the respondent's feelings of anxiety by letting him or her know what is to come. This orientation to the interview situation and procedures is called structuring.

Several examples of structuring taken from the first few minutes of interviews are listed below. In all of the interview excerpts contained in this and following chapters, the letter *I* will be used to designate the Interviewer, and *R* will designate the Respondent.

Example A

I: The purpose of this interview is so I can get to know Patrick better through you. I'm interested in anything you can tell me about your son.

Example B

I: We will have about a half hour to talk so maybe we could begin with you describing the problem as you see it.

Example C

I: I was happy to make the arrangements for this appointment, Mrs. Brown. You mentioned over the phone that you needed some advice concerning the establishment of a scholarship fund. Tell me more about it, and I'll see if I can be of help.

Let us take a closer look at these examples to note how these variations in structuring are designed to influence the course of the interview. In Example A, the interview has apparently been initiated by the interviewer. The interviewer's statement is directing the discussion to the subject of the respondent's son, Patrick. The statement acknowledges that the respondent is able to give worthwhile information regarding her son. It focuses on the respondent's perceptions of the son and their relationship. It enlists the cooperation of the respondent in what, at this point, appears to be an information-getting interview. It gives the respondent complete flexibility to discuss whatever she wishes about Patrick.

In Example B, the structuring actually indicates the time limitation within which the interview must take place. It is not clear who initiated the interview. The interview focuses on a *problem* and assumes that the respondent will be able to define and verbalize the problem. It seems to be a prelude to working toward a solution of the problem but does not give an indication as to who will assume the major responsibility for the solution. Again, it focuses on the respondent's perceptions and invites the respondent to verbalize those perceptions. The setting of the time limit may also invite the respondent to make the best use of the time by quickly getting to the major aspects of the problem.

In Example C, we get the feeling immediately that the appointment was respondent-initiated. The interviewer may or may not be the appropriate person to accomplish the purpose the respondent has in mind for the meeting. At this point, it appears that the basic purpose of the interview may be information-giving on the part of the interviewer concerning specific questions raised by the respondent. The interviewer is willing to listen, and to provide needed information if it is available to him. The implication here is that this interviewer may not have the answers and the respondent may have to talk to someone else.

In all three examples, structuring signals the end of small talk as far as the interviewer is concerned and invites the cooperation of the respondent in getting to the business at hand.

There is, of course, a limit to what can be contained in one or two sentences. Further orientation to the interview situation or procedures can be accomplished by additional statements. These three examples are certainly appropriate ways to structure an interview, particularly if the interviewer wishes to give considerable latitude to the respondent concerning the material to be discussed as the interview begins. There are other interview situations in which such latitude would be inappropriate. Consider the following instances:

Example D

I: We need to answer all the questions on this form in order for you to get food stamps.

Example E

I: O.K., Smith; I go to lunch in five minutes and I want this settled once and for all! Take down these three points and make sure that when you put them in your report this time, they're *accurate*.

Example F

I: Mrs. Danbury, you have gained five pounds again this week. In our session today, we are going to review your diet plan and make some adjustments.

As with our earlier examples, all three of these instances of structuring could be appropriate in certain circumstances. In Example D, it is obvious that a certain procedure must be accomplished before a desired outcome can be achieved. If obtaining food stamps is the major purpose for the interaction, it would be foolish to delay completing the required paperwork. In Example E, we get the feeling that a deadline is imminent and the boss's patience is at an end. She is making it clear to the employee that attention and cooperation are expected and that the session will be completed quickly. The counselor in Example F has determined what the major topic of discussion in the interview will be and appears to be forestalling any distraction maneuvers on the part of the client.

In these latter three examples, the interviewer structures the interview more precisely and narrows the focus. This results in a more obvious degree of directiveness on the interviewer's part. If we consider the dimensions of interactions discussed in Chapter 4, we can note some apparent differences in our six interview examples. In regard to a dominance-submission dimension, only Example E gives any real indication of the relative status of the interviewer as compared to the respondent. The other examples can be considered neutral on that dimension. This is also true in considering a friendliness-unfriendliness dimension. Only Example E gives any indication in its verbal content of unfriendliness on the part of the interviewer.

In summary, structuring can serve to accomplish one or more of the following:

To influence the behavior of the respondent

To move the interview from nonpertinent small talk to the business at hand

To indicate to the respondent what the interviewer considers an advisable way to proceed

To indicate the perceptions of the interviewer regarding the roles of the interview participants

To alleviate fears of the unknown by previewing the general nature of the session

To allay the "structure hunger" of both participants

Often, the purpose of an interview is understood by both participants even before the interview begins. In that case, a comment or two of structuring on the part of the interviewer will lead the participants directly into the main business of the interview. In other interviews, the purpose or purposes may be vague and not clearly defined. In these cases, discussion may be necessary for the participants to determine the purpose of the interview. The time involved to establish the purpose of the interview and the *modus operandi* will vary greatly from interview to interview.

THE USE OF QUESTIONS

Our discussion of the first minutes of verbal interaction has thus far concerned the types of utterances we designate as nonpertinent small talk and structuring. Several other types of utterances are likely to appear within the first few minutes of an interview. To facilitate exchange of information and establish the purpose of the interview, questions are frequently asked. James Lahiff (1973, p. 334) makes the following comment:

> While it is inaccurate to regard an interview as nothing more than a series of questions and answers, it is the questions which largely determine the route to be followed to the goal as well as how many detours may be encountered enroute. The lack of adequate planning of questions by the interviewer is one of the most frequent causes of inferior interviews.

Let us look more closely now at various types of questions found in interviews. One type of question is the indirect question, which does not require question mark punctuation when it is transcribed, yet encourages discussion of a particular topic. Several examples of Indirect Question are as follows:

I: I wonder what it is like to have three children all in different schools.
I: I'm interested in knowing how much income you've derived from your telephone stock.
I: It must be at least a two-hour drive for you to get to the office.

Another type of question is the direct question, which employs the traditional interrogatory inflection—in American English, a rising intonation at the end of the utterance. We have found it useful to designate two types of direct questions: Direct Question I requests a specific, externally verifiable statistic and Direct Question II requests information, opinion, or conclusion other than an externally verifiable statistic. Examples of Direct Question I are as follows:

I: How old is Beth?
I: What company did you work for last?
I: Who was the doctor who did your surgery last year?

Examples of Direct Question II are the following:

I: Does your husband spend much time with you?
I: What do you think was the reason for that?
I: How is Erica doing in dressing herself now?

To clarify the difference between these sets of examples, you will note that the three examples of Direct Question I would be answered in exactly the same way regardless of who was supplying the information for the respondent, that is, Beth's birthdate, the name of the company, and the surgeon's name. The examples for Direct Question II, on the other hand, could be answered in a number of different ways depending on who was supplying the information. The respondent's interpretation of the question depends upon his or her perceptions of the words used and of the situation being discussed. For example, the response to the question "Does your husband spend much time with you?" requires interpretation of what is involved in "spending time" and of what constitutes "much time." Similarly, the other two examples listed under Direct Question II also call for a personal opinion that cannot be externally verified.

Two terms that are sometimes used to differentiate between Direct Question I and Direct Question II are the terms "closed" and "open," respectively. Alfred Benjamin (1974, p. 67) makes the following comments regarding open versus closed questions:*

> The open question is broad, the closed question narrow. The open question allows the interviewee full scope; the closed question limits him to a specific answer. The open question invites him to widen his perceptual field; the closed question curtails it. The open question solicits his views, opinions, thoughts, and feelings; the closed question usually demands cold facts only. The open question may widen and deepen the contact; the closed question may circumscribe it. In short, the former may open wide the door to good rapport; the latter usually keeps it shut.

Alfred Benjamin is writing particularly about helping interviews, in which it is often advisable to encourage the client to express personal opinions and judgments rather than limiting the conversation to externally verifiable statistics. Depending on the purpose of the interview, the choice of either type of question may be appropriate.

Another type of question sometimes found in interviews is known as the leading question. This can be defined as a direct question that indicates a specific answer is expected or preferred. Some examples of Leading Question are the following:

> I: You're getting a little old to apply for a job like this, aren't you?
> I: You have been taking your medicine regularly, haven't you?
> I: Shouldn't a mature, capable woman be able to balance a budget without help?

Because a leading question gives the impression that a specific answer

* Alfred Benjamin, *The Helping Interview*, 2d ed. Boston: Houghton Mifflin, 1974, p. 67. Reprinted by permission.

is expected or preferred by the interviewer, there is always the possibility that the respondent will give that answer whether or not it reflects his or her actual opinion or the actual facts of the situation being discussed. We must remember that the respondent has a need for the interviewer's approval and respect, and may not wish to jeopardize the relationship by disagreeing with the interviewer. Also, the respondent may not perceive his or her role in the interview as one which permits such disagreement. At times, the use of a leading question may not significantly alter the direction of the interview, but at other times it may prevent an honest expression of opinion or fact by the respondent that might trigger a very significant discussion. After these comments, you will surely think twice before you use leading questions, won't you?

Occasionally, an interviewer will ask more than one question before the respondent has a chance to answer. A common term for two questions asked in immediate succession is "double question." We distinguish between two types of double questions: Double Question I, which we define as "asking two questions, the second question identical or almost identical with the first"; and Double Question II, which we define as "asking two questions, the second question dissimilar to the first, or either question incomplete." Examples of Double Question I are as follows:

I: When is Betty's birthday? When is her birthday?
I: Are you going to tell her? Are you going to let her know?
I: How can you know? Well, how can you know that?

Examples of Double Question II are:

I: Where is the school? Is it far from here?
I: How are you feeling today? Did the nurse change the bandages yet?
I: Have you two discussed how you will handle your finances? Where are you living now?

Note how in these latter three examples, the respondent has to shift gears mentally to formulate answers to both questions. In the examples of Double Question I, a mental shift is not required—both questions call for the same answer. Because of the mental shift required in processing two dissimilar questions, the respondent will frequently answer only one. It is interesting to note that when a first question in a Double Question II is an open question, the second question is often closed. The second and third examples of Double Question II illustrate this.

Some interviewers will ask three or more questions before the respondent has an opportunity to answer any. We designate such instances as "bombardment" and define the term as "asking three or more questions of any type within one utterance." Examples of Bombardment are as follows:

I: I'd like to hear more about John's speech pathologist. What days
   does John go to the clinic—still the same as last year?

I: Do you still read to him? Are you home at night when he's there?
   What hours do you work?

I: Do you ski or paint or go to those singles bars?

Note that in all three of these examples, the interviewer is asking the
respondent to process three distinct questions. This can be true even
though all the questions are asked within a single sentence, as seen in the
third example. Note that the first example is considered Bombardment
(three or more questions) because the first sentence is an indirect question.
We have pointed out that when an interviewer uses Double Question II, a
respondent will frequently answer only one. This situation can also occur as
a result of bombardment. In some instances, the respondent will appear
to have no trouble processing two queries, but will respond to bombardment
with a look of puzzlement or a blank expression. At times the respondent
may say something such as "What was that?" or "What was the question
again?", or answer one of the questions and ignore the others.

   Thus far, all of the examples given for various types of questions have
been spoken by the interviewer. It is likely that the respondent will also
ask questions during the first few minutes of an interview. These questions may be concerned with the interview procedures, with the interviewer's
qualifications or experience, with possible interview outcomes, and so forth.
Consider the following examples:

R: How much time do we have for our meeting today?

R: I'd be interested in knowing where you received your training and
   how long you've been in practice.

R: You won't let anyone else listen to this tape recording, will you?

The way an interviewer answers such questions can reflect his or her
philosophy regarding the interview and the role of the participants, and
other organismic variables. Consider, for instance, the various ways in
which an interviewer could respond to the question "Where did you receive
your training?" The interviewer could respond in a matter-of-fact way with
"At South-State Medical School," in an apologetic fashion with "We
didn't have much money so I went to a small medical school near home,"
or with an attempt to focus on the respondent's motivation for asking the
question: "That's an interesting question. Why do you want to know?" It
has been our experience that it is best to answer the respondent's questions
in a matter-of-fact fashion. In any case, it behooves the interviewer to
listen to any question asked and to respond in a manner that will not
be detrimental to the developing relationship and yet not take an inordinate
amount of the available time.

INTERVIEW EXCERPTS

Up to this point, we have identified several types of utterances that may occur in the first few minutes of an interview: nonpertinent small talk, indirect question, direct questions I and II, leading question, double questions I and II, bombardment, and structuring. As noted, structuring is a particular type of information provided by the interviewer to orient the respondent to the interview situation and procedures to be followed. Throughout the interview, both participants will be providing other data, designated generally as "information."

Let us now examine excerpts of the first few minutes of three interviews, identifying the utterance types we have discussed.

Interview Excerpt 6–1

1. I: Hello, Karen. It's nice to see you again. (offering his hand). — (nonpertinent small talk)

2. R: Hello, Mr. Wixler. (shaking his hand) — (nonpertinent small talk)

3. I: I haven't seen your parents for some time. How are they? — (nonpertinent small talk including direct question II)

4. R: Fine, thank you. I told Dad that I had an appointment with you today and he told me to say "hello" to you. They're looking forward to seeing you at the golf tournament next week. — (nonpertinent small talk)

5. I: Karen, even though I've seen you many times at your folks' home I don't feel I know much about you. I understand you're looking for a job and I'll be happy to help you if I can. — (transition from nonpertinent small talk to information relating to purpose of interview)

6. R: I understand, Mr. Wixler. I appreciate your seeing me. I would never want to take advantage of your friendship with my parents, but I think I definitely do qualify for a position here at the bank. I'd like to be considered, but I certainly wouldn't want to be hired if I weren't qualified. — (information)

7. I: Fine, that's understood then. Tell me something about your background as it relates to banking and investment service. — (structuring)

8. R: Well, I graduated with honors from State   (information)
        University two years ago. My degree is in
        business, specializing in accounting and
        foreign trade.

9. I: And what have you done since your   (direct question II)
        graduation?

10. R: I've been working for the Dalray Company   (information)
        as an accountant, but it's a very small
        company and there's not much opportunity
        for advancement.

11. I: Are you an employee there now?   (direct question I)

12. R: Yes.   (information)

The tenor of this conversation is a cordial one. The preliminary small talk leads quickly into the general purpose of the meeting, facilitated by the fact that the participants were already acquainted—an apparently pleasant acquaintance—and by the interviewer's use of structuring. The interviewer is straightforward in his reminder that their acquaintance does not insure employment, and the respondent is quick to acknowledge that fact. In reference to the interaction dimensions of friendliness-unfriendliness and dominance-submission, both participants in this excerpt would be classified as equally friendly. The interviewer plays the more dominant role.

In this interview excerpt, there is reference to a particular aspect of social amenities, that of handshaking. Certain nonverbal behaviors are customarily part of social amenities. One of these is handshaking. The purpose and implications of handshaking vary among cultures and in different situations. Some investigators attach a great deal of significance to the handshake; they note, for example, who offers the hand first, the degree of firmness in the handshaking, the extent of time spent in shaking the hand, who withdraws first, and the verbal and nonverbal accompaniments. In an article describing the function of the ceremony of the handshake, Deborah Schiffrin (1974, p. 190) comments that the handshake

> . . . is in a class of rituals that serves to provide brackets around a spate of activity, an occasion, undertaken by several participants, a "meeting", "gathering", and "encounter". The handshake marks the beginning of the activity, or the period during which there is an increase in joint access. It also can be used at the end of such periods, as an indication that the access gained will extend over the following period of separation, and not be limited to that one occasion.

Eric Berne (1972, p. 8) has the following things to say regarding his perceptions of the handshake as it relates to his psychiatric practice:*

---

* Berne, Eric. *What Do You Say After You Say Hello?* New York: Grove Press, 1972, p. 8. Reprinted by permission of Random House.

Many patients who come to a psychiatrist for the first time introduce themselves and shake hands when he invites them into his office. Some psychiatrists, indeed, offer their own hands first. I have a different policy in regard to handshakes. If the patient proffers his hand in a hearty way, I will shake it in order to avoid being rude, but in a noncommittal fashion, because I am wondering why he is being so hearty. If he offers it in a way which merely suggests that he considers it good manners, I will return the compliment in such fashion that we understand each other: this pleasant ritual will not interfere with the job to be done. If he proffers it in a way which indicates that he is desperate, then I will shake it firmly and reassuringly to let him know that I understand his need. But my manner when I enter the waiting room, the expression on my face and the position of my arms, indicates clearly enough to most newcomers that this amenity will be omitted unless they insist upon it. This is intended to establish, and usually does establish, that we are both there for a more serious purpose than to prove that we are good fellows or to exchange courtesies. Mainly, I do not shake hands with them because I do not know them, and I do not expect them to shake hands with me, because they do not know me; also, some people who come to psychiatrists object to being touched, and it is a courtesy to them to refrain from doing so.

Nancy Henley (1977), in her book on nonverbal communication, and Leonard Zunin (1972), in his discussion of the first four minutes of a variety of human contacts, briefly trace the history of handshaking. They make some interesting comments on sexual and cultural variations on the custom. In his work with people who are trying to improve their relationships with others, Zunin conducts contact workshops. He states (p. 106):

We shake hands thousands of times in a lifetime, and it is unfortunate that most of us get little or no feedback on whether or not others like or dislike our handshake. In Contact workshops I direct large groups of individuals to circulate, shaking hands at random, being aware of eye contact and grading the handshakes immediately. On a scale of one to five, one is the least meaningful and five is the most warm, friendly, sincere—even enticing—handshake-eye contact combination. After shaking hands and exchanging numerical ratings, people discuss the reasons for their opinions. Many are astounded because they have always felt their handshake was adequate and may exclaim, "A dozen people rated it 'one' or 'two.'" From this feedback, people have the opportunity to develop a more effective handshake that better conveys real feelings, while learning to size up others.

Interview Excerpt 6–2

1. I: Thank you, Mr. Mason, for agreeing to meet with me today. As I mentioned to your wife over the phone, I'm very concerned about Paul's frequent absences from school and the effect that this is having on his grades.

(nonpertinent small talk and information concerning reason for arranging interview)

2. R: Yes, when my wife told me about your call   (information con-
        I made arrangements to keep this appoint-   cerning reaction to
        ment even though it was very short notice.   request for interview)
        I gathered there wasn't much flexibility
        as to when you would be available.

3. I: Well, I'm here all day but my mornings are   (information)
        taken up with student problems that
        can't wait. This was the only free time I
        had until next Thursday.

4. R: I had an important committee meeting   (information and
        that had to be cancelled so I could meet   direct question II)
        with you. Just what is it that you people
        can't handle?

5. I: I wouldn't say that we can't handle it, but I   (information and
        thought that you would at least want to   bombardment)
        be informed about Paul's problems. Do
        you know how many times he has been
        absent this year? How many times he's cut
        class? Are you aware of our school policy
        regarding truancy?

6. R: I've found in my many years of teaching as   (information)
        a professor at the University that if classes
        are interesting, the students attend.

7. I: Well, I've found that it doesn't matter how   (information)
        interesting the classes are if a student is as
        emotionally disturbed as your son seems
        to be.

8. R: That's the first time that I've heard that   (information)
        unwillingness to attend classes is a sign of
        emotional disturbance. I don't think that a
        school counselor is in any position to
        make that diagnosis.

9. I: You obviously aren't aware of the training   (information)
        that's required to qualify for a school
        counseling credential. I certainly am quali-
        fied to recognize emotional difficulties in
        children—*and* to recognize defensiveness
        and denial on the part of parents.

10. R: This is getting us nowhere! I plan to talk to   (information)
        the principal about this! (leaves abruptly)

As we read this second interview excerpt, we are struck by the buildup of hostility. Small talk and structuring are noticeably absent. The opening statement made by the interviewer touches on her reason for arranging the interview. When the parent (respondent) makes a negative comment regarding the appointment, the interviewer responds with defensiveness. The interaction continues to deteriorate to the point that the respondent terminates the interview. On the basis of this information, we would rate this as an unfriendly interaction, with both participants trying to achieve the dominant role.

Jack Gibb (in Trent, Trent, and O'Neill, 1973, p. 319) has made the following comment regarding the buildup of defensive behavior in an interview: "The defensive behavior of one person tends to create similarly defensive postures in others; and, if unchecked, the ensuing circular response becomes increasingly destructive."

Interview Excerpt 6–3

1.	I: Hello, Mrs. Karsen, I'm Mike Sterns. Thank you for letting me come to talk to you today.	(nonpertinent small talk)
2.	R: Oh yes, Mike. Come on in. I hope you didn't have too much trouble finding our house.	(nonpertinent small talk including indirect question)
3.	I: Oh no, it didn't take long at all. Your directions were fine.	(nonpertinent small talk)
4.	R: That's good. Tell me again—just what do you want to talk to me about?	(nonpertinent small talk and direct question II)
5.	I: I'd like your help. As I explained on the telephone, I work for the Association for the Handicapped. We're preparing a pamphlet for parents of young children who are multiply handicapped. I'm interested in any comments and suggestions you may have that you feel would be helpful to these parents. Our director told me that she has really been impressed with your daughter, Lisa, and the way you have raised her. She suggested that I talk to you.	(information and structuring)
6.	R: Well, that's nice. It's taken me years. It wasn't like I was born like this, believe me. Yea, Lisa and I at one time were almost, well I don't want to say enemies, but I did too much for her and I was killing her with kindness. When Lisa was eleven, we ran into a lot of trouble, and we all went for therapy.	(information)

7.	I:	What kind of things were emphasized?	(double question II)
		How often did you meet?	
8.	R:	We met once a week.	(information)
9.	I:	What did you do in therapy?	(direct question II)
10.	R:	Well, it was mostly you do the talking. It	(information)
		was mostly he listened. I didn't have much	
		to say so he just sat there and looked at	
		me. Well, the first year I cried.	
11.	I:	Your therapist didn't object to that, did he?	(leading question)
12.	R:	Oh, no. The poor man would sit and fall	(information)
		asleep, and he'd say he wasn't asleep, but I	
		know he was and I would just cry. And the	
		second year I started to talk, and the	
		third year we started getting someplace. So	
		I went three years altogether.	

Our third excerpt of an interview opening appears to be a friendly interaction. Both participants are neutral on the dominance-submission dimension. The respondent terminates the preliminary small talk by asking a question concerning the interview purpose. The interviewer replies with pertinent background information and structuring. The structuring gives the parent considerable leeway to respond with information she feels is suitable.

AID TO ANALYSIS

Respond to the following as the items relate to the first few minutes of an interview you have conducted recently:

1. Was the physical setting appropriate?
2. Did the respondent make any mention of the physical setting?
3. Did the respondent make any mention of my personal appearance?
4. Did the respondent indicate that he or she had formed any opinions of me or my agency prior to our meeting?
5. Did I make a taped recording or have observers present? If so, did I obtain the respondent's permission?
6. Did I use structuring to inform my respondent of what I hoped we would cover during the interview or how I hoped we would proceed?
7. Did I discourage a prolongation of small talk?
8. If the respondent initiated the interview, did I ascertain his or her reasons for the request?
9. What words did I use that the respondent seemed to have trouble understanding?

10. Did I respond with any stereotyped behaviors or comments?
11. What nonverbal behaviors did I notice on the part of the respondent? Did I mention them?
12. Am I satisfied with the relationship we established in the first minutes?
13. Did I use the opening minutes productively?

REFERENCES

Benjamin, Alfred. *The Helping Interview.* 2d ed. Boston: Houghton Mifflin Co., 1974.

Berne, Eric. *What Do You Say After You Say Hello?* New York: Grove Press, Inc., Bantam Books, 1972.

Corey, Gerald. *Theory and Practice of Counseling and Psychotherapy.* Monterey, Calif.: Brooks/Cole Publishing Co., 1977.

Henley, Nancy. *Body Politics: Power, Sex, and Nonverbal Communication.* Englewood Cliffs: Prentice-Hall, 1977.

Lahiff, James. "Interviewing for Results." In *Readings in Interpersonal and Organizational Communication,* 2d ed., edited by Richard C. Huseman, Cal M. Logue, and Dwight L. Freshley, pp. 332–353. Boston: Holbrook Press, 1973.

Schiffrin, Deborah. "Handwork as Ceremony: The Case of the Handshake," *Semiotica,* 12 (1974), 189–202.

Trent, Jimmie D.; Trent, Judith S.; and O'Neill, Daniel J. *Concepts in Communication.* Boston: Allyn and Bacon, 1973.

Zunin, Leonard. *Contact: The First Four Minutes.* New York: Ballantine Books, 1972.

The Body of the Interview

The interviewer has two major responsibilities during the body of the interview: maintaining effective interaction and working toward the interviewing goal. As the interview progresses into the major portion of the interaction, the interviewer will be employing much of the information that has been discussed in previous chapters. There are, in addition, other basic techniques that can be used effectively in any type of interview. These are mostly concerned with maintaining effective interaction and encouraging respondent participation.

MAINTAINING EFFECTIVE INTERACTION

Definition of Active Listening

One technique that effective interviewers use most routinely is that of "active listening." Active listening implies four characteristics:

1. Attentiveness to the speaker
2. Desire to understand the speaker's viewpoint
3. Willingness to suspend judgment or evaluation of the ideas or feelings expressed by the speaker
4. Willingness to check your understanding by putting into words what you feel the speaker has conveyed

109

Carl Rogers (1961, pp. 331–332) describes active listening or listening with understanding as:*

> ... to see the expressed idea and attitude from the other person's point of view, to sense how it feels to him, to achieve his frame of reference in regard to the thing he is talking about.

This definition of active listening is also an acceptable definition of "empathy."

Thomas Gordon (1977, p. 72) emphasizes that active listening conveys acceptance rather than evaluation of the respondent's statements:

> Active Listening communicates, "I hear what you're feeling," neither agreement or disagreement, no judgment whether the feelings are right or wrong. The listener only conveys acceptance that the feelings exist. This kind of acceptance can be very disarming because people so seldom encounter it.

The rarity of truly satisfying communication is discussed by Dean Barnlund (1968, pp. 613–614):

> Incomplete communication between people seems to be the rule rather than the exception. It is said that if in a lifetime one meets even two or three persons with whom he feels completely free and completely understood, he is fortunate. The list of complaints is endless: people do not take time, do not listen, do not try to understand, but interrupt, anticipate, criticize, or disregard what is said; in their own remarks they are frequently vague, inconsistent, verbose, insincere, or dogmatic. As a result, people often conclude conversations feeling more inadequate, more misunderstood, and more alienated than when they started them ...
>
> Interpersonal communications are destructive when they leave participants more vulnerable than before to the strains of future interactions; they are neutral when they add information but do not affect underlying values or attitudes; they are regarded as therapeutic when they provoke personal insight or reorientation, and when they enable persons to participate in more satisfying ways in future social encounters.

Roger Kroth (1975) categorizes listeners into four general categories: (1) passive listeners, (2) active listeners, (3) passive nonlisteners, and (4) active nonlisteners. He (1975, p. 38) describes them as follows:

> There would appear to be four types of "listeners" in a communication interaction. One is the passive listener, the individual who attends to the speaker primarily on a nonverbal level. The active listener seems to work at helping the speaker clarify his thoughts, attitudes, and feelings about the

---

* Carl R. Rogers, *On Becoming a Person*. Boston: Houghton Mifflin, 1961, pp. 331–332. Reprinted by permission.

subject being discussed. The passive non-listener does not attend to messages on a feeling level, although she may be able to repeat words that were spoken during the interview. The active non-listener appears to take "equal time" in any conversation, possibly with material unrelated to the basic discussion. On a more difficult level the active non-listener may pick at the threads of a conversation and seemingly avoid the central issue being discussed.

Techniques for Active Listening

There are a number of techniques for active listening interviewers can use in maintaining effective interaction. These include the *mm-hm* response, restatement of content, reflection of feeling, and use of silence.

Mm-hm Response

In any conversation, one of the most frequent behaviors is the *mm-hm* response. The *mm-hm* response indicates that a listener is tuned in and following the conversation. Sometimes the *mm-hm* response is nonverbal, such as a nod of the head. At other times, it will take the form of an actual utterance: "Mm-hm, I see," "That's interesting," "You don't say," or "Yes, I see what you mean." Research on communication indicates that these verbal and nonverbal *mm-hm* responses serve to regulate the give-and-take of conversation by signaling to the speaker that he or she still has the floor. When we first listen to tape recordings of our interviews, we are often struck by the frequency with which *mm-hm* responses are used by both participants. If you don't *hear* many *mm-hm* responses, chances are the participants were using nonverbal equivalents.

Restatement of Content

One of the four characteristics of active listening is willingness to check our understanding by putting into words what we feel the speaker has conveyed. Sometimes we will want to respond to the factual content of the speaker's message; at other times we will attempt to verbalize feelings expressed by the speaker. Repeating or summarizing actual material or data expressed verbally by the respondent is "restatement of content." An interviewer may wish to restate essential content to confirm his or her understanding of what the speaker has said. One example is this interchange between an architect and his client:

R: We've decided that we'd like to have two bedrooms on the second floor with a connecting bath, plus the master bedroom and mother's room.

I: I see. You want four bedrooms altogether on the second floor.

At other times, an interviewer may repeat or summarize a portion of the speaker's message in order to direct the interview along particular lines. This technique is used in the following interchange between a speech/language pathologist and the parent of a child who stutters. You will note that the mother includes a great deal of information in her utterance but the speech/language pathologist restates only that portion referring to interruptions. It would be expected that the mother would respond with further explanations of the family's tendency to interrupt the child.

> R: One difficulty we have in the family is interruptions with . . . you know, everyone tends to interrupt to say what they want to. Suddenly you're aware of this small person who's been trying to say something. We've tried to be more aware and let him finish what he's trying to say and he's made some progress. He went through therapy at school which was sort of haphazard. He might go twice within one week and then go two weeks with none. He went to one summer session after first grade for six weeks.
>
> I: You say you've been trying to let Johnny say what he wants to without interrupting him so much.

Reflection of Feeling

We have noted that sometimes an interviewer will respond to the factual content of a speaker's message. At other times, an interviewer will attempt to verbalize current emotions expressed either verbally or nonverbally by the respondent. This is called "reflection of feeling." Let us contrast two possible responses that might be made by an interviewer—the first involves restatement of content and the second involves reflection of feeling. The responses are to the following statement made by a patient in his doctor's office.

> R: I'm still getting those awful back pains. I think I'll have to go in for that surgery you told me about. I've been doing those exercises regularly but there's been no change. And the traction last summer was worthless. I hate to think about being away from my job again. My boss is getting fed up with me and my problems.

The doctor might respond to this by restating the content:

> I: So everything we've tried so far hasn't helped, and you're thinking we should contact the orthopedic surgeon.

or she might respond by reflecting the feeling she detects:

> I: You feel that surgery is the only hope, but you're worried about taking more time off work.

In either case, the conversation will no doubt continue along the same general topic. But in the first instance, it is likely to focus on the proposed surgery—the factual content of the exchange. If the feelings are reflected, it is likely that some time will be spent discussing the patient's anxiety concerning his work situation.

The dictionary is filled with many words describing emotional states. Basically, however, we can classify feelings as positive, negative, or ambivalent. These categories of expressed feelings can be defined as follows:

> *Positive Feelings:* a currently felt emotion within the category commonly designated as "pleasant" (for example, expressions of happiness, pleasure, satisfaction, pride, delight, tenderness, desire, love, and joy)
>
> *Negative Feelings:* a currently felt emotion within the category commonly designated as "unpleasant" (for example, expressions of unhappiness, dissatisfaction, annoyance, irritation, frustration, anger, disgust, rage, fear, and grief)
>
> *Ambivalent Feelings:* expression within one utterance of both positive and negative emotions directed toward the same person, object, idea, or activity

An example of each of these feeling categories follows:

Positive Feeling

R: I'm thrilled with the idea of going on a vacation.

Negative Feeling

R: I'm so mad at that sales person I feel like writing a letter to the president of the company.

Ambivalent Feeling

R: I'm happy with my new job but all that responsibility is frightening.

You may recall that in Chapter 2 we mentioned research indicating certain universal emotional responses, including happiness, sadness, fear, anger, disgust, and surprise. One—happiness—is clearly positive. Four—sadness, fear, anger, and disgust—are all classified as negative emotions. The surprise response can be triggered by both pleasant and unpleasant situations and must be followed by another emotional expression before we can identify the response as either positive, negative, or ambivalent.

Emotions can, of course, be indicated verbally or nonverbally. We have already noted that messages sent both verbally and nonverbally can be congruent or incongruent. Sometimes, verbally expressed feelings are contradicted by the nonverbal clues we observe. Imagine, for instance, the tensed jaw, controlled facial expression, and forced attempt at pleasantness of a wife saying, "Pleased to meet you" as she is introduced to a woman she strongly suspects is her husband's current mistress.

In an interview, we want to be alert to both verbal and nonverbal expressions of feelings. We also want to try to identify towards what or whom the feelings are directed. Sometimes the feelings the respondent evidences are vague and without an expressed target—as in the following examples:

R: I'm really disgusted with the way things are going.
R: I feel like crying most of the time.
R: I don't know why, but I feel really great today.

An interviewer may reflect these feelings as follows:

I: You really wish things were different than they are.
I: You seem very depressed.
I: You sound on top of the world.

Or the interviewer may wish to help the respondent identify more particularly what is causing the emotion. An appropriate question may be used to accomplish this, as in the following examples:

I: What in particular is making you feel disgusted?
I: Can you tell me more about that?
I: Any special reason?

Both restatement of content and reflection of feeling are important interviewing techniques. They enable us to check whether or not we have actually understood what the respondent is trying to tell us. These techniques force us to be alert and maintain active listening because we must offer verbal feedback concerning what we think we are hearing and what we think the respondent is feeling. When using restatement of content and reflection of feeling, it is important to note the reaction of the respondent. We need to know if our restatement or reflection was on target. The following interview excerpt shows how one interviewer made use of restatement of content and reflection of feeling.

Interview Excerpt 7–1

The interviewer in this interview excerpt is a counselor in a women's re-entry program.

1. R: You reach a point where you just feel sort of
      trapped and you don't know what to do next—
      and I'm at that point now.

2. I: It's hard to find a new direction for yourself. (restatement of content)

3. R: We all like security.

4. I: Of course.

5. R: And—I don't feel very secure right now. I don't
      know what the future holds. I think if I knew, I
      would *really* feel a whole lot better about life.

6. I: You'd like to have some direction—something to (restatement of content)
      work toward.

7. R: Right. I really have to have a sense of myself. (agreement)
      Life is just passing me by.

8. I: You feel that you have to do something *now*, (reflection of feeling)
      that if you don't get out of this rut, you're going
      to be lost.

9. R: That's it. I've let too much time go by already. (agreement)
      I've got to make some plans.

10. I: OK. Let's talk about that.

Sometimes our restatement of content is off-target. The respondent
who disagrees with our restatement will usually attempt to clarify his or her
meaning for us. An example of this is apparent in the following excerpt.

Interview Excerpt 7–2

This interview excerpt was conducted by the director of a rest home.

1. R: My wife insisted that I talk with you today. She
      says that my father can't live with us anymore and
      we have to make other arrangements.

2. I: So you and your wife want to arrange for your (attempted
      father to come into our facility. restatement of content)

3. R: No, I'm not in favor of it at all. I'm just here (disagreement)
      because my wife is pushing me. I don't think it's
      right to put old people away in a rest home.

4. I: Our guests certainly are provided with all possible
      comforts. Our food is top quality, and we have a
      fine recreation room.

5. R: I vowed that I'd always make a home for my
       folks. Now my wife says that if my dad doesn't
       leave, she will. It's just impossible for me to put my
       father in a place like this.

6. I: You think it's impossible, but you may be sur-   (restatement of
       prised. We have a brochure prepared that discusses   content)
       financial arrangements that can be made
       incorporating social security and state benefits.

7. R: I didn't mean financially impossible. That's not   (disagreement)
       it at all! I mean, how can I turn my own father
       out of my home? What kind of a son am I?

Reflection of feeling can be in response to verbal or nonverbal messages. In the next interview excerpt, the interviewer responds to a long pause
and emphasis on certain words by reflecting a feeling the respondent has not
actually put into words. Her attempt is not exactly on target, and the
respondent disagrees and clarifies. The interviewer's second attempt at
reflection meets with agreement. The third attempt at reflection meets with
disagreement. When we reflect a feeling, the respondent may or may not
acknowledge or "own" the feeling. If he does own the feeling, our reflection may encourage further discussion of that feeling. If the respondent denies the feeling, we may be in error in our identification. On the other hand,
the respondent's denial may be an indication that he or she is not ready
to accept a verbalization of the feeling. Note the interchange in Utterances
10 and 11.

Interview Excerpt 7–3

The interviewer in this excerpt is the personnel director of a manu-
facturing firm.

1. R: I asked for this appointment today because I'd
       like a transfer from quality control to the produc-
       tion department.

2. I: I see. Why do you want to make the change?

3. R: I've been in quality control for two years now,
       and I think it's time I learned about another
       department.

4. I: Right now, there are no openings in production.
       We really need you where you are.

5. R: Well, the way things are going in Q.C. . . . (10
       second pause)

6. *I:* You're not happy with your job in quality   (reflection of
    control.   feeling)

7. *R:* No, it's not the job; it's Bill Clark. I don't think   (disagreement)
    I can work for him one more day.

8. *I:* You don't like having Bill Clark for your boss.   (reflection of
                                                             feeling)

9. *R:* No, I don't. He has no right telling me what to   (agreement)
    do. I've been here longer and I know ten times
    more than he does. It's too bad that *who* you
    know counts more than *what* you know!

10. *I:* You feel that you should have gotten the job   (reflection of
    instead of Clark.   feeling)

11. *R:* Well, I didn't say that. But almost anybody could   (disagreement)
    do a better job than Clark.

Active listening is a skill that is easier to describe than to accomplish. If you are interested in perfecting this skill, you might try this exercise, keeping in mind the four characteristics of active listening: attentiveness to the speaker; desire to understand the speaker's viewpoint; willingness to suspend judgment or evaluation of the ideas or feelings expressed by the speaker; and willingness to check your understanding by putting into words what you feel the speaker has conveyed. Sit down with a friend and carry on a conversation with this one rule: after one person speaks, the listener must verbally summarize that message to the speaker's satisfaction before making a reply of his or her own. To make this a more difficult exercise, direct the conversation to a topic that can arouse strong feelings. The listener must then satisfactorily verbalize not only the content of the speaker's message but also the feelings being expressed either verbally or nonverbally. After you have honed your skill in practice situations, the real test will be if you can follow this rule in a real-life argument or a highly charged confrontation. Of course, in your interviews you will not feel obliged to use restatement or reflection after every comment a respondent makes. However, if you develop this skill, you will be able to use it appropriately to facilitate understanding and continued respondent participation. By what you choose to restate or reflect, you can often encourage continued discussion of particularly significant or pertinent topics.

Carl Rogers is one of many counselors who stress the importance of restatement of content and reflection of feeling without judgmental evaluation. In fact, Rogers (1961, p. 332) states that achieving this listening with understanding can be a potent force in effecting personality change.*

* Carl R. Rogers, *On Becoming a Person.* Boston: Houghton Mifflin, 1961, p. 332. Reprinted by permission.

It is the most effective agent we know for altering the basic personality structure of an individual, and improving his relationships and his communications with others. If I can listen to what he can tell me, if I can understand how it seems to him, if I can see its personal meaning for him, if I can sense the emotional flavor which it has for him, then I will be releasing potent forces of change in him. . . . We know from our research that such empathic understanding—understanding *with* a person, not *about* him—is such an effective approach that it can bring about major changes in personality.

Uses of Silence

In discussing techniques the interviewer can use to further the interview and encourage respondent participation, we have described several ways in which the interviewer can behave verbally. In Chapter 6, we discussed structuring and the use of questions. So far in this chapter, we have talked about the *mm-hm* response, restatement of content, and reflection of feeling. It is now time to mention another important technique: the use of silence. Inexperienced interviewers often appear frightened or uneasy with silence. They feel compelled to fill even slight pauses by the respondent with further comments or questions. To combat this tendency we should be aware of what purposes silence can serve.

The respondent who has been doing the talking must sometimes pause to organize his or her thoughts in order to continue the discussion. If you want the respondent to continue, sitting quietly with an expectant look on your face signals to the respondent that he or she still has the floor, and that you are waiting for him or her to go on. If you have asked a respondent a question, silence may follow for one of several reasons:

1. He or she may need time to process your questions—and that can take quite a while if your question has been complicated, or your language or your vocabulary unfamiliar.
2. He or she may need time to organize his or her thoughts in order to frame an answer.
3. Your question may touch on a sensitive area, and the respondent may be deciding whether or not he or she is going to give the information requested.

Double questions and bombardment often result from an interviewer's fear of these natural pauses. The interviewer may feel that the question needs clarification—as the interviewer is asking the question, he or she may feel the need to rephrase it or soften it because the interviewer feels the respondent may not answer.

Silence may also occur after the interviewer has made a restatement of content. In that case, the respondent must not only recollect his or her own statement but must also decide if the interviewer's restatement is accurate. After a reflection of feeling on the part of the interviewer, the respondent has to decide not only if the interviewer has accurately verbalized what he or she is feeling but also if he or she wants to acknowledge or admit to that feeling. The restatement or reflection may trigger a desire to share more information, which the respondent must then organize to frame a response.

Sometimes silence occurs because one or both of the interview participants is experiencing strong emotions. Usually it is the respondent who is experiencing these emotions. In this case, it is often appropriate for the interviewer to wait quietly while the respondent gains sufficient control to continue. The interviewer's silence implies willingness to let the respondent experience the emotion without trying to minimize it or turn it off by changing the subject or making some other remark.

In situations such as we have described, the respondent will usually break the silence if the interviewer waits an appropriate length of time. Waiting does not imply inattention. The interviewer is, of course, attentive to the respondent during these moments of silence.

Use of silence on your part requires confidence: confidence that your respondent wishes to participate in the interview and will talk if given the opportunity; confidence in the adequacy of your single questions to bring forth a reply; and confidence that you can handle what may follow a silence.

There will be times in interviews when a silence will have to be broken by you. The respondent may not have anything more to say on a particular topic. It may then be time for you to redirect the interview. Or a prolonged silence on the part of the respondent may indicate resistance to the topic, you, or the entire interview situation. In that case, undue prolonging of the silence may only antagonize the respondent further. We certainly do not advocate that an interview ever deteriorate into a stare down or contest as to who is going to be the first to give in and break the silence. We *are* suggesting that many times an interview can be facilitated by appropriate uses of silence.

You may find yourself in an interview in which the situation is the reverse of the one described above: the respondent is doing *too much* talking. In this case, "too much talking" indicates that the respondent's discussion is off-target and not relevant to the interview purpose. Jean Converse and Howard Schuman (1974, p. 46) have some interesting comments on this problem:

> How to get the respondent to *stop* talking is rarely given as much attention in the literature or the training as how to prime the conversation and keep it flowing. . .
> Knowing how is especially difficult for beginning interviewers. In their zeal to gain rapport, they often have to labor *not* to give sympathetic, wide-eyed listening to everything the respondent says, relevant or irrelevant alike.

When the respondent lingers with his reverie or digression, experienced interviewers resort to methods ranging from soft gestures to straight talk. Some form of gentle inattention sometimes does it—putting down the pencil, looking away for a moment, even leafing through the questionnaire. If the respondent is too preoccupied with his own thought, such soft flutterings may go undetected, and the interviewer may have to escalate up to direct interruption.

The rate of the conversational exchange plus the length and frequency of pauses and silences contribute to the pace or timing of an interview. An experienced interviewer quickly senses the time and pace a respondent requires to participate most easily in the give-and-take of the conversational exchange. In one situation, the participants may engage easily in a rapid-fire exchange of ideas and comments. In another situation, an interviewer may feel the need to slow down considerably before the respondent can participate comfortably in the interaction. In still another situation, an alert, energetic respondent may leave an interview feeling frustrated because the interviewer talked and moved so slowly that the interview didn't get anywhere. In interviewing, as in athletics, comedy, parachuting, love making, and a host of other activities, timing is of utmost importance.

WORKING TOWARD THE INTERVIEWING GOAL

We have already noted in Chapter 1 that interviews can be described as fulfilling one or more of the following goals:

1. Information getting
2. Information giving
3. Expression and exploration of feeling
4. Problem solving
5. Planning for future action

There is no question that many interviews can accomplish more than one of these purposes. Many interviewing techniques are appropriate for interviews of any type. For purposes of illustrating these techniques, we will present some interview excerpts in which we will identify the utterances. You may wish to reread the section in Chapter 1 concerning the five purposes of interviews before moving on to the specific techniques discussed in the remainder of this chapter.

Information Getting

When we talk about getting information in order to work toward the interviewing goal we have to be clear in our own minds what information we want. We must decide what information would be helpful to us in the work we are trying to do. Sometimes some of the work has been done for us. For instance, there are case history forms or medical intake forms that have been compiled by experts. These forms include areas that have proved to be important. A rapid give-and-take of questions and answers may be quite appropriate in responding to some of these questionnaires. For example, factual information such as name, address, birthdate, and so forth can be asked and answered very quickly. Those would be Direct Question I, as you learned in Chapter 6. Questions that we referred to earlier as Direct Question II take a little more time to respond to because they are not strictly factual. The answer depends more on how the respondent feels or interprets the questions. One thing the interviewer must be alert to in an information-getting interview is whether or not the information he or she is getting is really important. It is easy to start asking questions. The respondent's answers can then trigger more questions. The conversation can continue in that fashion, and it may be quite a while before the interviewer realizes that the information he or she has obtained is not all that significant. The interviewer who does not keep the goal of the interview in mind may reach the end of the time allotted for the interview and find that many important questions have been left unanswered. Thus, in an information-getting interview, structuring can be very important.

Often, achievement of the interviewing goal is expedited by the interviewer's sharing with the respondent reasons why he or she is after certain information. Sometimes the interviewer simply fires questions at the respondent and gets answers. However, the answers might be much more meaningful or significant if the respondent understood why the information was necessary. The respondent may also be much more willing to respond to questions if he or she clearly understands why the questions are being asked. We often assume that the person is going to understand the reasons for our curiosity along certain lines. A patient might feel, for example, that a physician is prying unduly into personal subject matter; the respondent may not realize these details are crucially related to his or her condition.

The respondent will often look to us for assurance that the information he or she is giving to us is appropriate. According to the principles of behavior modification, behavior that we approve is likely to recur or become more frequent. The interviewer, then, can encourage information-giving with approval. What we have to beware of, though, is *what* we approve. If the respondent is giving us a variety of information, and obviously one type of information or certain facts are meeting with our approval, he or she is likely to give more similar facts. The respondent is likely to refrain from giving any contradictory information or something that might throw a different light on the matter. And yet we want him or her to keep sharing information with us. The trick then in approval is to approve the attitude of the respondent—his or her willingness to share with us—without actually approving the specific statements or information he or she is giving and making judgments about them.

Let us now consider two excerpts from predominantly information-getting interviews. As we have done in previous excerpts, we will identify the utterances by notations in the right hand margin.

Interview Excerpt 7–4

In this interview excerpt, a newspaper reporter is interviewing a prisoner recently released from jail in a foreign country.

1. *I:* How long were you held prisoner?   (direct question I)
2. *R:* Five months and seventeen days.   (information)
3. *I:* Were you allowed to contact anyone for   (direct question I)
   help?
4. *R:* Not for over three weeks. Then they agreed   (information)
   to let someone from the embassy talk to me.
5. *I:* What happened after you talked to the man   (direct question II)
   from the embassy?
6. *R:* I don't know all the details. All I know is that   (information)
   after almost five months they came and told
   me I was released. Frank Gray from the
   embassy had an airplane ticket for me, and
   I took the next flight home.
7. *I:* I think that our readers would like to know   (structuring)
   how you managed to get through those long
   months in prison.
8. *R:* I'm not sure I really know. I couldn't move   (information)
   around much in the cell but I tried to get
   what exercise I could. And I tried to think of
   good things that had happened to me, and
   other times when things were bad and I got
   through them.
9. *I:* Good. This is the sort of thing I'd like to   (approval)
   hear more about.
10. *R:* I started remembering songs and hymns I   (information)
    hadn't thought about since I was a kid.
    There were a couple that really helped.

Interview Excerpt 7–5

In this interview, a working mother is interviewing a potential babysitter.

1.	I: Have you done much babysitting?	(direct question II)
2.	R: Well, I raised three children of my own.	(information)
3.	I: That's good. That sure gives you a lot of experience with kids. Do they live here in San Francisco?	(approval and direct question I)
4.	R: One does—my daughter. My two sons live in the East	(information)
5.	I: I'll bet it's hard for you having them so far away.	(indirect question)
6.	R: *Mm-hm*—I wish I could see them more often.	(*mm-hm* response and information)
7.	I: Did you have a job when your children were little?	(direct question I)
8.	R: No . . . My one boy was always in trouble and needed real discipline.	(information)
9.	I: You don't believe in spanking, do you? I could never have anyone take care of Amanda who might hit her.	(leading question and information)
10.	R: Well . . . (pause) . . . if that's the way you feel . . . I'd go along with it.	(information)

In the first interview excerpt (7–4), we find examples of both direct question I (utterances 1 and 3), and direct question II (utterance 5). There is evidence of structuring (utterance 7) when the reporter indicates what he would like to have happen in the interview. In utterance 9, he approves the choice of topic and the nature of the respondent's remarks. This approval may have contributed to the respondent's further remarks on the topic.

In the second interview excerpt (7–5), we find examples of indirect question (utterance 5), direct question I (utterances 3 and 7), direct question II (utterance 1), and a leading question (utterance 9). We also have an instance of approval on the part of the interviewer (utterance 3). In general, the information obtained from the respondent would be of interest to a parent. However, if the time available for the interview is limited, the information obtained as a result of the interviewer's questions in utterances 3, 5, and 7 is not particularly helpful in deciding whether or not to hire this applicant. Information regarding the prospective babysitter's way of disciplining youngsters might be very important in making employment decisions. However, the interviewer's use of the leading question in utterance 9 indicates to the applicant what response would be best received.

Information Giving

In Chapter 1, in the section on information-giving interviews, we stressed the importance of presenting information in a clear manner, being accurate in the information presented, and being comfortable in acknowledging when we do not have the necessary information. Sometimes, the information we give will be readily accepted by our respondent. At other times, strong emotions associated with the topic—or aroused by the interviewer—may interfere with the listener's ability to process and accept the information offered. The interviewer must be alert to emotional reactions on the part of the respondent. These reactions cannot be ignored if the interviewer hopes to get the message across. In some situations, the emotions may have to be explored and dealt with before information-giving can proceed. In other circumstances, a modification or rephrasing of the information may be sufficient.

Let us now consider two excerpts from predominantly information-giving interviews.

Interview Excerpt 7–6

In this interview excerpt, a travel agent is interviewing a prospective client.

1.	*I:* We have several very fine tours of Hawaii. Let me tell you about them and then you can decide which one sounds best.	(information)
2.	*R:* OK.	(*mm-hm* response)
3.	*I:* The first—Hawaiian Highlights—is a three-week tour, and you visit four islands. This gives you an excellent idea of what the islands are like.	(information)
4.	*R:* What are the accommodations like? I don't want to stay in some small dark room blocks away from the beach.	(request for information; information; and negative feeling toward cramped hotel room distant from beach)
5.	*I:* Oh no, I agree. The rooms are very nice. In fact, on two islands—Kauai and Maui—you stay in condominiums that have kitchen and living room areas. They're right on the beach.	(agreement and information)
6.	*R:* That sounds great.	(approval)

7.   I: Yes. This tour is excellent. A luau on   (information)
         the beach is included and you can
         have the use of a rental car for a small
         additional payment.

8.   R: The rental car isn't included?   (request for information)

9.   I: No—but the price is nominal—much   (information)
         less than you'd pay on your own.

Interview Excerpt 7–7

The interviewer in this interview excerpt is a language pathologist speaking
to the wife of a patient who has suffered a stroke.

1.   I: Bob had a good session today. He was   (information)
         able to go through most of the
         activities without getting frustrated.

2.   R: That's good. He gets so upset and   (approval and information)
         angry at home.

3.   I: We also worked on the dysarthria. He   (information)
         had some difficulty with the lingual
         alveolar phonemes but many of the
         plosives were correct.

4.   R: Dysar . . .? Plosives?   (request for information)

5.   I: Yes . . . Well, you know we did spend   (information)
         most of the time on those but I
         was so pleased that he was doing so
         well that we worked on that longer
         than I originally planned.

6.   R: How long do you think it will take 'til   (request for information;
         he's back to himself? I just don't   information [problem area];
         know how much longer I can go on   negative feeling toward
         like this—we can't even talk to each   husband's condition)
         other.

7.   I: Well, today was a good session. We   (information)
         have to be thankful for every step
         forward.

8.   R: How can you tell when there's   (request for information;
         progress? I get so discouraged.   information [problem area];
                                                          negative feeling toward
                                                          husband's condition)

9.   I: That's natural. Most people in your   (reassurance)
         situation feel like that.

In the first excerpt of these information-giving interviews (7–6), a travel agent is providing information to a prospective client. Every one of the interviewer's utterances contains information—all of which is pertinent to the topic. The respondent gives evidence of listening: by an *mm-hm* response in utterance 2; by requests for further related information in utterances 4 and 8; and by approval of the offered information in utterance 6. The interviewer is alert to the respondent's questions and promptly supplies the requested information. You will note that the respondent expresses feeling in this excerpt—a negative feeling toward a certain type of hotel accommodation. The interviewer immediately acknowledges the concern and provides information to allay it.

Interview Excerpt 7–7 provides an example of what can go wrong in an information-giving interview. There is no doubt the interviewer is providing information (utterances 1, 3, 5, 7, and 9). However, much of the information provided does not really address the respondent's requests. In utterance 4, the respondent is asking for clarification of terms used that she does not understand—a request that is ignored by the interviewer. In utterances 6 and 8, the requested information is a result of the emotional state of the respondent—negative feeling toward her husband's condition and progress. It is especially important to an interviewer to be alert to the type of information contained in utterances 6 and 8. Because of this importance, we have found it helpful to use a special designation to identify this type of utterance. Information which identifies or indicates a situation that is currently causing stress or concern is designated as "problem area" to call special attention to it. This designation is used only when the stress or concern is *currently* felt by the respondent—not when a respondent is relating past feelings. The interviewer in this excerpt overlooks both the request for information and the expression of feelings in utterances 6 and 8. Thus, what is clearly a current problem for this respondent seems minimized by the interviewer.

There is another type of information that is introduced in this excerpt that is useful to identify. You will note that we have identified the information provided by the interviewer in utterance 9 as "reassurance." One definition of reassurance is "information that confirms or validates a respondent's stated information or supposition." The respondent's expression of discouragement in utterance 8 is acknowledged by the interviewer stating that many people in that situation feel that way; this can be considered reassurance. How effective such reassurance is in this case, however, can be questioned.

Expression and Exploration of Feelings

The expression and exploration of feelings can be the major goal of an interview. It may be difficult to accomplish other goals of an interpersonal relationship until certain feelings are verbalized, acknowledged, and dealt with. We have already discussed the fact that many counselors and psychotherapists feel that the free-flowing expression of emotions is in itself therapeutic. Psychotherapists employ a variety of techniques to encourage expression of emotion. One therapist might be especially alert to a client's nonverbal indication of emotion. The therapist might then encourage the client to exaggerate the behavior while the client verbalizes what he or she is feeling. Another therapist might hand an inhibited client a heavy pillow to punch while engaging in imaginary dialogue with the object of repressed feelings. A third therapist might endeavor to arouse a respondent's emotions by assuming the posture, tone of voice, and other characteristics of a significant person in the respondent's life. The list can be extended almost indefinitely: dream work; expression of emotion through dance or painting; primal therapy; hypnosis; rolfing; and so forth. For information regarding therapeutic techniques, the reader is referred to the works of representative therapists such as: Fritz Perls (1969), Gestalt therapy; Eric Berne (1961), transactional analysis; Muriel James and Dorothy Jongeward (1971), combining Gestalt techniques with transactional analysis; Albert Ellis (1973), rational-emotive therapy; Carl Rogers (1951), client-centered therapy; Eric Fromm (1941), psychoanalysis; William Glasser (1965), reality therapy; and J. L. Moreno (1934), psychodrama.

A word of caution is certainly in order here: effective use of specialized psychotherapy techniques requires extensive training and preparation under competent and recognized leadership. Reading one book on the subject or attending one weekend workshop does not make an expert! As interviewers, though, we can all make use of certain techniques designed to facilitate honest communication of feeling rather than hamper it.

Let us look now at excerpts from two interviews involving primarily expression of feeling.

Interview Excerpt 7–8

In this interview excerpt, a junior-year university student is meeting with her faculty adviser.

1. R: I have, I mean, I, uh, I'm (sighs) uh, I've been getting this thing that, uh, I should take a semester off and just, uh, not go straight on. Part of me says that's a smart thing to do and part of me says that's a dumb thing to do. (deep sigh)

   (problem area; ambivalent feeling toward continuing studies)

2. I: You haven't decided whether you'll be back in school in the fall?

   (restatement of content)

3. R: I mean, I'm, uh, you know, I'll mail in my   (problem area;
    computer registration form, but I'm not sure   negative feeling
    I can go through with it. I'm in a really   toward continuing
    strange space this semester. I can't bring   studies)
    myself to study anywhere near as much as I
    should.

4. I: You feel that you have to really force   (reflection of
    yourself to study.   feeling)

5. R: Yeah—and when I do study, I really can't   (agreement;
    get interested at all. I catch myself doing   problem area)
    really dumb things! I've got a term paper due
    in two days, and I haven't even started it yet.

6. I: It sounds as though you're setting yourself   (interpretation)
    up to fail so you won't have to go on in
    the fall.

7. R: Maybe that's true. But that would be a crazy   (partial agreement;
    thing to do. I'm two-thirds of the way   problem area;
    through to my credential. I just don't know   negative feeling
    what's the matter with me.   toward self as
                                                          student)

8   I: It's hard to keep your enthusiasm up and   (reflection of
    have the self-discipline to go one step by one   feeling)
    step by one step and do everything that's
    required of you.

9. R: It sure is. If I can make it through this   (agreement;
    semester that will help. I think I'll try to   planning)
    get away for a while this summer. Maybe
    that will get me going again.

10. I: If you can hang on for the rest of the   (reflection of
    semester, you think you can make it the rest   feeling)
    of the way.

Interview Excerpt 7–9

The interviewer in this excerpt is a staff worker in a child development clinic who is speaking with the mother of a developmentally disabled son.

1. I: We are recommending placement of Ronnie   (information)
    in the Developmental Center preschool
    program.

2. R: I won't agree to that. Ronnie is just fine, and you people are making some big deal out of these tests. First the pediatrician, then my in-laws, and now you! (disagreement; problem area; negative feeling toward people's judgment of Ronnie's condition)

3. I: We're all just trying to find out what would be best for Ronnie—to give him the best possible chance to develop. (information)

3. R: You act like he's some kind of moron. My husband didn't talk until he was almost two years old and there's nothing the matter with him! Taking him around to these places; sitting and waiting until somebody gets good and ready to see us. It's damned annoying! (information; problem area; negative feelings toward professional concern and procedures)

5. I: Well, you had to wait because there are several parts to the tests and different people administer them. (information)

6. R: I hope they know more than that pediatrician does. With all the shots and vaccines and vitamins and now these tests—before you know it, there *will* be something the matter with Ronnie! (problem area; negative feelings toward pediatrician and professional procedures)

7. I: Mrs. Monner, your son is mentally retarded. There's no doubt about that. But if he's going to get the best possible training, we want to have as much information about his condition as we can. (information)

8. R: What do you mean, retarded? That's a terrible thing to say about a little fellow only four years old. He's a lot smarter than some of the people we've come across in the last six months! (problem area; negative feelings toward interviewer's diagnosis and toward other professionals)

9. I: It's foolish for you to act this way about the situation. People are trying to help and you refuse to face the facts. (information; negative feeling toward mother's attitude)

10. R: Nobody has given me any facts. They're too busy playing God! (problem area; negative feeling toward professionals)

In excerpt 7–8, the respondent is giving information that indicates a problem area. Ambivalent feelings regarding the continuation of her studies are expressed by the student in Utterance 1, and negative feelings toward the continuation of her studies are expressed in Utterance 3. She also expresses negative feeling toward herself as a student in Utterance 7. Her adviser focuses on the emotions she expresses, helping her to stay with the feeling.

The techniques used by the interviewer include restatement of content and reflection of feeling without making any judgment concerning the student's expressed feelings. Utterance 2 points out that a restatement of content or reflection of feeling may take the form of a question. It is not uncommon for an interviewer to use a question form to check perceptions. In restatement and reflection, we are, in effect, asking the respondent if our perceptions are accurate; in these circumstances, we identify the technique rather than the form in which the technique is expressed. Athough we identify Utterance 2 as restatement of content, it borders on reflection of feeling. You will note that when the interviewer comments again in Utterance 4, there is no doubt that the focus is on the student's feelings.

Utterance 6 introduces a technique that has not yet been mentioned. This utterance is identified as interpretation, an utterance that suggests possible motivation (not verbally expressed by the respondent) to account for the respondent's expressed action or feeling. An interviewer will sometimes use interpretation in an effort to increase the respondent's insight into the reasons for feelings or behavior. In this example, the student's response to the interpretation is a partial agreement with the interviewer's statement, but we do not have any indication that the student has experienced any genuine insight. To be designated as insight, the respondent must express, in the utterance, awareness of motivation or consequences of behavior not previously understood or verbalized.

In interview excerpt 7–9, the respondent is the mother of a developmentally disabled child. This excerpt is an example of an interaction with a respondent who may well be in one of the stages of the process of mourning. Elisabeth Kübler-Ross (1969) has described various stages through which a person passes in coping with death and dying: denial, anger, bargaining, depression, and finally acceptance. The concept of this "grief work" has been extended to include the reactions of people to all types of loss, such as the loss of a limb in amputation; the loss of the use of the body in spinal cord injury; and the loss of the "perfect child" when a child is handicapped. An interviewer must understand that a respondent may be in one of these stages as they attempt to deal with a loss. In this particular excerpt, the mother is exhibiting both denial and anger, and is expressing strong negative feelings toward professionals evaluating her son and the procedures they use in this evaluation. In Utterance 6, she goes so far as to say that some of the procedures used to help her son may in fact be harmful. From a psychoanalytical standpoint, this utterance could be seen as the mother's unconscious attempt to rationalize her son's condition if she will no longer be able to repress or deny it.

The interviewer in this excerpt begins by giving the mother information regarding the son's evaluation and the recommended placement. She continues to give information despite the mother's expressions of feeling and rejection of the diagnosis and recommendation. Before any constructive action can take place, some of these feelings must be dealt with. In her continuing attempt to clarify the information, the interviewer uses highly charged vocabulary (as seen in Utterance 7). We cannot tell if the interviewer is aware that the mother is evidencing mourning; we do know that she makes no attempt to deal with the feeling. She identifies the feeling as foolish, passing judgment on the mother's behavior. This excerpt is an example of how the purpose of a particular interview may have to be changed in order to achieve an ultimate goal.

Problem Solving

Many interviews are conducted in order to resolve a problem that may exist for one or both of the interview participants. The major goal, therefore, in these interviews is problem solving. Robert Rutherford and Eugene Edgar (1979, p. 35) describe this process: "Problem solving involves a systematic procedure for resolving differences, reaching solutions, or discovering sources of difficulties." They describe this systematic procedure as a four-step process that includes: defining the problem, developing the solution, implementing the solution, and evaluating the results. They compare this four-step process with techniques of applied behavior analysis, interpersonal communication, and assertiveness. Their comparisons show that these basic steps in problem solving are used regardless of the particular techniques the interviewer prefers.

Naomi Brill (1978, pp. 90–91) discusses how the scientific method can be applied in working with people as they attempt to solve problems:

The classical "scientific method" involves recognition and systematic formulation of a problem, collection of data through observation and experiment, and the formulation and testing of hypotheses, or tentative explanations of the problem . . . The orderly framework for working with people is an adaptation of this . . .

1. Engagement—involving oneself in the situation, establishing communication, and formulating preliminary hypotheses for the problem.
2. Assessment—appraising the situation on the basis of data—facts, feelings, persons, circumstances.
3. Definition of the problem—formulating the need.
4. Setting of goals—the end toward which the effort is to be directed.
5. Selection of alternative methods and an initial mode of interven-

tion—looking at all the possible ways of tackling the problem and selecting the most propitious one.

6. Establishment of a contract—agreeing on a definition of the roles and responsibilities of the participants.

7. Action leading toward the desired goal—the work that is necessary.

8. Evaluation—weighing the outcome of action in terms of success or failure.

9. Continuation of working plan, abandonment of unsuccessful intervention and selection of a different approach, or termination—continuation and selection of a different interventive strategy are based on a repetition of this process.

Robert Carkhuff and William Anthony (1979) have developed a procedure for choosing a course of action when there are several possible solutions to a problem. Their procedure can be particularly helpful if there is a dilemma about which solution is best. They suggest the construction of a matrix in which the various alternatives are listed and the respondent (or helpee) assigns a numerical weight to each solution based on personal values. Once the preferred solution is identified, implementing the solution can begin. You may find it helpful to take a closer look at this procedure for assigning priorities when no one solution to a problem is clearly the best.

A review of the problem solving literature as it relates to the counseling process has been published by P. Paul Heppner (1978). You may also wish to examine this article.

Now let's take a look at interview excerpts from two problem-solving interviews.

Interview Excerpt 7–10

In this interview excerpt, a counselor is interviewing a client at a treatment center for those who wish to quit smoking.

1. I: Tell me what you hope to accomplish by coming to the Smith Treatment Center. (structuring)

2. R: I have to stop smoking and I've tried everything—nothing seems to work. My doctor told me that I have to stop if I want to live. I have emphysema and I smoke two and one-half packs a day. Is there any hope for such a heavy smoker? (problem area; request for information)

3. I: Many people have done it. We have several plans to help people stop smoking. Not everybody can do it the same way. One way that we've had a lot of success is the "cold turkey" plan. (information)

4. R: That's no good for me. I've tried that. Two days was the most I ever could go without a cigarette. (information)

5. I: Another plan is to keep a record of when you smoke the most during the day. Then we can help you plan things to do to avoid temptation during those times. (information)

6. R: *Mm-hm.* (*mm-hm* response)

7. I: Another way is by using hypnosis. One of our staff members specializes in this. Through what we call posthypnotic suggestion, your habit of smoking is more easily broken. You can also try what we call aversion therapy. This includes a very slight electric shock every time you reach for a cigarette. (information)

8. R: It's hard to know what to do. I don't like the idea of electric shock. And I don't see how keeping a record will help me stop. I've never been hypnotized. Do you think I could be? (information; negative feeling toward two of the plans; request for information)

9. I: Dr. Jones has some tests he gives to determine whether or not hypnosis might work for you. You could see him today. (Information; advice and suggestion)

10. R: Maybe that would help my will power. (agreement; positive feeling toward hypnosis)

11. I: After you've talked with Dr. Jones you can come back here and we can draw up a contract. It's important to make a firm commitment, no matter what plan you choose. (structuring; information)

Interview Excerpt 7–11

The interviewer in this interview excerpt is a priest speaking with a young man.

1. R: I wanted to talk to you today, Father, because I've been really trying to decide what to do about my religion. I feel like I'm Catholic, but I haven't gone to church for a long time. My life is getting pretty messed up and I need some help. I've been spend- (problem area; ambivalent feeling toward religion)

ing a lot of time talking about religion
with a friend. He's got me started reading
the Bible. There's a lot more there than
I ever thought.

2.   I: Is your friend Catholic?   (direct question I)

3.   R: No, he's Protestant.   (information)

4.   I: You'd better talk to some Catholics. You've   (advice or suggestion;
         talked to your parents, haven't you?   leading question)

5.   R: Yeah, they know what I've been doing.   (agreement plus
         That's why they made me come to see you.   information)
         The church is fine for them. They accept
         everything the church tells them.

6.   I: That shows how strong their faith is. You   (information)
         wouldn't be so upset if you came to Mass
         regularly.

7.   R: When I've come to Mass, it just hasn't   (disagreement;
         helped. What's in the church and what's in   information)
         real life are two different worlds.

8.   I: You need the sacraments to give you faith.   (information)

9.   R: But how will faith help me with all the   (request for
         problems I face every day?   information)

10. I: You should look to the life of Christ for   (advice or
         guidance.   suggestion)

11. R: You can't compare my problems with life   (disagreement)
         two thousand years ago.

In interview excerpt 7–10, the use of structuring by the interviewer leads the respondent to the statement identifying the problem (Utterances 1 and 2). The problem in this interview is clearly defined—the respondent smokes and says she must stop smoking. Because the problem is immediately defined, the interview can progress quickly to developing the solution. The treatment center has a number of plans already developed that are available to the respondent. The interviewer provides information regarding these plans (Utterances 3, 5, and 7). The respondent expresses negative feeling regarding three of the plans described and requests information on the fourth plan. In effect, she is assigning priorities to these solutions—cold turkey does not work; the value of keeping a record is questioned; electric shock is not viewed with favor. That leaves hypnosis. The interviewer does not attempt to dispute these reactions. Rather, he provides the requested information about hypnosis and then makes a specific suggestion (Utterance 9). This technique of advice or suggestion can be defined as recommending a course of action to be followed by the respondent other than during the interview. In this particular case, it appears that the respondent will follow through on the suggestion.

Interview excerpt 7–11 concerns a problem that is not clearly defined. The young man in this interview describes his life as "messed up," but he is not specific and can only verbalize that he needs help (Utterance 1). The interviewer does not attempt to help the respondent to define the problem. He ignores the ambivalent feelings expressed toward religion and responds with a direct question I (Utterance 2). No further emotions are expressed by the young man, although the interview may have included more exploration of feeling if the interviewer had encouraged this. The information the interviewer does provide could be considered his beliefs and attitudes, but these are likely to be heard as religious platitudes by the young man. The platitudes result in encouragement of antagonism, but not necessarily expression of feelings that are contributing to the young man's frustration. The priest is judgmental, which provokes defensiveness. His needs include the desire to instill respect for the church and the teachings of the church.

We can consider this excerpt from the perspective of various personality theorists. For example, in transactional terms, the priest is operating from a parent ego state, assuming the role of parent—telling the young man what he should and should not do. The young man, however, is attempting adult-adult transactions. This crossed transaction is creating problems. In terms used by Robert Havighurst, the developmental task that is posing problems for the young man in this interview is concerned with formulating a set of values to guide his behavior. We can consider the excerpt in light of the dimensions of dominance-submission and friendliness-unfriendliness. The priest is assuming a dominant role. The young man has come to the priest, apparently acknowledging the priest's role of leadership in religious matters. The solutions suggested by the priest are not acceptable to the young man, because he does not see their relevance to the realities of his life. It is difficult on the basis of this excerpt to make any comment regarding the friendliness-unfriendliness dimension within the interview.

Planning for Future Action

In Chapter 1, we pointed out the the desirability of setting up specific long-range and intermediate goals when planning for action. The nature of these goals will, of course, depend on circumstances prompting the action. Workers in many fields have made specific suggestions regarding the establishment of objectives and methods of evaluation appropriate for those fields. In the field of education, for example, Robert Mager (1962) detailed procedures for establishing instructional objectives.

Several psychotherapy approaches emphasize the planning and practice of new behaviors by clients as they progress in therapy. These therapists stress the importance of developing insight into problems and awareness of alternate ways of behaving. They feel, however, for this insight and awareness to be effective, it is necessary to achieve behavioral change. For example, homework assignments are routinely included in Rational-Emotive Therapy. Clients practice new behaviors, which are then evaluated and discussed with the therapist. In discussing this aspect of Rational-Emotive Therapy, Gerald Corey (1977, p. 154) states:*

> The homework-assignment method is well suited to enabling clients to practice new behaviors and assisting them in the process of their reconditioning. Reality therapy, behavior therapy, and Transactional Analysis share with RET this action orientation. Clients can gain a multitude of insights and can become very aware of the nature of their problems, but I question the value of self-understanding unless specific plans that lead to behavioral changes desired by the client are implemented. RET insists on this action phase as a crucial part of the therapy process.

Nena and George O'Neill (1974) have done considerable work assisting people in acquiring new behaviors and changing their life style. The O'Neills refer to these significant changes in life direction as shifting gears. One of their major points is that we must take the risk of new behavior in order to grow. They point out the paradox of the human being's need for security—which implies maintenance of the familiar—and our need for challenge—which implies going into the unknown and taking risks. They also point out that often significant life changes can be made in a series of small achievable steps. They (1974, pp. 183, 186–187) discuss the importance of genuine commitment to action:**

> You find yourself in crisis. You face up to the existence of the crisis, achieving awareness, which is the first step in the process of shifting gears. By focusing and centering you refine that awareness, evaluating your situation and exploring possible alternatives. You make a decision to change, to seek a specific new path to self-fulfillment. But if you stop there, you have not shifted gears nor resolved the crisis. To resolve the crisis you must now take the risk of committing yourself to action, of testing your competence in a new situation . . .
>
> When we commit ourselves fully to a new course of action, when we take the step, we bring our total selves into play—our past experiences (including some that may have seemed "wasted"), our developed abilities, our latent or hidden capacities. It is as if the active commitment itself releases these capacities and makes it possible to utilize many resources we were unaware of. But we use these parts of ourselves in new ways, reorganizing and reintegrating the various parts of ourselves to apply to the particular

---

* From *Theory and Practice of Counseling and Psychotherapy*, by G. Corey. Copyright © 1977 by Wadsworth, Inc. Reprinted by permission of the publisher, Brooks/Cole Publishing Company, Monterey, California.
** From *Shifting Gears: Finding Security in a Changing World* by Nena O'Neill and George O'Neill. Copyright © 1974 by Nena O'Neill and George O'Neill. Reprinted by permission of the publisher, M. Evans and Company, Inc., New York, N.Y.

focus we have decided on. And as this reintegration occurs, we grow, inevitably. The degree to which we grow will depend on how much of ourselves we bring to the commitment, will depend on the level of interaction and exchange we can stimulate between our inner selves and the external situation or relationship to which we have committed ourselves.

Interview excerpts 7–12 and 7–13 provide examples of planning for future action.

Interview Excerpt 7–12

In this interview excerpt, a physician is in his office discussing proposed surgery with a patient.

1. *I:* Irma, your x-ray shows that your gall- (information;
   bladder is full of stones, as we   advice or suggestion)
   suspected. Those are what are causing
   you all this pain. I think you should
   have surgery as soon as possible to get
   the gallbladder out.

2. *R:* Isn't there something you could do   (request for information)
   besides surgery?

3. *I:* Well, you could try to wait it out.   (information;
   Some people with gallbladder trouble   advice or suggestion)
   get by for years on a strict low-fat diet.
   But you've been having a lot of discomfort in recent years, and it has
   really flared up now. You could wait a
   while to have the surgery, but I'm
   afraid if you don't do it now, the
   bladder will become infected. Then
   you'd have to have surgery to drain the
   infection, and surgery again a few
   months later to remove the stones. I
   advise that you have the surgery
   immediately.

4. *R:* Is the surgery dangerous?   (request for information)

5. *I:* Well, there is always some danger with   (information)
   surgery, particularly with the use of
   anesthesia—but the risk is minimal
   compared to letting the infection
   develop.

6. *R:* I'll let them know at work right away—   (planning; information;
   I have plenty of sick leave coming.   request for information)
   How long will I have to be off work?

7. I: I'd say about a week in the hospital—   (information)
    and at home, two more weeks—about
    three weeks altogether.

8. R: I hope my insurance covers it.   (information)

9. I: It probably does—if you have a fairly   (information;
    comprehensive plan. If you show me   advice or suggestion;
    your policy, I can tell. Or the hospital   direct question II;
    has someone on the staff who can   information)
    figure it out for you and give you all the
    information. Shall I go ahead and
    check with the surgeon and see if we
    can schedule surgery the day after
    tomorrow? That means you'd check
    into the hospital tomorrow. I can call
    you at home this afternoon to confirm
    that surgery is scheduled.

10. R: You might as well. If it has to be, it has   (information; planning)
    to be. I'll call work as soon as I get
    home. And then when I hear from you
    this afternoon I'll call my sister. She can
    probably drive me to the hospital
    tomorrow morning after her boy goes
    to school.

Interview Excerpt 7–13

The interviewer in this excerpt is a psychiatrist meeting with a female
patient.

1. I: So we've agreed that it doesn't do   (information;
    either you or Joe any good if you don't   advice or suggestion)
    tell him how angry you are. Your anger
    is eating a hole in your stomach.
    You've got to behave differently when
    he does those things that annoy you so.

2. R: Well, what should I do?   (request for information)

3. I: What do you think you should do?   (forcing client
                                                    responsibility)

4. R: Speak up and tell him I'm not a door   (information; negative
    mat to be walked over. I have some   feeling toward husband's
    rights too.   attitude)

5. I: That should shake Joe up!   (information)

6. R: But that'll just start an argument and those don't do my stomach any good either. It always ends up the same. (deep sigh) — (Problem area; negative feeling toward arguments)

7. I: Maybe you could reach some sort of agreement, a compromise. What decisions *you* can make and what decisions *he* can make. — (advice or suggestion)

8. R: Yeah—he decides how to spend all our money and I decide what toilet paper to buy. — (agreement; information)

9. I: Why don't you tell him that from now on, you will keep your paycheck and buy all the groceries with it? That will be a start. — (advice or suggestion)

10. R: I *could* do that. But what if I get laid off? — (partial agreement; request for information)

Note that in interview 7–12, the discussion moves quickly from identification of a problem through enumeration of possible solutions, to planning for future action. Using the results of diagnostic tests, the physician identifies the problem for the patient: gallstones. He immediately recommends what he considers the preferred solution: surgery. The patient wants to know if any other course of action would solve the problem. Another possible solution is explored—a low-fat diet—but surgery is medically preferred. Acceptance of the advice offered by the physician (Utterances 1, 3, and 9) leads to planning on the part of the respondent (Utterances 6 and 10). Planning can be defined as "the respondent verbalizing his or her own planned future behavior." Both interview participants have responsibilities in carrying out the proposed action. These are verbalized and confirmed in Utterances 9 and 10. Evaluation of the results of the action will be evidenced in the performance of surgery and the subsequent relief of the patient's symptoms.

In interview excerpt 7–13, it is apparent that previous discussion has centered around problem solving—probably accompanied by expression and exploration of feelings. As is often the case in psychotherapy, the psychiatrist is now encouraging a change in behavior that will lead to the client's more effective functioning. He is trying to help the client plan more appropriate behavior and be responsible for carrying it out. We have an example in this interview excerpt of a technique that is known as "forcing client responsibility," which is defined as "immediately redirecting the respondent's question back to the respondent."

When the psychiatrist suggests a specific plan of action (Utterance 7), the client does not appear to take the suggestion seriously. The psychiatrist follows up with an even more specific suggestion (Utterance 9). The respondent's reply (Utterance 10) gives evidence of what transactional analysts consider game playing. If actual behavioral change on the part of the respondent is going to take place, the respondent will have to agree to a specific attainable goal and act accordingly. As we have noted, one of the principles of planning for future action is to make the behavioral goals as specific and attainable as possible. In this excerpt, the psychiatrist is attempting to do that as the interview proceeds. However, he may be getting caught up in the respondent's game playing.

You will note that we have identified several utterances (Utterances 4 and 6) as containing expressed feelings. As was the case in past interview excerpts, we prefer to identify expressed feelings only when the emotions are clearly evident.

A word of caution is in order. Interviewers may be faced with respondents who are docile and dependent in their behavior, asking help from the interviewer and expressing admiration and respect for the interviewer's knowledge and good judgment. Leary's circumplex of interpersonal reflexes reminds us that such behavior on the part of the respondent is likely to encourage an increased amount of directiveness on the part of the interviewer, who may be tempted to outline specific plans of action without encouraging the respondent to participate in the development of the plans. When the responsibility for future action rests primarily on the respondent, the action is more likely to be carried out if the respondent has taken an active role in formulating the plan.

AID TO ANALYSIS

In Chapter 1, we presented a series of questions specific to the five purposes of interviews. These questions can be useful for you as you analyze a particular interview. For example, if an interview you are analyzing is predominantly an information-getting interview, the questions in Chapter 1 specific to this purpose could be reviewed. This also would be the case for each of the other interview purposes.

In addition to the questions related to specific purposes, the following aid to analysis can be applied to the body of an interview. Respond to the following as the items relate to the body of an interview you have conducted recently.

1. Was I genuinely attentive to the respondent?
2. Did I show a desire to understand the respondent's viewpoint, even if it differed from my own?
3. Was I willing to suspend judgment or evaluation of the ideas expressed by the respondent? Was I willing to suspend judgment or evaluation of feelings expressed?
4. What kind of questions did I use during the body of the interview?

Did my respondent seem to have any difficulty in understanding them?

5. Did my respondent indicate any current problem area? What was my reaction to this information?

6. Did I check my understanding of what the respondent said by restating content when appropriate?

7. Did the respondent express any feelings, either verbally or non-verbally? Was I able to determine whether the feelings expressed were positive, negative, or ambivalent?

8. How did I react to expressions of feeling? Did I attempt to verbalize current emotions expressed either verbally or nonverbally by the respondent—in other words, to reflect those feelings?

9. Did my restatements of content and reflections of feeling further the purpose or purposes of the interview?

10. Did I pay attention to whether my respondent agreed or disagreed with my restatement or reflection? What did I do if the respondent disagreed?

11. Did I feel comfortable if there were periods of silence? Did I allow the respondent sufficient time to answer my questions or make other remarks?

12. Was I able to keep the interview moving satisfactorily and in the appropriate direction?

13. Did the pace and timing of my participation in the interview seem appropriate?

14. Did I use approval? What did I approve? Did I express disapproval? What did I disapprove?

15. Did I use interpretation during the interview—in other words, did I suggest possible motivations (not verbally expressed by the respondent) to account for the respondent's expressed actions or feelings?

16. What was the general tenor of the interview—friendly or unfriendly, "in depth" or superficial?

17. How would I describe my role and my respondent's role on the dominance-submission dimension?

18. Did either the respondent or I exhibit any of the styles of communication described by Virginia Satir: placating, blaming, computing, distracting, or leveling?

REFERENCES

Barnlund, Dean C. *Interpersonal Communication: Survey and Studies.* Boston: Houghton Mifflin Co., 1968.

Berne, Eric. *Transactional Analysis in Psychotherapy*. New York: Grove Press, 1961.

Brill, Naomi I. *Working with People*, 2d ed. Philadelphia: J. B. Lippincott Co., 1978.

Carkhuff, Robert R., and Anthony, William A. *The Skills of Helping*. Amherst, Mass.: Human Resource Development Press, 1979.

Converse, Jean, and Schuman, Howard. *Conversations at Random: Survey Research as Interviewers See It*. New York: John Wiley and Sons, 1974.

Corey, Gerald. *Theory and Practice of Counseling and Psychotherapy*. Monterey, Calif.: Brooks/Cole Publishing Co., 1977.

Ellis, Albert. *Humanistic Psychotherapy: The Rational-Emotive Approach*. New York: Julian Press, 1973.

Fromm, Erich. *Escape from Freedom*. New York: Farrar and Rinehart, 1941.

Glasser, William. *Reality Therapy*. New York: Harper & Row, 1965.

Gordon, Thomas. *Leader Effectiveness Training (L.E.T.)*. New York: Bantam Books, 1977.

Havighurst, Robert. *Developmental Tasks and Education*, 3rd ed. New York: Longman, 1972.

Heppner, P. Paul. "A Review of the Problem-Solving Literature and Its Relationship to the Counseling Process." *Journal of Counseling Psychology*, 25 (1978), 366–375.

James, Muriel, and Jongeward, Dorothy. *Born to Win: Transactional Analysis with Gestalt Experiments*. Reading, Mass.: Addison-Wesley Publishing Co., 1971.

Kroth, Roger L. *Communicating with Parents of Exceptional Children*. Denver: Love Publishing Co., 1975.

Kübler-Ross, Elisabeth. *On Death and Dying*. New York: Macmillan Publishing Co., 1969.

Mager, Robert F. *Preparing Instructional Objectives*. Palo Alto, Calif.: Fearon Publishers, 1962.

Moreno, J. L. *Who Shall Survive?* New York: Nervous and Mental Disease Publishing Co., 1934.

O'Neill, Nena, and O'Neill, George. *Shifting Gears: Finding Security in a Changing World*. New York: M. Evans and Co., Avon Books, 1974.

Perls, Frederick. *Gestalt Therapy Verbatim*. Lafayette, Calif.: Real People Press, 1969.

Rogers, Carl R. *Client-Centered Therapy: Its Current Practice, Implications, and Theory*. Boston: Houghton Mifflin Co., 1951.

Rogers, Carl R. *On Becoming a Person*. Boston: Houghton Mifflin Co., 1961.

Rutherford, Robert B., Jr., and Edgar, Eugene. *Teachers and Parents: A Guide to Interaction and Cooperation*, abridged edition. Boston: Allyn and Bacon, 1979.

8

The Last Minutes
of the Interview

The last few minutes of an interview are special. The interview must be brought to a close; more than that—it should be brought to a satisfying close. Both interview participants have the need for completion of task. The gestalt psychologists have made us aware of the human need for closure—perception of an item as an organized whole. An unsolved problem or an uncompleted task can be considered an incomplete gestalt. As such, it can cause tension and frustration in an individual—a tension that can be relieved or discharged only when the incompleteness is somehow resolved, and the situation can be perceived as an organized whole. In an interview, this feeling of satisfying closure can be achieved if the purpose of the interview is accomplished.

We must be aware that the purpose of some interviews is such that it is not possible to make both participants happy with the interview outcome. Consider, for example, an interview set up to inform an employee that he or she is fired, or an interview to tell a patient that the results of a physical examination reveal a serious medical problem. In such cases, the interviewer can still aim for the most satisfying close possible under such circumstances. As with all effective interviews, this entails the interviewer's awareness and consideration of the respondent's basic human needs.

Many interviewers find that feelings of closure can be achieved by the use of summarizing, evaluating, or planning. A helpful way to look at this is attention to the immediate past, present, and future: summarizing what has happened in the interview; evaluating the present or current feelings of the participants toward the interview; and planning what may take place following the interview. The time devoted to each of these activities will vary

143

considerably depending upon the purpose, the length, and the complexity of the interview. The degree to which the interview participants will share in summarizing, evaluating, or planning will also vary. The extent to which this occurs will be largely dependent upon the interviewer's use of structuring.

USING THE LAST MINUTES EFFECTIVELY

In Chapter 6, we discussed the importance of structuring in getting the interview off to a satisfying start. During the main portion of the interview, structuring is often necessary to bring the interview back on course. As the time approaches to end the interview, structuring again is necessary. Often the interviewer reminds the respondent of the time remaining and what he or she would like to accomplish in this time.

The respondent's reaction to this reminder may take one of several directions, depending on what has transpired in the interview up to this point. The reminder may create a sense of urgency to bring up a critical issue that has not yet been discussed. Interviewers are frequently advised to avoid bringing up new material during the last few minutes of a session. The reason for this advice is that there may not be enough time to discuss the new issue. We run the risk of arousing new and strong emotions or raising an important problem that cannot be resolved or even explored satisfactorily in a few minutes.

The interviewer cannot prevent the respondent from bringing up new material, however. If the respondent introduces a new issue, the interviewer can proceed in one of several ways: ignore the new material; acknowledge it and dismiss it; discuss the material in the time remaining; or postpone the discussion until a future meeting.

Consider the following instance in which the interviewer reminds the respondent that five minutes remain in the interview. The respondent replies by bringing up a new topic:

> I: It's almost two-thirty. We have five minutes left and I want to be sure we're all set to go on this report. I'd like to review the list of people who should receive a copy.
> R: Only five more minutes? I wanted to talk with you about a whole new idea I have for the McGorry account. I was thinking of a TV campaign tied in with a direct mailing of free samples.

The interviewer's response to the introduction of this new topic can be in any one of the four ways listed above. For example, the interviewer can ignore the new material:

> I: I think we've got this report in good shape now. Have Doris type up the draft. We'll ask Lem Clarsen to look it over before we make the final copy. Now, who should get copies?

Or the interviewer can acknowledge the new material but dismiss it:

> *I:* I've just given that account to Higgins. We'll see what *he* comes up with. Now, let's get back to this report.

Or the interviewer can discuss the material in the time remaining:

> *I:* Say, that sounds like something I want to hear more about. Give me a quick run-down in the few minutes we have left.

Or the interviewer can postpone the discussion until a future meeting:

> *I:* Let's talk about that. We don't have time today—but I'm free for lunch tomorrow. We can get together then. Now what about the copies for this report?

Sometimes, an issue raised by the respondent is of such a crucial nature that the interviewer will extend the time for the interview. A depressed respondent may threaten suicide. A previously calm and collected respondent may suddenly break into tears or violent sobs. A previously uncommunicative respondent may suddenly disclose a piece of information that can shed an entirely new light on an important situation. There are times when schedules must be broken. This is one of the decisions that an interviewer must make.

Reminding the respondent of the time remaining in the interview does not always result in the introduction of important material. Rather than bring up a new topic, the respondent may interpret the reminder as a signal to stop serious discussion. He or she may then revert to small talk and social amenities. The interviewer may do likewise if he or she feels that the purpose of the interview has been met.

There is a happy medium between the two extremes of introducing new material or immediately shifting to small talk. Most often, the last few minutes involve efforts on the part of the interviewer to bring the session to a satisfying close through the use of summary, evaluation, and/or planning.

Using Summary

The degree to which the last few minutes will be spent in summary depends on the nature of the interview and the complexity and importance of the material discussed. In an information-getting interview, if the accuracy of the information obtained is so important that errors could prove disastrous— or even fatal—the interviewer might very well wish to repeat certain information in detail.

> *I:* I want to make sure I have this right. When the red light flashes and the buzzer sounds, we have two minutes to clear the building.

Or:

> I: I want to check again on your answers to two of these questions.
> You *are* allergic to penicillin?
> R: That's right. I had a terrible reaction when they gave it to me
> once.
> I: But you are *not* to erythromycin?
> R: No. I've had that several times and it didn't bother me.

As interviewers, we don't wish to spend any more time in summary than we feel is important to achieve the interview goal. A mere rehash of the preceding discussion may be time-consuming and frustrating—and accomplish nothing. However, there are other times when highlighting a particular portion of the interview can be effective. It can reemphasize a significant revelation or decision or can recall an important insight. For example,

> I: You realized something important about your relationship with
> your parents today. As you said, you can be angry with them and
> still love them.

Sometimes, the interviewer may prefer to summarize the important material. At other times, it is more effective to have the respondent do so.

> I: We have a few minutes left. Let's review what you think are the
> most important points we discussed today.

Some interviewers find it helpful to provide paper and pencil in case the respondent wishes to make notes. This can be particularly helpful if there are specific details or information that the respondent wishes or needs to remember. For instance, Alan Zalkowitz (1980, p. 133), a physician, makes the following statement:*

> Two of the most important pieces of equipment in my office are the pad
> and pencil in my consultation room. They're put to work near the end of
> each office visit, when my patient, examination concluded, is sitting across
> the desk from me waiting to hear what I have to tell him about his medi-
> cation or therapy. Before I begin, I hand him the paper and pencil and ask
> him not only to listen to what I say but to write it down.

Using Evaluation

One purpose in evaluating an interview during the last minutes can be to find out the respondent's reaction to what has transpired. In some settings, an actual checklist is provided for the respondent. This is a formalized way of evaluating the session. More often, the assessment will be done informally. For example:

> I: We met today to discuss ways to help John improve his reading. How do you feel about the ideas we've come up with?

Or:

> I: Did we cover what you hoped to cover in our discussion today? Please don't hesitate to speak frankly.

When we invite the respondent's evaluation, we should take care how we word the request. A leading question or verbalized assumption on our part may produce the hoped-for response, but may not reveal how the respondent truly feels. For example:

> I: Well, we've certainly accomplished a lot today, haven't we?

Or:

> I: I imagine getting this all off your chest makes you feel a lot better.

It can often be appropriate for the interviewer to provide his or her own evaluation of the interview. This can prove reassuring to the respondent if the evaluation is favorable. For example:

> I: I think we've accomplished a lot today. The information you've given me about Suzie will be very helpful in working with her.

Or our evaluation can provide selective reinforcement for certain types of behavior that occurred during the interview:

> I: Generally, I feel good about our meeting today. We got bogged down at the start in that hassle about duty and responsibility, but then we came up with these four procedures that should solve the problem.

What can we do if the respondent expresses a feeling that the interview has not been satisfactory or productive? We can acknowledge the respondent's dissatisfaction, trying not to be defensive. We can try to determine the reason for dissatisfaction. Even if there is no immediate remedy, we may get some important feedback from the respondent regarding our role in the interview. Perhaps we didn't provide enough direction to keep the interview on target. Perhaps there was too much small talk, or talk on topics that were of minor importance. Perhaps we, as the interviewer, did too much talking; the respondent may feel he or she did not get enough chance to talk. Perhaps we did not make the respondent feel sufficiently comfortable to want to share information or feelings. This is not to say that the interviewer is always responsible for an unsatisfying session. We know that there are any number of organismic variables that can affect the course of an interview.

Using Planning

Often the closing minutes involve planning what may take place after the interview. These plans may involve action by the interviewer, the respondent, or both. Based on discussion in the interview, the respondent may agree to do certain things. For example:

> R: The next step, then, is for me to take Peter to the orthodontist. I can call tomorrow to make an appointment.

We don't always know whether the respondent will do as he or she has planned. This will largely depend on the importance of the action to the respondent in relation to the difficulty in carrying it out. We may want to have some check to determine if the respondent followed through—if such follow through is related to our own responsibilities.

The interviewer may promise to do certain things. For example:

> I: I'll see that this report gets typed up and in the mail by Friday.

A conscientious interviewer will make only those promises that he or she intends to, and is able to, carry out. In the words of Robert Service (*The Cremation of Sam Magee*), "a promise made is a debt unpaid." It is easier to make a promise than to fulfill it.

Sometimes, interviewers may take on responsibility that rightfully belongs to the respondent. Personality theorists have various explanations for this dependence-encouraging behavior. The interviewer may be assuming a parent role in order to nurture or dominate the respondent. The interviewer may have been hooked into a respondent's game playing. Or this behavior may reflect the interviewer's philosophy regarding people's ability to take charge of their own lives.

As plans are discussed, the interview participants may schedule additional meetings, which may or may not involve arrangements for others to participate. At times, referrals to other people or agencies may be in order. These referrals may be general. For example:

> I: It seems to me that you and your husband would benefit from family counseling. I recommend that you look into it.

On the other hand, these referrals may be very specific:

> I: Our test results show that you will definitely benefit from a hearing aid. Here are the names and addresses of three hearing aid dealers and a copy of my recommended specifications for the hearing aid.

A specific referral may be the result of a respondent's request. If we feel that a specific referral will make a follow-up more likely to occur, we may well want to be specific. Making effective referrals will, of course, depend on thorough and accurate knowledge of available resources.

Ending the Interview

If both interview participants are aware of the time limit, there usually is no difficulty in ending an interview. On occasion, a person may want more time. If the interviewer's schedule is flexible, and he or she wishes to take more time, that is the interviewer's prerogative. The interviewer may not have the time or inclination to extend the interview. In that case, we have found that frankness and firmness work well. For example:

> R: It is such a treat for me to be able to talk to you. Did I tell you about our meeting at the Senior Center last week? We made some important decisions.
> I: I'm glad to hear that you're going to the Senior Center. I'd like for us to talk about that meeting, too, but there just is no more time. Keep up your good work at the Center!

As the interview comes to a close, you may wish to provide the respondent with some take-home materials. These can include previously prepared materials, an appointment card reminder of the next scheduled meeting, a listing of referral sources, and so forth. Whenever we provide a respondent with written material, we must of course make sure that the language and level of these materials is appropriate.

Occasionally, an interview comes to a close earlier than expected by either participant. It may be that the business of the interview is accomplished more quickly than anticipated. Or it may turn out that an immediate referral to a more appropriate person or agency is indicated. The meeting may be ended prematurely because one of the participants becomes ill, or an emergency message or telephone call is received. In such circumstances, the participants may quickly resolve the business at hand or may have to arrange for another meeting.

We need to allow a few moments at the end of the interview for good-byes. The actual form of leave-taking and social amenities that will end each interview will depend on the circumstances and the roles and personalities of the participants.

INTERVIEW EXCERPTS

Let us examine excerpts of the closing minutes of two interviews. We can note the use of summary, evaluation, and planning in these excerpts.

Interview Excerpt 8–1

Consider the following excerpt from an interview in which the owner of a natural food store is engaged in an unpleasant task: that of firing an elderly maintenance man. The man has been on this job for five years. The reason for firing is that the maintenance man is no longer able to meet the owner's standard of cleanliness for the store.

1. I: John, I have to get to the warehouse to pick up that shipment—so I can't talk with you much longer. I'm sorry it has to be this way, but the store has to be spotless. As I said, I think it's just getting to be too much for you.
    (structuring and information; negative feeling toward firing)

2. R: I have to have a job. And where can I go at my age?
    (problem area; negative feeling toward job outlook)

3. I: Well, John—as you said—I'm sure your sister will want you to keep your room at her house. She's mentioned to me how much you help her around the place. The way we figured it—with your social security and veteran's pension, you should be able to get by.
    (restatement of content)

4. R: Yeah, when you added it up that way for me, it doesn't sound too bad. But I still think there's a lot of work left in me.
    (agreement and information; ambivalent feeling toward retirement)

5. I: I'm sure that's true, John. It's just that *this* job is very demanding. I'm sure there are fellows a lot younger than you who wouldn't be able to handle it.
    (reassurance and information)

6. R: Yeah, but that doesn't help me much.
    (agreement and problem area)

7. I: No, I understand that. (pause) But we talked about those things you'll have more time to do now—like fishing. As you said, it's not all bad. The hard part is having it come a little sooner than you expected.
    (reassurance; restatement of content; reflection of feeling)

8.	R: It sure did. (pause) I guess that's it, then. I'll finish out the week, the way you want me to.	(agreement and planning)
9.	I: That'll be fine, John. I'll have your check ready on Friday. I'll see you then.	(approval and information)
10.	R: All right. (leaves the office)	(*mm-hm* response)

In Excerpt 8–1, the interviewer is faced with a difficult task. He must attempt a satisfying close in a situation which is basically unsatisfying to the respondent. No one likes to be fired; and most of us don't like to fire people. In this situation, the cause of the respondent's incapacity is advanced age—a life stage which brings with it certain inevitable problems.

In Utterance 1 of the excerpt, the employer uses structuring to alert the respondent that the interview is coming to a close. He also expresses his feeling of regret that he must fire the employee. He reiterates his reason for having to do so. As the respondent expresses his regret at being forced to retire, the interviewer summarizes the positive aspects of early retirement. He also acknowledges the current feelings that John is expressing. The employer is considerate of John's basic need for respect and self-esteem. He is sensitive to the fact that John is beginning to feel a sense of uselessness. He points out that John can continue to hold a useful role—that of helping his sister maintain her home. The employer does not deny or play down the feelings that John is expressing. Nor does he succumb to the temptation of giving false assurances that John could easily find and hold another job. From a transactional standpoint, it can be difficult in a situation such as this to maintain adult-adult transactions. The temptation exists to transfer to a parent-child relationship, with the employer assuming the parent role.

Note the absence of small talk. This is probably due to the seriousness of the topic for both participants. As the session ends, John verbalizes acceptance of the loss of his job. Plans are then made for the remaining work days.

Interview Excerpt 8–2

In this excerpt, the decorating consultant at a department store is talking with a prospective customer.

1.	I: Mrs. Brockton, we have been talking for over an hour, and you'll have to make a decision. I have an appointment with an architect across town in just thirty minutes.	(structuring)
2.	R: I don't like to be rushed, Mr. Finch. This is a very important decision for me.	(information)

3. I: It shouldn't take this much time to decide   (disapproval and
        on one chair. I've shown you the only chair   information)
        that will work in that room.

4. R: Are you sure that bright red is the only   (request for
        color that would work? I'm afraid we might   information and
        get tired of that after a while.   problem area;
                                                          negative feeling
                                                          toward chair color)

5. I: I've explained to you several times that you   (advice or
        must have bright red to make that room   suggestion)
        come alive. Nothing else will do.

6. R: We have to live with this a long time.   (problem area)
        I don't want to make a mistake.

7. I: Mrs. Brockton, if you follow my advice   (information)
        you won't make a mistake. After all, that's
        why you came to me.

8. R: But, bright red! I just don't know.   (problem area)

9. I: If you don't get the bright red, it will be a   (information)
        nothing room. You told me you wanted
        something dramatic.

10. R: I just don't know what my husband would   (problem area)
        think about something so bright.

11. I: I don't presume to know what your hus-   (information;
        band would think. I *do* know what's right   negative feeling
        for that room. I can't spend any more time   toward customer's
        now. You have my card. You can phone me   indecision)
        if you want to order the chair. (He stands
        up to leave)

12. R: This is frustrating. I want a chair, but I need   (problem area;
        more time to think about it.   negative feeling
                                                          toward making
                                                          decision)

13. I: That's entirely up to you. (leaves the office)   (information)

In contrast to interview excerpt 8–1, the circumstances surrounding interview excerpt 8–2 are not basically unpleasant. The customer wishes to purchase furniture. This has prompted her to seek the services of a store decorating consultant. It is clear that the decorating consultant has recommended the purchase of a particular chair. In Utterance •1 of this excerpt, the interviewer notifies the client that the interview must soon end. He presses her for a decision regarding the purchase. When the client expresses negative feelings toward the recommendation, the decorator refuses to suggest alternatives. He adamantly states there is one and only one suitable selection. In response to the customer's continued uncertainty, the decorator merely repeats his only recommendation. He does not provide other choices; nor does he provide clear reasons for his recommendation.

This closing is an unsatisfying one for both participants. The customer requested the interview, no doubt hoping that she would be given information and assistance in selecting appropriate furniture for her home. At the close of the interview, she expresses frustration. The singlemindedness of the consultant—his refusal to provide choices—contributes to her frustration.

Consider this brief exchange on the basis of the dominance-submission and friendliness-unfriendliness dimensions. We get the impression that the interviewer views his role as the dominant one. However, it is not clear that the respondent accepts the submissive role. She neither accepts nor rejects his recommendation—resulting in postponement of any decision. On the friendliness-unfriendliness dimension, we get the distinct impression that the interview ends on an unfriendly note.

It is certainly the decorator's prerogative to make one and only one recommendation. He may do this because he feels that his recommendation is absolutely correct. However, he must then accept the possibility that the customer will reject that one recommendation. In life, we may find ourselves in many situations where we initially feel that only one solution is acceptable. Experts on problem solving remind us that there are usually several acceptable solutions or resolutions of a problem. As this interview illustrates, unwillingness to consider alternatives can lead to frustration and dissatisfaction.

IMMEDIATELY FOLLOWING THE INTERVIEW

In our discussion of scheduling interviews in Chapter 5, we mentioned the advisability of allowing some time between interviews for necessary details before moving on to the next appointment. If we have tape recorded the interview, we will want to mark the tape with identifying information and put it in a place where confidentiality will be insured. If we have made the tape for purposes of analysis, we may find it helpful to listen to the tape and analyze it as soon as possible after the interview. This is particularly true if there were difficulties in communication—a language barrier, for instance.

Methods of recording interview information were also discussed in Chapter 5. After the interview is completed, the interviewer may wish to take a few minutes to review and organize his or her notes. There may be time to carry out promises made during the interview. If that is not possible, the interviewer should have some procedure for completing these tasks as soon as possible. A tickler file or memo listing "things to do" can be helpful if the interviewer can't immediately complete the necessary chores or delegate them to someone else. In some settings, a report or summary of the interview must be prepared and placed in the client's file. The particular procedure after an interview will depend upon the interviewer's personality, setting, and responsibilities.

A common problem for interviewers in many settings is effective use of time. Alan Lakein (1973), Donna Goldfein (1977), Michael LeBoeuf (1979), Helen Reynolds and Mary Tramel (1979), and others have written books containing excellent suggestions. You may wish to take advantage of their expertise.

AID TO ANALYSIS

Listen to a taped interview, and ask yourself the following questions regarding the last minutes of the session.

1. Was there enough time to end the session so that there was not an abrupt cut-off without any warning?
2. Did we look back on the interview in any way? By summarizing the most important information or feelings? By summing up decisions or what was accomplished?
3. Did we evaluate the interview in any way? By expressing feeling as to whether or not we accomplished the goal of the interview or achieved its purpose? Did I—as the interviewer—share my feelings regarding the interview with the respondent? Did I make it easy for the respondent to express his or her evaluation in a frank manner? Did I avoid leading questions that would invite flattery at the expense of honesty?
4. Did we look to the future in any way? By noting, for instance, any effect the interview might have on future behavior or activities? By planning specific actions? By arranging another meeting?
5. Did I structure the last few minutes of the interview so that the respondent had opportunity to add any desired information or comments?
6. If the respondent introduced a new topic in the last few minutes, how did I handle it? By ignoring it? By acknowledging it and dismissing it? By discussing it in the remaining time? By postponing discussion until a future time?
7. Did either the respondent or I commit ourselves to any specific future action? If so, did we provide for a way to check up on whether the action or plan is carried out?
8. Did I—as the interviewer—make any promises to the respondent? Have I kept those promises?
9. What was the general mood or tone of the closing minutes? Optimistic? Pessimistic? Frustrated? Hostile? Congenial? Relieved? Other?
10. Focusing on the respondent, were there any indications of the

respondent's feelings concerning the interview? What were they?

11. Did I provide any take-home materials for the respondent? Any notes, printed materials, samples, or the like that would be helpful to the respondent? Were these materials appropriate for this particular respondent? Did I consider reading ability, visual ability, and so forth?

12. Did I make any referrals? Were they appropriate? Did I provide the respondent with necessary information?

13. Was there any small talk in the last few minutes? Did it seem appropriate? What purpose did it serve?

14. Is there evidence of concern for the respondent's basic needs? Did I foster respondent independence and self-esteem?

REFERENCES

Goldfein, Donna. *Everywoman's Guide to Time Management*. Millbrae, Calif.: Les Femmes Publishing, 1977.

Lakein, Alan. *How to Get Control of Your Time and Your Life*. New York: The New American Library, 1973.

LeBoeuf, Michael. *Working Smart*. New York: Warner Books, 1979.

Reynolds, Helen, and Tramel, Mary E. *Executive Time Management*. Englewood Cliffs, N.J.: Prentice-Hall, 1979.

Zalkowitz, Alan. "When I Give Instructions, My Patients Take Notes," *Medical Economics*, 18 (August 1980), 133–138.

9

The Molyneaux/Lane Interview Analysis

SURVEY OF SYSTEMATIC INTERVIEW ANALYSIS METHODS

In the preceding chapters, we have looked at the various portions of an interview: the opening minutes, the body of the interview, and the closing minutes. In each of these chapters, we have included questions that an interviewer might ask concerning these portions of the interview. Within the past three decades, a number of investigators have developed more formal systems of analysis designed to study interpersonal communication. Their investigative purposes have included:

1. Analyzing the interactions of teachers and students in the classroom setting (Flanders, 1960; Wilhelms, 1973; Gazda et al., 1977)
2. Analyzing small group interactions (Bales, 1950)
3. Evaluating the effectiveness of poll-takers in household interviews (Cannell, Lawson, and Hausser, 1975)
4. Studying the dynamics of family communication (Bateson, 1951; Mark, 1971; Watzlawick and Weakland, 1977)
5. Evaluating the effectiveness of training methods in developing counseling techniques and helping skills (Carkhuff, 1969; Danish and Hauer, 1973; Volz et al., 1978)
6. Analyzing clinician-client interactions (Aronson and Weintraub, 1972; Siegman and Pope, 1972; Boone and Prescott, 1974; Brookshire et al., 1978; Oratio, 1979; Stiles and Sultan, 1979; Stiles, McDaniel, and McGaughey, 1979)

7. Analyzing and comparing the verbal behavior of counselors representing various theoretical orientations (Hill, 1978; Brunink and Schroeder, 1979; Hill, Thames, and Rardin, 1979; Meara, Shannon, and Pepinsky, 1979)

These systems are similar in that they all study some aspect of interpersonal communication and employ a coding system to assist in that study. They differ in many ways, including: the types of coding used; the focus of the analysis; the population for which the analysis was designed; the number of participants permitted; the complexity of the system; the degree of subjective judgment required; attention to verbal and/or nonverbal communication; and the applicability of the analysis method to a variety of interpersonal communications. Each of these systems has merit. If you are interested in details of any of these systems, you may wish to look up the references listed at the end of this chapter. For a review of studies published between 1954 and 1968 analyzing the content of psychotherapeutic sessions, you may wish to examine Gerald Marsden's work (1971).

DEVELOPMENT OF THE MOLYNEAUX/LANE INTERVIEW ANALYSIS

In 1966, the authors were given the responsibility of developing and teaching a university seminar in parent counseling. Much of the seminar was devoted to helping students acquire the skills and techniques we have talked about in previous chapters of this book. Throughout the semester the students would be given the opportunity to practice some of these skills, either with classmates in role-playing situations or in brief real-life interview sessions.

As the culminating experience, each member of the class interviewed a parent of a child with communication problems. Each student tape recorded his or her interview and prepared a typed verbatim transcription. The students then analyzed their interviews to determine what interactions had taken place. They made notations in the margins identifying techniques used in particular utterances. The student interviewers also identified feelings expressed by the parents and toward what or whom the feelings were directed.

The instructor read the transcripts and reviewed the students' identifications of utterances noted in the margins. A personal conference was then scheduled with each student interviewer to discuss particular aspects of the interview and what had occurred. The aim of the personal conference was to help the student gain insight into his or her particular style of interviewing.

As a result of our experience in teaching the seminar, we became convinced that there was a need for a more efficient and consistent way of identifying what went on in an interview. We were interested in identifying two types of information: the particular types of utterances made by the interviewer and the respondent, and the feelings expressed. To achieve this goal, we needed a systematic procedure that would allow us to make these identifications. Naturally, in this advanced technological age, we sought a system that would allow computer analysis of any information we obtained. We wanted to use the system to analyze the more than 200 typed verbatim interview transcriptions we already had on file. A search of the literature did not reveal any existing method that would meet our particular needs.

We therefore developed a five-digit coding system that was refined and revised over a period of two years. The first digit in the five-digit code indicates the speaker designation. A 1 identifies the interviewer as the speaker; a 2 indicates the respondent as the speaker when there are two interview participants. A 3 would be used to indicate a second respondent, and so forth. The second and third digits are code numbers for the type of utterance. All utterances made by the interviewer are coded 01 to 20. All respondent utterances are coded 50 to 64. The designations were selected to focus on specific behaviors identified as critical interview techniques or responses. See Table 9–1 for the listing of utterance designations and their code numbers and definitions.

TABLE 9–1   Utterance Codings, Designations, and Definitions

Digit	Function	Indicator	Definition
1	Speaker designation	1 Interviewer 2 Respondent	(Additional numbers assigned if more than two interview participants)
2–3	Interviewer utterance designation	01 Indirect question	Does not require question mark punctuation yet encourages discussion of a particular topic
		02 Direct question I	Requests specific externally verifiable statistic
		03 Direct question II	Requests information, opinion, or conclusion other than an externally verifiable statistic
		04 Leading question	Direct question indicating that specific answer is expected or preferred
		05 Double question I	Asks two questions, the second question identical or almost identical with the first
		06 Double question II	Asks two questions, the second question dissimilar to the first or incomplete
		07 Bombardment	Contains three or more questions of any type
		08 *Mm-hm* response	Indicates that listener is tuned in and following conversation
		09 Approval	Expresses agreement with or favorable judgment of respondent's statement, action, and/or reported behavior when respondent has not expressed a judgment

TABLE 9–1 (*Continued*)

Digit	Function	Indicator	Definition
		10 Disapproval	Expresses negative evaluation of respondent's statement, action, and/or reported behavior
		11 Forcing client responsibility	Immediately redirects respondent's question back to respondent
		12 Information	Provides data
		13 Reassurance	Confirms or validates respondent's stated information or supposition
		14 Restatement of content	Repeats or summarizes actual material or data expressed verbally by respondent
		15 Reflection of feeling	Attempts to verbalize current emotions expressed either verbally or nonverbally by respondent
		16 Structuring	Orients respondent to interview situation or prescribes procedure to be followed during interview
		17 Interpretation	Suggests possible motivation (not verbally expressed by the respondent) to account for respondent's expressed action or feeling
		18 Advice, suggestion, or command	Recommends or orders course of action to be followed by the respondent other than during the interview
		19 Nonpertinent small talk	Consists of irrelevant comments and/or social amenities
		20 Other	Any utterance not defined above
2–3	Respondent utterance designation	50 Agreement	Confirms interviewer's statement or leading question
		51 Disagreement	Denies or differs with interviewer's statement or leading question
		52 Request for information	Seeks data from interviewer
		53 Information	Provides data
		54 Problem area	Identifies or indicates situation as currently causing stress or concern
		55 Insight	Expresses awareness of motivation or consequences of behavior at time of utterance not previously understood or verbalized
		56 Planning	Verbalizes own planned future behavior
		57 *Mm-hm* response	Indicates listener is tuned in and following conversation

TABLE 9–1 (Continued)

Digit	Function	Indicator	Definition
		58 Advice, suggestion, or command	Recommends or orders a course of action to be followed by the interviewer or the interviewer's agency
		59 Agreement with restatement, reflection, interpretation, or leading question, plus asking for information (agreement plus asking)	Confirms interviewer's statement and seeks data from interviewer
		60 Agreement with restatement, reflection, interpretation, or leading question, plus giving information (agreement plus giving)	Confirms interviewer's statement and provides data
		61 Disagreement with restatement, reflection, interpretation, or leading question plus asking for information (disagreement plus asking)	Denies or differs with interviewer's statement and seeks data from interviewer
		62 Disagreement with restatement, reflection, interpretation, or leading question, plus giving information (disagreement plus giving)	Denies or differs with interviewer's statement and provides data
		63 Nonpertinent small talk	Consists of irrelevant comments and/or social amenities
		64 Other	Any utterance not defined above

The fourth and fifth digits code the feelings expressed. The fourth digit indicates whether the feeling is positive, negative, or ambivalent. The fifth digit indicates toward what or whom the feeling is directed. Two zeros as the fourth and fifth digits of the code number indicate that no feelings are expressed in the utterance. See Table 9–2 for the listing of codings used for expressed feelings. It can be noted that the designations for the fifth digit— toward what or whom the feeling is directed—are specifically related to feelings expressed by parents of children with communication problems. These designations are appropriate for interviews in our setting, a communicative disorders clinic. Interviewers in other fields may wish to establish designations more applicable to their settings.

TABLE 9–2   Codings for Expressed Feelings

Digit	Function	Indicator			
4–5	Designation of expressed feelings	00			No feelings expressed
		(+)	(−)	(±)	
		11	31	51	Feelings toward self (respondent) as parent
		12	32	52	Feelings toward self (respondent) other than as parent
		13	33	53	Feelings toward spouse (child's natural parent)
		14	34	54	Feelings toward spouse (if other than child's natural parent)
		15	35	55	Feelings toward child's (clinic enrollee) speech and/or language skills and development to date
		16	36	56	Feelings toward child's (clinic enrollee) skills, development, personality, and interests other than speech and language
		17	37	57	Feelings toward child's (clinic enrollee) future
		18	38	58	Feelings toward child's siblings and/or child's relationships with siblings
		19	39	59	Feelings toward children other than immediate family
		20	40	60	Feelings toward adult relatives (other than spouse) and/or baby sitters or adult acquaintances
		21	41	61	Feelings toward bearing and/or raising children
		22	42	62	Feelings toward schools and/or teachers
		23	43	63	Feelings toward language, speech, or hearings services and/or therapists
		24	44	64	Feelings toward medical agencies (including school medical services) and/or physicians or dentists
		25	45	65	Feelings toward psychological or social services including school psychologists, school counselors, and/or social workers
		26	46	66	Other

TABLE 9–2 (Continued)

Definitions of Categories of Expressed Feelings

Positive Feeling (+): a currently felt emotion within the category commonly designated as pleasant (for example, expressions of happiness, pleasure, satisfaction, pride, delight, tenderness, desire, love, and joy)

Negative Feeling (−): a currently felt emotion within the category commonly designated as unpleasant (for example, expressions of unhappiness, dissatisfaction, annoyance, irritation, frustration, anger, disgust, rage, fear, and grief)

Ambivalent Feelings (±): expression within one utterance of both positive and negative emotions directed toward the same person, object, idea, or activity

RESEARCH FINDINGS

By 1976, the coding system was established and we began our interview research project. All the interviews had been conducted by graduate students in Communicative Disorders enrolled in the seminar in parent counseling. All the respondents were parents of children with language, speech, and/or hearing disorders enrolled in the San Francisco State University Communicative Disorders Clinic. The interviews were basically information-getting interviews. The students were instructed to obtain information concerning the child that might be helpful to the child's clinician. However, no specific format or questions were prescribed. An eclectic counseling approach was advocated in the seminar. However, client-centered principles of creating a nonjudgmental atmosphere, using open rather than closed questions, and recognizing and reflecting feelings expressed by the respondents were encouraged.

We found that 150 of the 200 interviews were suitable for inclusion in the research project in that they met the following criteria: each interview was conducted by a different student interviewer; and each interview was conducted with a different respondent. The only available transcribed interviews not included in the research project were second or third interviews with a particular parent or interviews in which both parents were present and participating in the interview.

To facilitate statistical analysis, we decided to use the utterance as the unit for study. An utterance was defined as "everything expressed by one speaker before another person speaks." One five-digit code number was assigned to each utterance. The first digit of the code number was easily assigned, since identification of the speaker was always clear-cut. Coding the second and third digits (the type of utterance) was more difficult. There were some utterances that could be appropriately coded by more than one designation. For example, restatement of content and reflection of feeling occasionally took the form of a question. Therefore, the following two rules for coding digits two and three were adopted: if an *mm-hm* response or nonpertinent small talk response is combined with any other utterance, code the remainder of the utterance; if two or more designations are appropriate, choose the one with the higher code number. The fourth and fifth digits coded expressed feelings. In occasional instances where more than one feeling was expressed within an utterance, the coding assigned was based on the dominant feeling expressed.

All of the 150 transcribed interviews were coded by the authors. Initial inter-rater reliability between the two authors was 86 percent based on independent coding of the first few interviews. As subsequent interviews were coded, occasional questions arose regarding appropriate coding for a particular utterance. A mutually agreed-upon coding was determined following brief discussion and review of definitions. This occurred for approximately four or five utterances per interview. Upon completion of the coding of the 150 interviews, the five-digit coded utterances were then keypunched for computer analysis. Computer analysis was completed on the CDC 3150 using a specially designed FORTRAN program. Statistical procedures included Biomedical Computer Program 08M (factor analysis), 09M (canonical correlation analysis) as described in Dixon (1977). Pearson product moment r correlation and t-test were also obtained.

These procedures provided the following data. Tabulations using the second and third digits of the code number revealed the number of times a particular type of utterance appeared in each interview and the proportion (percentage) of that type to the total number of utterances in one interview. We also obtained information regarding the means and standard deviations of each type of utterance (the utterance designation was the second and third digit of the code number) in the total number of 150 interviews.

Tabulations using the fourth and fifth digits of the code number revealed the number of times expressed feelings were identified within each interview and toward what or whom those feelings were directed. Again, in addition to statistics for each interview, we obtained information regarding the incidence and nature of expressed feelings in the total 150 interviews. Pearson product moment correlations were calculated to determine whether the percentage of feelings expressed by the respondents correlated with types of interviewer utterances.

Factor analysis was then performed using two different rotations— varimax and oblimin. The data were also analyzed using Johnson hierarchical clustering. The factors extracted provided evidence regarding the characteristics demonstrated by interview participants. Canonical correlation analysis of the first order factors for both interviewers and respondents were utilized to determine second order factors. These second-order factors provide information regarding relationships among interviewer and respondent factors.

These statistical analyses resulted in some interesting findings that we will now briefly summarize. Detailed tables of our findings are included in Appendix B for readers who would like more information.

As might be expected in a group of information-getting interviews, we found that the largest percentage of *interviewer* utterances was in the category designated direct question II (code number 103) at 26 per cent.

You will recall that direct question II is defined as a question that requests information, opinion, or conclusion other than an externally verifiable statistic. The next higher percentage of utterances obtained was the *mm-hm* response (108) at 15 percent. This utterance designation indicates that the listener was tuned in and following the conversation. The types of utterances having the next highest percentage of occurrence were information (112) utterances at 13 percent and restatement of content (114), also at 13 percent. Information is defined as providing data; and restatement of content is defined as repeating or summarizing actual material or data expressed verbally by the respondent. These four utterance designations accounted for 67 percent of all utterances produced by the interviewers. In contrast, the utterance designations disapproval (110), forcing client responsibility (111), and interpretation (117) occurred infrequently. (Refer to Table B-1 in Appendix B for the occurrence, mean percentage, and interquartile range for each of the utterance types made by the interviewers in the total 150 interviews.)

The largest percentage of *respondent* utterances were information (code number 253), utterances where the parents provided data. This utterance designation comprised 55 percent of the total number of utterances made by the respondents in the 150 interviews. The next highest percentage was 17 percent for utterances indicating a problem area (254). This designation is used to code an utterance in which a parent identified a situation as currently causing stress or concern. The next most frequently occurring utterances were agreement (250) utterances at 9 percent and agreement with restatement, reflection, interpretation, or leading question, plus giving information (260) utterances, also at 9 percent. These four utterance designations account for 90 percent of all utterances made by the parents. We see that the analysis indicated that the interviews were, by and large, information-getting interviews; the interviewers asked questions, which the respondents then answered. (Table B–2 in Appendix B lists the occurrence, mean percentage, and interquartile range of each of the utterance types made by the respondents in the 150 interviews.)

Of the utterances made by the respondents, 22 percent were identified as containing expressed feelings. We found that the 150 interviewers seldom expressed feelings. Almost half of the feelings expressed by parents directly concerned their child. The largest percentage of such feelings expressed concern about their child's future. This concern for their child's future accounted for one-third (32 percent) of all utterances in which feelings were expressed. The feelings expressed by the parents were almost equally divided between positive feelings regarding their child's future and negative or ambivalent feelings in this area. Parents also expressed feelings about their child's skills, development, personality, and interests other than speech and language. These expressed feelings accounted for 15 percent of all utterances in which feelings were expressed. Again, the parents expressed positive, negative and ambivalent feelings in this area. One-third of their expressed feelings were positive, and two-thirds were negative or ambivalent. (Table B-3 in

Appendix B lists the percentage of feelings expressed by the respondents occurring in at least 1 percent of the utterances.)

As we mentioned, the Pearson product moment correlation was computed to determine whether the percentage of feelings expressed by the respondents correlated with any particular interviewer utterances. Two statistically significant correlations were obtained: restatement of content (114) with expressed feelings, significant at the .02 level ($t = 2.416$); and, of course, reflection of feeling (115) with expressed feelings, significant at the .01 level ($t = 5.914$).

Nine factors were extracted in the analysis of the interviewer utterances, and five factors were extracted in the analysis of the respondent utterances. (Tables B-4 and B-5 in Appendix B indicate factor loadings obtained using the oblimin rotation.) All three methods of analysis—varimax, oblimin, and Johnson hierarchical clustering—resulted in the extraction of essentially the same factors. The fact that the designated utterance types clustered into discernible factors provides insight into nine distinct interviewer styles and five distinct respondent styles.

The use of questions appeared in most of the interviewer factors, but with subtle differences. For instance, the styles of several groups of interviewers involved use of open questions (direct question II) that had been encouraged in the parent counseling seminar. The differences that distinguished these interviewing styles were related to the extent to which interviewers also used restatement of content and reflection of feeling (factor 2), or used the *mm-hm* response (factor 3), or the extent to which they provided information (factor 9).

Three of the five factors that characterized respondent utterances involved information-giving, but again with a difference. One group of parents provided information in answer to interviewer questions but did not appear personally responsive to other interviewer utterances (factor 1). The information given by other respondents involved more detailed elaboration (factor 2). Other respondents gave information but did not discuss current problem areas (factor 5).

Three canonical correlations significant at the .01 level were obtained in the analysis of relationships between interviewer factors and respondent factors. These second order factors, sometimes termed "super-factors," are detailed in Table B-6 of Appendix B.

Super-factor I characterized interviews in which the interviewer was businesslike and used a high percentage of open questions, as well as restatement of content and reflection of feeling. This style reminds us of the traditional Rogerian client-centered interviewer. The respondent in this interaction provided information along with elaboration of detail, and was present-oriented rather than future-oriented.

Super-factor II, on the other hand, describes an interviewer who primarily used open questions without restatement of content or reflection of feeling, and without providing information or additional input. The respondent in this interview situation gave information but did not elaborate, and was unresponsive to other interviewer comments.

The interviewers who clustered in super-factor III were businesslike and provided the respondent with considerable information. The respondents, on the other hand, did not provide information. Perhaps they did not have an opportunity to do so.

Our experience in this research project proved to us that it was helpful to have specific designations to identify types of utterances made in interviews. Formulating discrete definitions for these designations insures considerable agreement among a number of people using the same system. Since the completion of the research project, we have been teaching students to use the interview analysis method. We have found that student inter-rater reliability on three different studies was 84 percent, 86 percent, and 93 percent. Preliminary intra-rater reliability studies indicated an 83 percent intra-rater percentage of agreement on interview excerpts coded three months apart. Several other research projects using the interview analysis are under way. These involve the analysis of various types of interviews conducted by professional interviewers. One of the projects also involves the coding of interviews with three or more participants. The first digit of the code number is, of course, particularly necessary for these interviews because it identifies the various participants.

Use of the numerical coding system made computer analysis possible —an important consideration when vast amounts of data are being analyzed. Of course, the numerical coding system can conveniently be used to analyze individual interviews without relying on a computer. Using the first three digits of the five-digit code provides a handy method for designating the speaker and the type of utterance. If analysis of feelings is desired, a fourth and fifth digit can be used to identify that information.

Information obtained by using the interview analysis method may be helpful in determining interviewing style, whether or not the goals of the interview were met, and if the types of utterances used were those that the interviewer considered appropriate and effective. A tally of the interviewer and respondent utterances can provide information regarding the interaction of the participants and perhaps a clearer picture of how their utterances affected the course of the interview.

Some professionals are acknowledged to be excellent interviewers. They appear to be able to work effectively with respondents in achieving a variety of interviewing goals. An analysis of a series of interviews conducted by acknowledged experts may reveal interviewing strategies and provide models for less advanced interviewers.

Uses of the interview analysis method include the following:

To analyze your own interviews
To determine personal interviewing strengths and possible weaknesses
To assist in improving interviewing style and technique

To aid in supervision of student interviewers
To document interviewer and/or respondent change
To facilitate a variety or research

In Chapters 10 and 11, we have provided materials to assist you in working with the Molyneaux/Lane Interview Analysis.

REFERENCES

Aronson, H., and Weintraub, W. "Personal Adaptation as Reflected in Verbal Behavior." In *Studies in Dyadic Communication* edited by A. W. Siegman and B. Pope. New York: Pergamon Press, 1972.

Bales, R. F. *Interaction Process Analysis: A Method for the Study of Small Groups.* Cambridge, Massachusetts: Addison-Wesley, 1950.

Bateson, G. "Information and Codification: A Philosophical Approach." In *Communication: The Social Matrix of Psychiatry*, edited by J. Ruesch and G. Bateson. New York: W. W. Norton and Co., 1951.

Boone, D. R., and Prescott, T. E. *Speech and Hearing Therapy Scoring Manual: A Manual for Learning to Self-Score the Events of Therapy.* Washington, D.C.: U.S. Department of Health, Education and Welfare, Division of Research Bureau of Education for the Handicapped, Office of Education, 1974.

Brookshire, R. H.; Nicholas, L. S.; Krueger, K. M.; and Redmond, K. J. "The Clinical Interaction Analysis System: A System for Observational Recording of Aphasia Treatment," *Journal of Speech and Hearing Disorders*, 43 (1978), 437–447.

Brunink, Sharon A., and Schroeder, Harold E. "Verbal Therapeutic Behavior of Expert Psychoanalytically Oriented, Gestalt, and Behavior Therapists," *Journal of Consulting and Clinical Psychology*, 47 (1979), 567–574.

Cannell, C. F.; Lawson, S. A.; and Hausser, D. L. A *Technique for Evaluating Interviewer Performance.* Ann Arbor, Mich.: The University of Michigan, 1975.

Carkhuff, R. R. *Helping and Human Relationships: A Primer for Lay and Professional Helpers*, Vol. I and II. New York: Holt, Rinehart, and Winston, 1969.

Danish, S., and Hauer, A. *Helping Skills: A Basic Training Program.* New York: Behavioral Publications, 1973.

Dixon, W. J., editor. *BMD Biomedical Computer Programs.* Berkeley: University of California Press, 1977.

Flanders, N. *Interaction Analysis in the Classroom.* Minneapolis, Minn.: University of Minnesota, 1960.

Gazda, G. M.; Asbury, F. R.; Balzer, F. J.; Childers, W. C.; and Walters, R. P. *Human Relations Development: A Manual for Educators*, 2d ed. Boston: Allyn and Bacon, 1977.

Hill, Clara E. "Development of a Counselor Verbal Response Category System," *Journal of Counseling Psychology*, 25 (1978), 461–468.

Hill, Clara; Thames, Terri B.; and Rardin, David K. "Comparison of Rogers, Perls, and Ellis on the Hill Counselor Verbal Response Category System," *Journal of Counseling Psychology*, 25 (1979), 198–203.

Mark, R. A. "Coding Communication at the Relationship Level," *Journal of Communication*, 21 (1971), 221–232.

Marsden, Gerald. "Content-Analysis Studies of Psychotherapy: 1954 through 1968." In *Handbook of Psychotherapy and Behavior Change*, edited by Allen Bergin and Sol Garfield, pp. 345-407. New York: John Wiley & Sons, 1971.

Meara, Naomi M.; Shannon, Joseph W.; and Pepinsky, Harold B. "Comparison of the Stylistic Complexity of the Language of Counselor and Client Across Three Theoretical Orientations," *Journal of Counseling Psychology*, 26 (1979), 181–189.

Oratio, Albert R. *"Pattern Recognition"*: *A Computer Program for Interaction Analysis of Intervention and Training Processes in Speech and Hearing*. Baltimore: University Park Press, 1979.

Siegman, A. W., and Pope, B. *Studies in Dyadic Communication*. New York: Pergamon Press, 1972.

Stiles, William B.; McDaniel, Susan H.; and McGaughey, Kim. "Verbal Response Mode Correlates of Experiencing," *Journal of Consulting and Clinical Psychology*, 47 (1979), 795–797.

Stiles, William B., and Sultan, Faye E. "Verbal Response Mode Use By Clients in Psychotherapy," *Journal of Consulting and Clinical Psychology*, 47 (1979), 611–613.

Volz, H. B.; Klevans, D. R.; Norton, S. J.; and Putens, D. L. "Interpersonal Communication Skills of Speech-Language Pathology Undergraduates: The Effects of Training," *Journal of Speech and Hearing Disorders*, 43 (1978), 524–541.

Watzlawick, P., and Weakland, J. H., eds. *The Interactional View*. New York: W. W. Norton and Co., 1977.

Wilhelms, F. T. *Supervision in a New Key*. Washington, D.C.: Association for Supervision and Curriculum Development, 1973.

Identifying Interview Utterances

In the earlier chapters of this book, you have been introduced to techniques and terms used in interviewing. You have also been introduced to the designations and numerical coding used in the Molyneaux/Lane interview analysis. In this chapter, we will provide an opportunity for you to identify and code sample interviewer and respondent utterances.

The first practice exercise is limited to interviewer questions for you to identify. The second exercise involves interviewer questions and respondent replies. In Exercise Three, we have included longer interview excerpts and a greater variety of interviewer and respondent utterances to be identified. In Exercise Four, you have the opportunity to identify feelings in addition to the utterance designations.

Each practice exercise will indicate the speaker (I = Interviewer or R = Respondent) and what he or she has said. Space is provided next to each utterance for you to write down the appropriate designation as you identify each utterance. Space is also provided for you to write down the appropriate code number, if you wish. Remember, the first digit of the code number is always 1 when the Interviewer is speaking and always 2 when the Respondent is speaking. The complete listing of the utterance designations, code numbers, definitions, and examples is found in Appendix A. You may find it helpful to make a copy of those pages for handy reference as you do the exercises.

IDENTIFYING INTERVIEWER QUESTION TYPES

Exercise One

Instructions

Place the appropriate utterance designation opposite each utterance in the Utterance Designation column. The three digit code number may also be listed in the Code Number column. The first digit of the three-digit number is the speaker designation. In this exercise, it will always be 1 since these are all interviewer utterances. The second and third digits code the utterance designation. The utterances in this exercise are all interviewer questions. They should be coded as follows: 01, indirect question; 02, direct question I; 03, direct question II; 04, leading question; 05, double question I; 06, double question II; or 07, bombardment.

For example, if the interviewer asks:

	Utterance Designation	Code Number (3-digit)
I: What is the date of your next appointment?	_____	_____

The utterance designation is Direct Question I, and the code number is 102. This information would be placed on the appropriate line.

Utterance	Utterance Designation	Code Number (3-digit)
1. I: What things have been going on at that workshop you've been attending?	_____	_____
2. I: Did John talk much to you when he was little, or did you notice that he seemed to have trouble hearing you?	_____	_____
3. I: What are some of the problems you feel Mary Ann should be disciplined for— that she should be disciplined for?	_____	_____
4. I: I'd be interested in knowing how the prices of homes here compare with those in the city you just moved from.	_____	_____
5. I: Are there some differences in the way of life, or had you visited here before?		

		Utterance Designation	Code Number (3-digit)

	Utterance		
	The children are still pretty young though, aren't they?	_____	_____
6.	*I:* Are there any other comments you'd like to make?	_____	_____
7.	*I:* What is your home address?	_____	_____
8.	*I:* You wouldn't want Joe to go that far by himself, would you?	_____	_____
9.	*I:* What do you think we can do for her here?	_____	_____
10.	*I:* Who is your supervisor?	_____	_____
11.	*I:* How do you feel about your classes? This is your first semester here?	_____	_____
12.	*I:* What does your husband think about your getting a job? What does he think about your working?	_____	_____
13.	*I:* You and your husband take your vacations together, don't you?	_____	_____
14.	*I:* I imagine you don't have much trouble finding a job in your field.	_____	_____
15.	*I:* John, wilt thou have Clara here present, to be thy wedded wife, to live together after God's ordinance in the holy estate of matrimony? Wilt thou love her, comfort her, honor her, and keep her in sickness and in health, and, forsaking all others, keep thee only unto her so long as ye both shall live?	_____	_____

Did you designate the first utterance as direct question II (103)? And what about the second example? Did you code that double question II (106)? If you wish to check your answers for the remainder of this exercise, you will find our suggested designations and code numbers at the end of this chapter. If your codings are different from the ones listed, you may want to recheck the definitions and examples in Appendix A.

IDENTIFYING INTERVIEWER QUESTIONS AND RESPONDENT UTTERANCES

Exercise Two

Instructions

Place the appropriate utterance designation opposite each utterance in the Utterance Designation column. The three-digit code number may also be listed in the Code Number column. Remember, the first digit of the three digit code number is the speaker designation. (1 = Interviewer; 2 = Respondent). The second and third digits code the utterance designation. The interviewer utterances in this exercise are again all interviewer questions (01, indirect question; 02, direct question I; 03, direct question II; 04, leading question; 05, double question I; 06, double question II; or 07, bombardment.) The utterance designations for the respondent utterances are all one of the following: 50, agreement; 52, request for information; 53, information; or 54, problem area. If you feel more than one designation may be appropriate, remember the rule: "In case two designations are appropriate, choose the one with the higher code number."

	Utterance Designation	Code Number (3-digit)
Interview Segment 1.		
I: What is your birthdate?	_____	_____
R: January 2, 1953.	_____	_____
Interview Segment 2.		
I: Do you have time to answer some questions? Can you spare the time?	_____	_____
R: I have ten minutes before I have to leave for a dental appointment.	_____	_____
Interview Segment 3.		
I: You've had experience using a duplicating machine, haven't you?	_____	_____
R: What kind?	_____	_____
Interview Segment 4.		
I: How do you feel you and your husband are getting along now?	_____	_____
R: Not well at all. It just seems to get worse and worse. I don't know what to do anymore.	_____	_____

	Utterance Designation	Code Number (3-digit)

Interview Segment 5.

    I: Did you follow the instructions closely? Did you have all the parts? What about those small bolts?   _____ _____

    R: Here are the small bolts.   _____ _____

Interview Segment 6.

    I: I wonder how the mother of a large family like yours manages these days.   _____ _____

    R: It isn't easy. Sometimes, I use up the grocery money by Wednesday. We have a tough time getting food for the rest of the week.   _____ _____

Interview Segment 7.

    I: You make sure all the offices are locked every night before you leave, don't you?   _____ _____

    R: Yes, of course.   _____ _____

Interview Segment 8.

    I: Have you ever been to Australia? What time of year will you be making your trip?   _____ _____

    R: My vacation is the first two weeks in August.   _____ _____

Interview Segment 9.

    I: What do you think about the teacher your son had last year?   _____ _____

    R: She was wonderful. He still talks about her.   _____ _____

Interview Segment 10.

    I: How have your exercise classes been going?   _____ _____

    R: I enjoy them, but I haven't lost any weight. I seem to be eating more than ever.   _____ _____

Again, our suggested codings for the above exercise are listed at the end of this chapter. If your designations or code numbers differ from ours,

you may want to review the list of definitions and examples found in
Appendix A. Did you differentiate between Respondent Information (253)
and Respondent Problem Area (254)? In the latter case, the information
supplied identifies or indicates a situation that is *currently* causing stress or
concern. The higher-code-number rule applies here.

IDENTIFYING INTERVIEWER AND RESPONDENT UTTERANCES

Exercise Three

Instructions

Place the appropriate utterance designation opposite each utterance in
the Utterance Designation column. The three-digit code number may also
be listed in the Code Number column. Remember, the first digit of the
three-digit code number is the speaker designation (1 = Interviewer; 2 =
Respondent). The second and third digits code the utterance designation.
Examples of all the interviewer and respondent utterance types listed in
the interview analysis are included in this exercise. You will need to use
the list of utterance designations found in Appendix A. You will have to remember the following two rules:

1. In case of two appropriate designations, choose the one with the
   higher code number.
2. If an *mm-hm* response or nonpertinent small talk is combined with
   any other utterance, code the remainder of the utterance.

Don't panic! Take your time and review the definitions and examples
when necessary. Following each interview excerpt, we will alert you to particular circumstances that may have caused problems for you in identifying
the utterances. Our suggested utterance designations and code numbers for
all the excerpts are listed at the end of the chapter.

	Utterance Designation	*Code Number (3-digit)*

Interview Excerpt 10–1

1.   *I:* We have this time today to discuss any-
         thing you'd like that you think would be
         helpful to us in working with Patty.   _____   _____

2.   *R:* What sort of things would you like me to
         tell you about?   _____   _____

	Utterance Designation	Code Number (3-digit)

3. I: What sort of things do you think are important for us to know?

4. R: Well, I think you might want to know about the things she's doing in school. It seems to me that that's important.

5. I: I agree. That information would be very helpful to us.

In Interview Excerpt 10–1, Utterance 3 is an instance where the higher number rule is applied. In this utterance, the interviewer asks a question: "What sort of things do you think are important for us to know?" Taken by itself, this utterance would be identified as a direct question II, and the three-digit code number would be 103. However, note that this question is in response to the respondent's question: "What sort of things would you like me to tell you about?" So, in this case, this utterance can be identified as forcing client responsibility, with a three-digit code number of 111. The interviewer is immediately redirecting the respondent's question back to the respondent. Did you find the one utterance in this excerpt identified as reassurance?

	Utterance Designation	Code Number (3-digit)

Interview Excerpt 10–2

1. I: Did you get that prescription filled?

2. R: Yes, I've been taking it. But I'm kind of worried. For about an hour after I take it, I feel very sick to my stomach.

3. I: The medicine seems to make you nauseated.

4. R: Yes, that's right. Should I be taking the medicine on an empty stomach?

In Interview Excerpt 10–2, Utterance 4 may have caused you some difficulty in coding. Here, the respondent is requesting information. However, the request follows agreement with the doctor's restatement—"The medicine seems to make you nauseated." The respondent agrees with this restatement, verifying that it is correct. The patient continues immediately after agreeing and asks a question—"Should I be taking the medicine on an empty stomach?" This utterance should be identified as agreement with re-statement, reflection, interpretation, or leading question, plus asking for information, which is code number 259. This utterance designation can be abbreviated as agreement plus asking.

	Utterance Designation	Code Number (3-digit)

Interview Excerpt 10–3

1. *I:* Is there any kind of rivalry between John and Lucy? _____ _____

2. *R:* Between the two, very little. Except when one tries to take a larger glass of orange juice or have an extra piece of cookie. We don't encourage it. _____ _____

3. *I:* Hmmm. That's good to hear. That's the best way to handle it. _____ _____

4. *R:* Do many parents have problems with brother and sister rivalry? _____ _____

5. *I:* Yes, some do. _____ _____

6. *R:* Perhaps you could have a discussion of that at one of your parent meetings. _____ _____

In Interview Excerpt 10–3, have you remembered the two rules? You must apply at least one of them in Utterance 3.

	Utterance Designation	Code Number (3-digit)

Interview Excerpt 10–4

1. *I:* How does your husband feel about your therapy? How does he feel about it? _____ _____

2. *R:* Oh, he approves of it. Anything that can help me he's all for it. He's the ideal husband. _____ _____

3. *I:* Mm-hm. _____ _____

4. *R:* In fact, now that I think about it, I realize that I can't manage without his help. _____ _____

In Interview Excerpt 10–4, Utterance 4 is identified as insight, code number 255. Here the respondent is expressing awareness of motivation or consequences of behavior at the time of her utterance that was not previously understood or verbalized. You may also note that feelings are expressed in this excerpt. You will have an opportunity to code feelings in Exercise Four.

	Utterance Designation	Code Number (3-digit)

Interview Excerpt 10–5

1. *I:* Does Sally seem to be getting more self-reliant? Does she play well alone? How is her relationship with the other children?

2. *R:* Very good. Very, very good.

3. *I:* I suppose they use sign language mostly when they talk to her, don't they?

4. *R:* No, I won't allow them to; you know, uh, I've asked them to use as little uh, you know, gestures as possible. But she seems to understand so much better when they use it. I, uh, just don't know what's best.

5. *I:* Perhaps you could talk to her teacher at school about that.

In Interview Excerpt 10–5, did you find an utterance that is appropriately labeled advice, suggestion, or command?

	Utterance Designation	Code Number (3-digit)

Interview Excerpt 10–6

1. *R:* This is what really bothers me. Sam doesn't listen when I tell him what's to be done.

2. *I:* Hm, is it just to you, do you think? Or do you think that . . .

3. *R:* Well, Charlie has complained about him too. He had to redo three of his orders last week.

4. *I:* It sounds like Sam is really getting to you. You seem really upset.

5. *R:* Yes, I *am* upset. No one else has given me as much trouble as he has.

In Interview Excerpt 10–6, did you find an instance of agreement with restatement, reflection, interpretation, or leading question, plus giving information (agreement plus giving), code number 260?

	Utterance Designation	Code Number (3-digit)

Interview Excerpt 10–7

1. I: If you want to leave specific jewelry to specific heirs, it is necessary to list each item and the person you wish to leave it to. _____ _____

2. R: That will be tough. I want to leave the ruby ring to my daughter—but I suppose my sister will say it belongs to her. _____ _____

3. I: You say the ring was originally your sister's. _____ _____

4. R: No, I didn't say that, but *she* probably will. The ring belonged to our mother. Can she say she should get it if I die? _____ _____

5. I: I'm wondering if your mother had a will. _____ _____

6. R: No, she didn't. _____ _____

In Interview Excerpt 10–7, did you find the disagreement plus asking utterance? Did you remember the utterance designation indirect question?

	Utterance Designation	Code Number (3-digit)

Interview Excerpt 10–8

1. R: I think I'll return the *damn hearing aid* to the dealer next week and get my money back. _____ _____

2. I: The hearing aid is not the problem. You just can't face the fact that you have a hearing loss. _____ _____

3. R: No, that's not it at all! _____ _____

4. I: Your idea about returning the hearing aid is a big mistake. _____ _____

Interview Excerpt 10–8 contains an utterance that should be identified as planning. Did you find it? Are there any instances of interpretation?

	Utterance Designation	Code Number (3-digit)

Interview Excerpt 10–9

1. R: When we're in the car Joe always likes to ask questions. "Where are we going? Why are we going?" He asks them continuously, and it's too much. I know it's the sign of a healthy, inquiring mind, but it's rather taxing on me. Sometimes it's all right, but when it's all the time, he just gets in the way. At those times you'd wish he wasn't around to bother you.

2. I: You know that it's good for Joe to ask lots of questions, but sometimes you need peace and quiet too.

3. R: That's it. That's it exactly.

4. I: You might try scheduling some time just for yourself during the late afternoon.

5. R: Do you have any children of your own?

Did you have any trouble deciding on the utterance designation for Utterance 2 in Interview Excerpt 10–9?

	Utterance Designation	Code Number (3-digit)

Interview Excerpt 10–10

1. I: Well, our time is almost up. Let's quickly review what classes you'll take next semester.

2. R: I'll take that English IA course, Spanish 2, Adolescent Psych, Women's Studies, and Swimming.

3. I: That should do it. I'll have my same office hours next semester, if you need to see me.

4. R: O.K.

5. I: It was good to see you. Have a good semester.

6. R: Thanks. You too.

In this last excerpt of Exercise Three, did you find instances of structuring and nonpertinent small talk?

IDENTIFYING INTERVIEWER AND RESPONDENT UTTERANCES AND EXPRESSED FEELINGS

Exercise Four

Instructions

Place the appropriate utterance designation opposite each utterance in the Utterance Designation column. We hope you are also becoming familiar with the three-digit code numbers. We find them a convenient short-hand method of identifying utterances. Remember, the first digit of the three-digit code number is the speaker designation (1 = Interviewer; 2 = Respondent). The second and third digits code the utterance designation. You will need to use the list of utterance designations found in Appendix A. You will also need to remember the two rules:

1. In case of two appropriate designations, choose the one with the higher code number.
2. If an *mm-hm* response or nonpertinent small talk is combined with any other utterance, code the remainder of the utterance.

In this exercise, you will have an opportunity to identify expressed feelings. If a *currently felt emotion* is expressed in an utterance, write the symbol + (positive), − (negative), or ± (ambivalent) in the column provided. This will designate the type of feeling expressed. Also indicate toward what or whom the feeling is directed. Be as specific as possible. If feelings are directed toward more than one person or object in an utterance, select and identify what you consider to be the dominant feeling. If no feeling is expressed in a particular utterance, or if you are uncertain as to whether or not a feeling is expressed, leave the column blank.

Please note: we have not made provision in this exercise to expand the three-digit code number to provide numerical coding for expressed feelings. We do not wish to overwhelm you with too many options as you practice the system. You may recall that in the computer research project described in Chapter 9, the authors used five-digit code numbers, in which the fourth and fifth digits coded feelings expressed in an utterance. If you are interested in using a five-digit code number in any research of your own, we recommend rereading the project description in Chapter 9.

Here is an example of how to record your identification of utterances and expressed feelings in Exercise Four:

	Utterance Designation/ Code Number	Feelings Expressed (+, −, or ±) Toward What or Whom?

Example

1. I: How does your husband feel about your therapy? How does he feel about it? _____ _____

2. R: Oh, he approves of it. Anything that can help me he's all for it. He's the ideal husband. _____ _____

3. I: Mm-hm. _____ _____

4. R: In fact, now that I think about it, I realize that I can't manage without his help. _____ _____

Following each interview excerpt, we will again alert you to particular circumstances to be considered in identifying the utterance designations and expressed feelings. As with the other exercises, our suggested utterance designations and code numbers are listed at the end of this chapter. Our suggested identifications of expressed feelings in Exercise Four are also listed. Of course, it is not necessary for you to use the same wording we did in the identification of "toward what or whom" the feelings are expressed. Wording that conveys a similar idea would be considered agreement with our identification.

Interview Excerpt 10–11

	Utterance Designation/ Code Number	Feelings Expressed (+, −, or ±) Toward What or Whom?

1. I: Mrs. Gains, I needed to talk with you this morning to find out why you haven't been making the payments on your Health Club contract. The last payment according to our records was two months ago. _____ _____

2. R: I know I'm two months behind. I'll bring in a check tomorrow for forty dollars. _____ _____

	Utterance Designation/ Code Number	Feelings Expressed (+, −, or ±) Toward What or Whom?

3. *I:* Well, of course, now that you've missed two months payments, the penalty clause is in effect.   _____   _____

4. *R:* What do you mean—penalty clause?   _____   _____

5. *I:* The additional hundred dollars. You must pay that for every month a payment is late. In your case—if you pay tomorrow—your check should be for $240.00.   _____   _____

6. *R: Two hundred and forty dollars.* You must be kidding! The contract I signed is for $20.00 a month! It's going to be hard enough covering a check for $40.00 by tomorrow. *That's* what I owe you.   _____   _____

7. *I:* Mrs. Gains, you signed that contract. Anybody with any sense reads a contract through before signing it. The way you talk, you obviously didn't read the penalty clause.   _____   _____

8. *R:* With three of you standing over me telling me that it was the last day of this wonderful introductory special, you didn't give me any time to really read the contract. I trusted you people and now you're trying to cheat me!   _____   _____

9. *I:* We didn't pressure you. And besides—you have your own copy of the contract. According to law, you had three days

	Utterance Designation/ Code Number	Feelings Expressed (+, −, or ±) Toward What or Whom?
in which to change your mind. Now, it's legally binding. Your best bet is to pay what you owe us immediately to avoid further penalty.	_____	_____
10. R: You guys are going to be lucky to get forty dollars! If you're smart you'll take that.	_____	_____
11. I: I'm not going to argue with you. If we don't have a check for $240.00 tomorrow, we'll turn this over to our collection agency.	_____	_____

The general tenor of Interview Excerpt 10–11 is one of unpleasantness. You might feel that every utterance basically contains negative feelings. This is heightened by the fact that you may have pictured yourself in a similar situation and imagined the negative feelings you would have. However, a general pervasive tone should not be identified as expressed feelings in every utterance. When you make an identification of feelings, it is important that these feelings be *expressed* in the *particular* utterance you are coding.

We have found that interview participants vary considerably in their actual expression of feelings. In some interviews, feelings are clearly expressed and easily identified. In others, the identification is more difficult. Use your own best judgment. We feel it is better to err on the side of *not* identifying feelings unless they are clearly expressed. This helps to avoid making assumptions about what another person may be feeling or reading into their utterances more than is actually expressed. It may also help to minimize projection of our own feelings into our analysis of the utterances made by the interview participants. When feelings are sufficiently strong, these will usually be clearly expressed in one or more utterances. Using these guidelines, we have identified two respondent utterances (Utterances 6 and 8) and one interviewer utterance (Utterance 7) as containing expressed feelings.

In regard to your answers in the Utterance Designation/Code Number column, you probably found it necessary to employ the higher-number rule. On occasion, both the interviewer and respondent supply information. However, some of these utterances also meet the criteria for designations with higher code numbers. For instance, in Utterance 1 the interviewer provides information but is also structuring the session. The respondent's reply provides information but also includes an expression of planned future behavior. You may wish to review all of your utterance identifications in this excerpt to make sure you considered this rule.

	Utterance Designation/ Code Number	Feelings Expressed (+, −, or ±) Toward What or Whom?
Interview Excerpt 10–12		
1. R: It's been a tough decision for me to make. You know I love teaching but I can't stand another year of it.	_____	_____
2. I: I'm very distressed at your decision. I hate to think of losing you. You're one of our best teachers.	_____	_____
3. R: I've tried to be, but it's just not worth the effort. These kids want everything to be easy. They don't want to study or learn. They act like they're doing me a favor just coming to class.	_____	_____
4. I: It sounds as though the students have really got you down.	_____	_____
5. R: Yes. Sometimes it's all I can do to get up in the morning and face another day of teaching.	_____	_____
6. I: Do you feel that way about all your classes? Are some worse than others?	_____	_____
7. R: They're all about the same. Teaching most of the students is a constant struggle—but there are some who are terrific. That's what makes this decision so hard.	_____	_____

	Utterance Designation/ Code Number	Feelings Expressed (+, −, or ±) Toward What or Whom?
8. *I:* Is there any chance you'll change your mind?	_____	_____
9. *R:* No. When I first came in to tell you, I still had mixed feelings about quitting. But as we've been talking, I realize what a relief it is not to have to come back. I know this is the right decision for me.	_____	_____

Several of the utterances in Interview Excerpt 10–12 contain expressed feelings. These center around the teacher's decision to resign from teaching. Some of his ambivalence toward leaving teaching is evident in the interchanges. The principal actually expresses feelings in only one utterance (Utterance 2), even though we get the impression throughout the interview excerpt that she is sorry one of her best teachers is leaving the profession. In Utterance 2, the school principal obviously expresses negative feelings toward the teacher's decision to leave. Her comment that the teacher is one of her best certainly indicates positive feeling toward the teacher's teaching ability. Either one of these identifications would be a valid one for you to make. Since the instructions for Exercise Four were to select the dominant feeling, we have selected the negative feeling expressed as the dominant feeling. The principal's positive feelings toward the teacher no doubt are an important factor in her distress regarding the teacher's decision.

A similar situation occurs in Utterance 7. The teacher expresses positive feelings toward teaching some students and negative feelings toward teaching others. These positive and negative feelings contribute to his ambivalence toward teaching. We have identified this ambivalence as the dominant feeling expressed.

Remember that any time an interviewer restates content, reflects feeling, attempts interpretation, or asks a leading question, you must pay special attention to whether or not the respondent agrees or disagrees. The special designation agreement plus asking (259), agreement plus giving (260), disagreement plus asking (261), or disagreement plus giving (262) may apply. One utterance in this excerpt falls in this category.

	Utterance Designation/ Code Number	Feelings Expressed (+, −, or ±) Toward What or Whom?

Interview Excerpt 10–13

1. *I:* I'm Inspector Holmes of the Public Health Department. I'm here for the annual inspection of your beauty shop.

2. *R:* It's that time already? What happened to Bill Simpleton, the inspector who used to come?

3. *I:* Simpleton is no longer with the Department. I have been assigned his cases. I've also done the rechecking that has been necessary in a number of instances.

4. *R:* I see. I'm with a customer right now. I'll have one of my other operators take my next customer. I'll be able to talk with you then.

5. *I:* All right. I'll examine the premises first while you finish with your customer. Then there are some questions you will have to answer.

6. *R:* I got a new sterilizer for the combs and brushes. That was the only thing Bill got me for last year.

7. *I:* You say that your only violation last year was for an unsatisfactory sterilizer. That was the only code violation the inspector informed you of?

8. *R:* Yes—that was the only one he found. He understood about the sterilizer, but said I should

	Utterance Designation/ Code Number	Feelings Expressed (+, −, or ±) Toward What or Whom?

	get a new one before this year's inspection.	_____	_____
9.	I: In other words, the sterilizer was unsatisfactory, but he permitted your license to be renewed last year.	_____	_____
10.	R: That's right.	_____	_____
11.	I: I'm getting fed up with these cases where violations are found but licenses are still reissued. As far as I'm concerned, that's illegal.	_____	_____
12.	R: Inspector, how about some coffee? I just brewed a fresh pot.	_____	_____
13.	I: Trying to butter me up isn't going to get your license renewed. That may have worked with Simpleton, but it can't work with me.	_____	_____

Interview Excerpt 10–13 happens to be an interview in which few feelings are expressed. There are many interviews in business and professional settings where this is the case. We have identified only two utterances in which feelings are expressed and these are both utterances made by the inspector. The comments we have made with regard to feelings in previous excerpts of this exercise should be considered for this excerpt also.

By this time, you are no doubt becoming more comfortable in identifying the utterance designations. You may no longer need to be reminded of the higher-number rule or the rule to ignore *mm-hm* responses or nonpertinent small talk in utterances where another designation can be applied. Both of these rules apply in this interview excerpt.

If any of your identifications in Exercise Four do not agree with those listed at the end of the chapter, you will probably want to check the definitions and examples found in Appendix A. If, after examining these, you still feel your identification is more appropriate, that is your prerogative. The important thing is to examine the utterances closely and give careful thought to your identification.

	Utterance Designation/ Code Number	*Feelings Expressed* $(+, -, \text{ or } \pm)$ *Toward What or Whom?*

Interview Excerpt 10–14

1. I: What is your husband's annual salary?

2. R: *Twenty-five thousand dollars* for sitting on his duff all day! His secretary does most of the work. I *know* I work harder than he does, and I make $12,400 a year!

3. I: $25,000 a year.

4. R: Aren't you going to write down how much I make?

5. I: That's not one of the questions.

6. R: That figures! I work *twice* as hard, get paid *half* as much, and your survey doesn't give me any credit at all!

This excerpt requires little, if any, comment. Did you note the instance where a restatement of content occurs, but the respondent neither agrees nor disagrees with it?

	Utterance Designation/ Code Number	*Feelings Expressed* $(+, -, \text{ or } \pm)$ *Toward What or Whom?*

Interview Excerpt 10–15

1. I: What is your major reason for wanting to adopt a child?

2. R: Ever since I was little, I always dreamed of having a big family. When I found out I couldn't have children, it almost destroyed me. When we started looking into adoption, I just knew that would be the answer.

	Utterance Designation/ Code Number	Feelings Expressed (+, −, or ±) Toward What or Whom?

3. *I:* Does your husband feel that way too? Does he feel the same way you do? _____ _____

4. *R:* Oh yes. He will make a great father. He loves children and he's wonderful with them. _____ _____

5. *I:* So you think your husband feels the same way you do about adopting a child. _____ _____

6. *R:* Oh yes. When we found out I couldn't have children, he's the one who suggested adoption. _____ _____

7. *I:* Mm-hm. _____ _____

8. *R:* He's seen me through some rough periods. I really am lucky to have him. _____ _____

9. *I:* You really appreciate him— having a husband who cares, really helps during rough times. _____ _____

10. *R:* Yes, it certainly does. Isn't that one of the things you look for in these interviews? _____ _____

11. *I:* It certainly is an important consideration. _____ _____

In Interview Excerpt 10–15, several positive feelings are expressed by the respondent. A word of caution is in order: remember that only the expression of *current* feelings should be identified in these exercises. The same guideline applies in identification of an utterance as indicating a problem area. Indication of an utterance as a problem area (254) applies only when the respondent identifies or indicates a situation as *currently* causing stress or concern. Any mention of feelings or problems occurring in the past should be considered information unless there is a definite indication that the feelings or problems continue into the present.

We hope that these exercises have helped you to become more skilled in identifying the various types of utterances that are common in many interviews. You may want to go back over these excerpts and consider them from other viewpoints we have discussed in previous chapters. You might, for instance, wish to consider each of the excerpts in regard to the dominance-submission and friendliness-unfriendliness dimensions. You may wish to consider the various roles the interview participants play and the basic human needs they are exhibiting.

It is our intention that, at this point, you feel sufficiently confident to analyze one of your own interviews according to the Molyneaux/Lane interview analysis. The next chapter will detail our suggested procedure.

ANSWERS FOR PRACTICE EXERCISES

Answers for Exercise One (Pages 172 to 173)

Utterance Designation	Code Number
1. direct question II	103
2. double question II	106
3. double question I	105
4. indirect question	101
5. bombardment	107
6. direct question II	103
7. direct question I	102
8. leading question	104
9. direct question II	103
10. direct question I	102
11. double question II	106
12. double question I	105
13. leading question	104
14. indirect question	101
15. bombardment	107

Answers for Exercise Two (Pages 174 to 175)

Utterance Designation	Code Number
1. I: direct question I	102
R: information	253
2. I: double question I	105
R: information	253
3. I: leading question	104
R: request for information	252
4. I: direct question II	103
R: problem area	254

Utterance Designation	Code Number
5. I: bombardment	107
R: information	253
6. I: indirect question	101
R: problem area	254
7. I: leading question	104
R: agreement	250
8. I: double question II	106
R: information	253
9. I: direct question II	103
R: information	253
10. I: direct question II	103
R: problem area	254

Answers for Exercise Three (Pages 176 to 181)

Utterance Designation	Code Number
Interview Excerpt 10–1	
1. I: structuring	116
2. R: request for information	252
3. I: forcing client responsibility	111
4. R: information	253
5. I: reassurance	113
Interview Excerpt 10–2	
1. I: direct question I	102
2. R: problem area	254
3. I: restatement of content	114
4. R: agreement plus asking	259
Interview Excerpt 10–3	
1. I: direct question II	103
2. R: information	253
3. I: approval	109
4. R: request for information	252
5. I: information	112
6. R: advice, suggestion, or command	258
Interview Excerpt 10–4	
1. I: double question I	105
2. R: information	253
3. I: *mm-hm* response	108
4. R: insight	255

Utterance Designation	*Code Number*
Interview Excerpt 10–5	
1. I: bombardment	107
2. R: information	253
3. I: leading question	104
4. R: disagreement plus giving	262
5. I: advice, suggestion, or command	118
Interview Excerpt 10–6	
1. R: problem area	254
2. I: double question II	106
3. R: information	253
4. I: reflection of feeling	115
5. R: agreement plus giving	260
Interview Excerpt 10–7	
1. I: information	112
2. R: problem area	254
3. I: restatement of content	114
4. R: disagreement plus asking	261
5. I: indirect question	101
6. R: information	253
Interview Excerpt 10–8	
1. R: planning	256
2. I: interpretation	117
3. R: disagreement	251
4. I: disapproval	110
Interview Excerpt 10–9	
1. R: problem area	254
2. I: reflection of feeling	115
3. R: agreement	250
4. I: advice, suggestion, or command	118
5. R: request for information	252
Interview Excerpt 10–10	
1. I: structuring	116
2. R: information	253
3. I: information	112
4. R: *mm-hm* response	257
5. I: nonpertinent small talk	119
6. R: nonpertinent small talk	263

Answers for Exercise Four (Pages 183 to 191)

Utterance Designation/ Code Number (3-digit)	*Feelings Expressed (+, −, ±) Toward What or Whom?*

Interview Excerpt 10–11
1. I: structuring/116
2. R: planning/256
3. I: information/112
4. R: request for information/252
5. I: information/112
6. R: problem area/254
7. I: interpretation/117   (−) toward Mrs. Gains' limited knowledge of contract
8. R: problem area/254   (−) toward Health Club personnel
9. I: advice, suggestion, or command/118
10. R: advice, suggestion, or command/258
11. I: information/112

Interview Excerpt 10–12
1. R: problem area/254   (±) toward teaching
2. I: information/112   (−) toward teacher's decision to leave
3. R: problem area/254   (−) toward students' attitudes and behavior
4. I: reflection of feeling/115
5. R: agreement plus giving/260   (−) toward teaching
6. I: double question II/106
7. R: problem area/254   (±) toward teaching
8. I: direct question II/103
9. R: insight/255   (+) toward decision to leave teaching

Interview Excerpt 10–13
1. I: information/112
2. R: request for information/252
3. I: information/112
4. R: planning/256
5. I: structuring/116
6. R: information/253
7. I: restatement of content/114
8. R: agreement plus giving/260
9. I: restatement of content/114
10. R: agreement/250

Utterance Designation/ *Code Number (3-digit)*	*Feelings Expressed* $(+, -, \pm)$ *Toward What or Whom?*
11. I: information/112	(−) toward reissuing of licenses when code violations are noted
12. R: nonpertinent small talk/263	
13. I: interpretation/117	(−) toward respondent's behavior

Interview Excerpt 10–14

1. I: direct question I/102	
2. R: problem area/254	(−) toward discrepancy between husband's salary and her own
3. I: restatement of content/114	
4. R: request for information/252	
5. I: information/112	
6. R: problem area/254	(−) toward survey

Interview Excerpt 10–15

1. I: direct question II/103	
2. R: information/253	
3. I: double question I/105	
4. R: information/253	(+) toward spouse as father
5. I: restatement of content/114	
6. R: agreement plus giving/260	
7. I: *mm-hm* response/108	
8. R: information/253	(+) toward spouse as husband
9. I: reflection of feeling/115	
10. R: agreement plus asking/259	
11. I: reassurance/113	

Analyzing Your Interview

In Chapter 9, we mentioned that one of our training methods includes the analysis of typed verbatim transcriptions of the students' tape-recorded interviews. We have found that this is an excellent procedure because it provides a number of interviewer and respondent utterances to identify. The typed transcription makes it possible to read the utterances and refer back to previous utterances, taking as much time as needed for identification. The utterance designations (or their code numbers) and identifications of expressed feelings can be noted in the margin of the transcription opposite each utterance. Once you have identified the interview utterances the information can be recorded on the Molyneaux/Lane interview analysis forms.

It is possible to analyze a tape recording of an interview without the intermediate step of preparing a type transcription. If you do the analysis directly from a tape recording, you will tally the utterance designations or types directly onto the analysis forms. You will probably have to play the tape at least twice. The first time, you can identify the utterance types. The second time, you can concentrate on identification of the feelings expressed.

As we have stated, the analysis forms provided in this chapter can be used by an interviewer in analyzing either a typed transcription or a tape recording. They can also be used by an observer or supervisor viewing or listening in on an actual interview session. We suggest that you make copies of these Molyneaux/Lane interview analysis forms. You can then use these forms to analyze one or more interviews. This chapter also includes a completed sample of each of the forms for your information.

THE INTERVIEW INFORMATION SHEET

Instructions

The Interview Information Sheet (Figure 11–1) provides space for necessary information concerning your interview. The first item on the sheet is Interview Identification. To complete this space, identify the interview by whatever method you or your agency have established. The next five items on the sheet are self-explanatory. The seventh item concerns the Purpose(s) of Interview. Your notations regarding the purpose(s) of the interview can be as general or specific as you wish. You may, for example, wish to use the terms we discussed previously: information getting; information giving; expression and exploration of feeling; problem solving; and planning for future action. You may wish to be more specific regarding what you hope you and your respondent will achieve during the session. For example, rather than note "problem solving" as the purpose, you might list "finding alternatives to current payroll procedures."

MOLYNEAUX/LANE INTERVIEW ANALYSIS
INTERVIEW INFORMATION SHEET

Interview Identification: _____

Interviewer Name: _____

Respondent Name: _____

Date of Interview: _____

Initiated by: _____

Place of Interview: _____

Purpose(s) of Interview:

Interviewing Improvement Goal(s):

Comments/Evaluation:

FIGURE 11–1   *Interview Information Sheet*

The space provided for Interviewing Improvement Goal(s) can be used to list one or more personal goals to which you wish to pay special attention as you conduct the interview. This space should be used to list what your objectives are for yourself as an interviewer. Your wording may take whatever form is most comfortable for you and/or required by your setting. You may list utterance types that you wish to use as frequently as possible: such as "increased reflection of feeling" or "encourage respondent expression of problem area." You may wish to remind yourself to *avoid* using certain utterance types, for example, "avoid bombardment."

The Comments/Evaluation section is to be completed following the interview. You may wish to indicate whether or not your interviewing purpose(s) and interviewing improvement goal or goals were achieved. You may want to complete this section after you have completed the other analysis sheets that follow.

Figure 11-2 provides a sample of a completed Interview Information Sheet.

MOLYNEAUX/LANE INTERVIEW ANALYSIS
INTERVIEW INFORMATION SHEET

Interview Identification: _____*A-43*_____

Interviewer Name: _____*Jenny Brown*_____

Respondent Name: _____*Mrs. Irene Green*_____

Date of Interview: _____*9-6-80*_____

Initiated by: _____*Interviewer*_____

Place of Interview: _____*Clinic Office*_____

Purpose(s) of Interview:
> *Information Getting re:*- *Johnny's school performance*
>   - *communication at home*
>   - *relationship with other family members*

Interviewing Improvement Goal(s):
> -*Encourage mother's expression of feeling regarding interview topics*
> -*avoid leading questions*
> -*avoid bombardment*

Comments/Evaluation:
> - *16 out of 77 respondent utterances were indication of problem area*
> - *mother expressed feelings in 7 of 77 utterances*
> - *no leading questions or bombardment!*
> *Should have explored further:*
>   *mother's ambivalence toward helping Johnny with his speech problem*

FIGURE 11-2   *Interview Information Sheet (Sample)*

THE UTTERANCE SUMMARIES FOR
INTERVIEWER AND RESPONDENT

The utterance summaries for the interviewer (Figure 11–3) and for the respondent (Figure 11–4) contain a listing of the utterance designations in the Molyneaux/Lane interview analysis. The utterance summaries provide an opportunity for you to analyze the relative proportion of different types of utterances occurring in your interview. For example, if you were particularly interested in attempting restatement of content, the utterance summary will show you what percentage of your total utterances were so designated.

Instructions

As you identify each utterance in the interview, place a tally mark in the space provided opposite the appropriate utterance designation. Note that all interviewer utterance types are tallied on the Utterance Summary—Interviewer (Figure 11–3); all respondent utterance types are tallied on the Utterance Summary—Respondent (Figure 11–4). If the utterance cannot be identified with one of the designations, place a tally mark in the space opposite that marked "Other." After you have assigned all the utterances, total the number of times each utterance type occurred. Place the total for each utterance type in the column marked "Total Number" opposite the appropriate utterance type.

Note that on the Utterance Summary—Interviewer, there is a blank where you can put the total number of all interviewer utterances. On the Utterance Summary—Respondent, there is a blank where you can put the total number of all respondent utterances. These totals are necessary in order to figure the percentages for each utterance type. Once you have determined the total number of interviewer utterances, you can compute the percentage of occurrence of each interviewer utterance type. (To do this, divide each utterance type total number by the total number of all interviewer utterances.) Place the percentage figure in the percent column opposite the appropriate utterance type. For example, if your tally indicated 4 indirect questions, and the total number of interviewer utterances was 80, you would divide 4 by 80, which equals .05 or 5 percent. This figure would be placed in the percent column opposite indirect question.

The same procedure is followed to compute the percentage of occurrence of the various respondent utterance types. Be certain you use the total number of *respondent* utterances as your divisor in figuring the percentage of occurrence of each respondent utterance type.

In Figures 11–5 and 11–6 we have provided samples of these forms completed as we have suggested.

MOLYNEAUX/LANE INTERVIEW ANALYSIS
UTTERANCE SUMMARY—INTERVIEWER

Interview Identification:

Interviewer Utterance Types	Tally of Occurrence	Total #	%[a]
01 Indirect Question			
02 Direct Question I			
03 Direct Question II			
04 Leading Question			
05 Double Question I			
06 Double Question II			
07 Bombardment			
08 Mm-hm Response			
09 Approval			
10 Disapproval			
11 Forcing Client Responsibility			
12 Information			
13 Reassurance			
14 Restatement of Content			
15 Reflection of Feeling			
16 Structuring			
17 Interpretation			
18 Advice, Suggestion, or Command			
19 Nonpertinent Small Talk			
20 Other			

[a]To compute Interviewer percentages: Divide each Interviewer Utterance Type Total # by total number of all Interviewer Utterances.

Total Number of all Interviewer Utterances: _____

FIGURE 11-3 *Utterance Summary—Interviewer*

MOLYNEAUX/LANE INTERVIEW ANALYSIS
UTTERANCE SUMMARY–RESPONDENT

Interview Identification:

Respondent Utterance Types	Tally of Occurrence	Total #	%[a]
50 Agreement			
51 Disagreement			
52 Request for Information			
53 Information			
54 Problem Area			
55 Insight			
56 Planning			
57 Mm-hm Response			
58 Advice, Suggestion, or Command			
59 Agreement Plus Asking			
60 Agreement Plus Giving			
61 Disagreement Plus Asking			
62 Disagreement Plus Giving			
63 Nonpertinent Small Talk			
64 Other			

[a]To compute Respondent percentages: Divide each Respondent Utterance Type Total # by total number of all Respondent Utterances.

Total Number of all Respondent Utterances: _____

FIGURE 11–4 *Utterance Summary—Respondent*

MOLYNEAUX/LANE INTERVIEW ANALYSIS
UTTERANCE SUMMARY—INTERVIEWER

Interview Identification: *A-43*

Interviewer Utterance Types	Tally of Occurrence	Total #	%[a]
01 Indirect Question	//	2	3
02 Direct Question I	⫲⫲ ⫲⫲ (11)	11	14
03 Direct Question II	/	1	1
04 Leading Question		0	0
05 Double Question I		0	0
06 Double Question II		0	0
07 Bombardment		0	0
08 Mm-hm Response	⫲⫲ ⫲⫲ //	17	22
09 Approval	////	4	5
10 Disapproval		0	0
11 Forcing Client Responsibility		0	0
12 Information	⫲⫲ ⫲⫲ ⫲⫲ ⫲⫲ ⫲⫲ ⫲⫲ ///	33	42
13 Reassurance	///	3	4
14 Restatement of Content	//	2	3
15 Reflection of Feeling		0	0
16 Structuring	//	2	3
17 Interpretation		0	0
18 Advice, Suggestion, or Command		0	0
19 Nonpertinent Small Talk	//	2	3
20 Other			

[a]To compute Interviewer percentages: Divide each Interviewer Utterance Type Total # by total number of all Interviewer Utterances.

Total Number of all Respondent Utterances: __77__

FIGURE 11-5 *Utterance Summary—Interviewer (Sample)*

MOLYNEAUX/LANE INTERVIEW ANALYSIS

UTTERANCE SUMMARY—RESPONDENT

Interview Identification: *A-43*

Respondent Utterance Types	Tally of Occurrence	Total #	%[a]
50 Agreement	///	3	4
51 Disagreement		0	0
52 Request for Information	ЖЖ ///	8	10
53 Information	ЖЖ ЖЖ ЖЖ ЖЖ ЖЖ ЖЖ ЖЖ ЖЖ	41	54
54 Problem Area	ЖЖ ЖЖ ЖЖ /	16	21
55 Insight		0	0
56 Planning		0	0
57 Mm-hm Response	ЖЖ	5	6
58 Advice, Suggestion, or Command		0	0
59 Agreement Plus Asking		0	0
60 Agreement Plus Giving	/	1	1
61 Disagreement Plus Asking		0	0
62 Disagreement Plus Giving		0	0
63 Nonpertinent Small Talk	///	3	4
64 Other			

[a]To compute Respondent percentages: Divide each Respondent Utterance Type Total # by total number of all Respondent Utterances.

Total Number of all Respondent Utterances: 77

FIGURE 11–6   *Utterance Summary—Respondent (Sample)*

THE EXPRESSED FEELINGS SUMMARIES FOR
INTERVIEWER AND RESPONDENT

Instances of expressed feelings in your interview can be summarized on the Expressed Feelings Summaries (Figure 11–7 for interviewer feelings and Figure 11–8 for respondent feelings). These sheets can serve as a summary of an important aspect of interview content: that which aroused expressed feelings on the part of either interview participant.

Instructions

Each instance of expressed feeling made by the Interviewer or Respondent must first be identified as positive (+), negative (−), or ambivalent (±). You must then describe toward what or whom the feeling is directed. This information is then written in the appropriate space on the Interviewer or Respondent Expressed Feelings Summary. Be as specific as possible in your identification of toward what or whom the feelings are directed. Each time a particular feeling is expressed, place a mark in the "Tally" column. More than one instance of the same feeling directed toward the same target can be indicated by additional tally marks. Once you have tallied all the feelings expressed in the interview, you can complete the "Total Number" column. The percentage of utterances in which feelings were expressed by the interview participants can then be determined and recorded on the appropriate forms. Figures 11–9 and 11–10 are samples of completed Expressed Feelings Summaries.

MOLYNEAUX/LANE INTERVIEW ANALYSIS
EXPRESSED FEELINGS SUMMARY—INTERVIEWER

Interview Identification:
Total Number of Interviewer Utterances:

Feel-ing	Toward What or Whom	Tally	Total #
+ Positive			
	Positive Feelings Total # = _____		
− Negative			
	Negative Feelings Total # = _____		
± Ambivalent			
	Ambivalent Feelings Total # = _____		

Positive Feelings Total # ÷ Total Number of Interviewer Utterances = _____ %
Negative Feelings Total # ÷ Total Number of Interviewer Utterances = _____ %
Ambivalent Feelings Total # ÷ Total Number Interviewer Utterances = _____ %

FIGURE 11–7 *Expressed Feelings Summary—Interviewer*

MOLYNEAUX/LANE INTERVIEW ANALYSIS
EXPRESSED FEELINGS SUMMARY–RESPONDENT

Interview Identification:
Total Number of Respondent Utterances:

Feel-ing	Toward What or Whom	Tally	Total #
+ Positive			
	Positive Feelings Total # = _____		
– Negative			
	Negative Feelings Total # = _____		
± Ambivalent			
	Ambivalent Feelings Total # = _____		

Positive Feelings Total # ÷ Total Number of Respondent Utterances = _____ %
Negative Feelings Total # ÷ Total Number of Respondent Utterances = _____ %
Ambivalent Feelings Total # ÷ Total Number Respondent Utterances = _____ %

FIGURE 11-8   *Expressed Feelings Summary—Respondent*

MOLYNEAUX/LANE INTERVIEW ANALYSIS
EXPRESSED FEELINGS SUMMARY – INTERVIEWER

Interview Identification: *A-43*
Total Number of Interviewer Utterances: *77*

Feel-ing	Toward What or Whom	Tally	Total #
+ Positive	*Mother's reading to Johnny*	*ll*	*2*
	Mother's consistency of discipline	*l*	*1*
	Mother's interest in J's progress in school	*l*	*1*
	Positive Feelings Total # =		*4*
— Negative			
	Negative Feelings Total # =		
± Ambivalent			*0*
	Ambivalent Feelings Total # =		*0*

Positive Feelings Total # ÷ Total Number of Interviewer Utterances = ___*5*___ %
Negative Feelings Total # ÷ Total Number of Interviewer Utterances = ___*0*___ %
Ambivalent Feelings Total # ÷ Total Number Interviewer Utterances = ___*0*___ %

FIGURE 11–9   *Expressed Feelings Summary—Interviewer (Sample)*

MOLYNEAUX/LANE INTERVIEW ANALYSIS
EXPRESSED FEELINGS SUMMARY–RESPONDENT

Interview Identification: *A-43*
Total Number of Respondent Utterances: *77*

Feel-ing	Toward What or Whom	Tally	Total #
+ Positive	*Johnny's speech-language clinician*	*I*	*1*
	Positive Feelings Total # =		*1*
– Negative	*J's repeating kindergarten*	*I*	*1*
	J's inability to sit still while being read to	*II*	*2*
	Negative Feelings Total # =		*3*
± Ambivalent	*grandmother's overprotection of J.*	*I*	*1*
	helping J. with his speech problem	*II*	*2*
	Ambivalent Feelings Total # =		*3*

Positive Feelings Total # ÷ Total Number of Respondent Utterances = *1* %
Negative Feelings Total # ÷ Total Number of Respondent Utterances = *4* %
Ambivalent Feelings Total # ÷ Total Number Respondent Utterances = *4* %

FIGURE 11–10 *Expressed Feelings Summary—Respondent (Sample)*

THE CUMULATIVE RECORD

The Cumulative Record (Figure 11–11) provides an opportunity for you to compare analyses of several interviews. These interviews may be a series of interviews conducted by one interviewer, with either the same respondent or different respondents. This record can also be used to compare the analyses of interviews conducted by various interviewers.

Instructions

Complete the space marked "Interview Identification" using the method you have selected to identify interviews. The percentages you will list for the various utterance types and expressed feelings will be those contained in the analysis sheets for each interview. Figure 11–12 is a sample of a Cumulative Record with three interviews recorded.

MOLYNEAUX/LANE INTERVIEW ANALYSIS
CUMULATIVE RECORD

Interview Identification:								
Utterance Types Interviewer	%	%	%	%	%	%	%	%
01 Indirect Question								
02 Direct Question I								
03 Direct Question II								
04 Leading Question								
05 Double Question I								
06 Double Question II								
07 Bombardment								
08 Mm-hm Response								
09 Approval								
10 Disapproval								
11 Forcing Client Resp.								
12 Information								
13 Reassurance								
14 Restate Content								
15 Reflect Feeling								
16 Structuring								
17 Interpretation								
18 Adv, Suggest, Command								
19 Nonpert. Small Talk								
20 Other								
+ Positive Feelings								
− Negative Feelings								
± Ambivalent Feelings								
Respondent								
50 Agreement								
51 Disagreement								
52 Request for Inform.								
53 Information								
54 Problem Area								
55 Insight								
56 Planning								
57 Mm-hm Response								
58 Adv, Suggest, Command								
59 Agree Plus Asking								
60 Agree Plus Giving								
61 Disagree Plus Ask								
62 Disagree Plus Give								
63 Nonpert. Small Talk								
64 Other								
+ Positive Feelings								
− Negative Feelings								
± Ambivalent Feelings								

FIGURE 11–11   *Cumulative Record*

MOLYNEAUX/LANE INTERVIEW ANALYSIS

CUMULATIVE RECORD

Interview Identification:	A-43	A-87	A-143					
Utterance Types Interviewer	%	%	%	%	%	%	%	%
01 Indirect Question	3	9	9					
02 Direct Question I	14	1	4					
03 Direct Question II	1	11	30					
04 Leading Question	0	0	0					
05 Double Question I	0	0	0					
06 Double Question II	0	2	0					
07 Bombardment	0	1	0					
08 Mm-hm Response	22	13	4					
09 Approval	5	2	0					
10 Disapproval	0	0	0					
11 Forcing Client Resp.	0	0	0					
12 Information	42	6	4					
13 Reassurance	4	0	0					
14 Restate Content	3	30	40					
15 Reflect Feeling	0	20	4					
16 Structuring	3	1	2					
17 Interpretation	0	1	0					
18 Adv, Suggest, Command	0	0	0					
19 Nonpert. Small Talk	3	2	2					
20 Other	0	0	0					
+ Positive Feelings	5	0	0					
− Negative Feelings	0	0	0					
± Ambivalent Feelings	0	0	0					
Respondent								
50 Agreement	4	10	13					
51 Disagreement	0	0	2					
52 Request for Inform.	10	1	0					
53 Information	54	41	41					
54 Problem Area	21	11	7					
55 Insight	0	0	0					
56 Planning	0	0	0					
57 Mm-hm Response	6	1	2					
58 Adv, Suggest, Command	0	0	0					
59 Agree Plus Asking	0	0	0					
60 Agree Plus Giving	1	30	35					
61 Disagree Plus Ask	0	0	0					
62 Disagree Plus Give	0	5	0					
63 Nonpert. Small Talk	4	0	0					
64 Other	0	0	0					
+ Positive Feelings	1	14	22					
− Negative Feelings	4	3	4					
± Ambivalent Feelings	4	9	0					

FIGURE 11–12 *Cumulative Record (Sample)*

THE STATISTICAL COMPARISON SHEET

The Statistical Comparison Sheet (Figure 11–13) permits comparison of your interview with those of the 150 graduate student interviewers participating in the research project described in Chapter 9. Keep in mind the interviews in the research project were primarily information-getting interviews. The percentages in your interview may vary considerably if the primary purpose of your interview was other than information getting.

You will notice two columns on the Statistical Comparison Sheet labeled "Mean" and "Interquartile Range." The mean, of course, is the average percentage of occurrence of each utterance type in the total 150 interviews. The interquartile range includes the middle 50 percent of the percentage scores in these 150 interviews. If you wish to compare your percentage scores with those obtained in the research population, there is a space provided for you to do so.

Instructions

The first step in using the Statistical Comparison Sheet is to transfer the figures in the "%" (Percentage) columns on the utterance summaries to the "%" column on the Statistical Comparison Sheet. This permits you to compare your percentages with the mean percentages obtained by the 150 interviewers in our research project.

The columns entitled "Below Interquartile Range" and "Above Interquartile Range" allow you to determine whether your percentages are either lower or higher than those obtained by the middle 50 percent of the interviewers. To make this comparison, place a check in the "Below Interquartile Range" column for any utterance type where your percentage is lower than the lowest percentage in the interquartile range. For example, if you had 2 percent indirect questions, that is below the interquartile range of 3 to 9 percent. You would therefore place a check in the "Below Interquartile Range" column opposite indirect question.

Place a check in the "Above Interquartile Range" column for any utterance type where your percentage is higher than the highest percentage in the interquartile range. For example, if 11 percent of your utterances were direct question I, place a check in the "Above Interquartile Range" column opposite direct question I (11 percent is above the interquartile range of 3 to 10 percent). If your percentage for any utterance type falls within the interquartile range for that utterance type, you need not make any notation. Figure 11–14 is a sample of a completed Statistical Comparison Sheet.

MOLYNEAUX/LANE INTERVIEW ANALYSIS
STATISTICAL COMPARISON SHEET

Interview Identification:

Utterance Types Interviewer	%	Mean %[a]	Interquartile Range[b]	Below Interq. Range	Above Interq. Range
01 Indirect Question		7%	3- 9%		
02 Direct Question I		8%	3-10%		
03 Direct Question II		26%	16-33%		
04 Leading Question		1%	0- 1%		
05 Double Question I		3%	0- 4%		
06 Double Question II		2%	1- 3%		
07 Bombardment		1%	0- 1%		
08 Mm-hm Response		15%	5-23%		
09 Approval		0%	0- 3%		
10 Disapproval		0%	0%		
11 Forcing Client Resp.		0%	0%		
12 Information		13%	5-18%		
13 Reassurance		2%	0- 3%		
14 Restate Content		13%	8-18%		
15 Reflect Feeling		2%	0- 2%		
16 Structuring		2%	1- 2%		
17 Interpretation		0%	0%		
18 Adv, Suggest, Command		1%	0- 1%		
19 Nonpert. Small Talk		2%	1- 3%		
20 Other					

Utterance Types
  Respondent

	%	Mean %[a]	Interquartile Range[b]	Below Interq. Range	Above Interq. Range
50 Agreement		9%	5-12%		
51 Disagreement		0%	0%		
52 Request for Inform.		4%	1- 6%		
53 Information		55%	46-64%		
54 Problem Area		17%	9-23%		
55 Insight		0%	0%		
56 Planning		0%	0%		
57 Mm-hm Response		4%	0- 4%		
58 Adv, Suggest, Command		0%	0%		
59 Agree Plus Asking		0%	0%		
60 Agree Plus Giving		9%	4-11%		
61 Disagree Plus Ask		0%	0%		
62 Disagree Plus Give		0%	0%		
63 Nonpert. Small Talk		2%	0- 3%		
64 Other					

[a] Mean is based on the analysis of performance of 150 interviewers enrolled in a graduate training program.

[b] The Interquartile Range is the range that includes the middle 50% of the percentage scores obtained by the sample population.

FIGURE 11–13 *Statistical Comparison Sheet*

MOLYNEAUX/LANE INTERVIEW ANALYSIS

STATISTICAL COMPARISON SHEET

Interview Identification: *A-43*

Utterance Types Interviewer	%	Mean %[a]	Interquartile Range[b]	Below Interq. Range	Above Interq. Range
01 Indirect Question	3	7%	3- 9%		
02 Direct Question I	14	8%	3-10%		✓
03 Direct Question II	1	26%	16-33%	✓	
04 Leading Question	0	1%	0- 1%		
05 Double Question I	0	3%	0- 4%		
06 Double Question II	0	2%	1- 3%	✓	
07 Bombardment	0	1%	0- 1%		
08 Mm-hm Response	22	15%	5-23%		
09 Approval	5	0%	0- 3%		✓
10 Disapproval	0	0%	0%		
11 Forcing Client Resp.	0	0%	0%		
12 Information	42	13%	5-18%		✓
13 Reassurance	4	2%	0- 3%		✓
14 Restate Content	3	13%	8-18%	✓	
15 Reflect Feeling	0	2%	0- 2%		
16 Structuring	3	2%	1- 2%		✓
17 Interpretation	0	0%	0%		
18 Adv, Suggest, Command	0	1%	0- 1%		
19 Nonpert. Small Talk	3	2%	1- 3%		
20 Other	0				

Utterance Types Respondent	%	Mean %[a]	Interquartile Range[b]	Below Interq. Range	Above Interq. Range
50 Agreement	4	9%	5-12%	✓	
51 Disagreement	0	0%	0%		
52 Request for Inform.	10	4%	1- 6%		✓
53 Information	54	55%	46-64%		
54 Problem Area	21	17%	9-23%		
55 Insight	0	0%	0%		
56 Planning	0	0%	0%		
57 Mm-hm Response	6	4%	0- 4%		✓
58 Adv, Suggest, Command	0	0%	0%		
59 Agree Plus Asking	0	0%	0%		
60 Agree Plus Giving	1	9%	4-11%	✓	
61 Disagree Plus Ask	0	0%	0%		
62 Disagree Plus Give	0	0%	0%		
63 Nonpert. Small Talk	4	2%	0- 3%		✓
64 Other	0				

[a] Mean is based on the analysis of performance of 150 interviewers enrolled in a graduate training program.

[b] The Interquartile Range is the range that includes the middle 50% of the percentage scores obtained by the sample population.

FIGURE 11–14 *Statistical Comparison Sheet (Sample)*

Our objectives in Chapters 10 and 11 have been:

To enable you to use the Molyneaux/Lane Interview Analysis
To provide practice in identifying utterance types
To provide practice in identifying expressed feelings
To introduce you to analysis forms for you to use in analyzing your
    own interviews

If you haven't yet taken time to code one of your own interviews, we encourage you to do so. The practical experience of coding a complete interview is an effective way of gaining insight into your own interviewing style. Your analysis will reveal utterance types and feelings expressed in your interview. This knowledge will help you in deciding whether or not your interview and interviewing techniques were effective. Once these techniques and behaviors are identified, you will be in a better position to make decisions regarding any desired changes in future interviews.

Maximizing Your Interviewing Effectiveness

Our primary objective in writing this book has been to help you increase your effectiveness in interviews. In order to do this, we have provided information which we hope will assist you in three processes:

1. Clarifying your interviewing philosophy
2. Developing insight into your interviewing style
3. Making desired changes

We shall discuss each of these processes briefly in this final chapter.

CLARIFYING YOUR INTERVIEWING PHILOSOPHY

Several earlier chapters were devoted to a discussion of basic principles of interpersonal communication and human motivation. To engage effectively in any process, one should know the fundamentals of that process. Since interviewing involves communication for a variety of purposes, a closer look at aspects of the communication process can be helpful to you as an interviewer.

You recall that in Chapter 2 we talked about the verbal and nonverbal aspects of communication. Verbal aspects of communication can be considered from the standpoint of the sounds of the language and whether or not other people can understand the sounds we make as we speak that

217

language. Verbal aspects of communication also involve the words and sentences we use as we communicate. They involve whether or not we make it easy for our respondent to follow our conversation and understand what we are trying to convey. The content of our speech can be clear or confusing, pertinent or nonpertinent, helpful or harmful. Which of these it turns out to be in any particular interaction is largely our responsibility. Nonverbal aspects of the communication process also play an important part in a communicative relationship. Our gestures and facial expressions; our tone of voice and the stress and emphasis we use as we speak; our use of space and time and touch as we interact with another person—all reveal some very fundamental attitudes of ours regarding the interview situation and our respondent.

What are some of the personal attitudes that are reflected in these verbal and nonverbal variables? For one thing, they may indicate where we stand on some of the dimensions of human interaction that were discussed in Chapter 4. Our verbal and nonverbal behavior may indicate to others

Whether we consider ourselves inferior, equal, or superior to them
Whether we wish to dominate them or work as equals with them
Whether we like or dislike them
Whether we accept or reject them
Whether we are spending time with them willingly or resentfully
Whether we are willing to share our thoughts and feelings with them
    or prefer to keep our thoughts and feelings hidden

Much of our behavior in personal interactions depends on our underlying attitudes regarding people and what makes them behave as they do. Our opinions regarding the basic worth or expendability of individuals, including our fundamental life-positions (such as "I'm OK—You're OK") play an important role in our perceptions and treatment of others. Our estimate of people's capacity and motivation for change will affect the outcomes we will expect from our interactions with people and the techniques we will use in our interviews. Our estimate of our respondent's potential and our potential for growth and achievement will affect what we attempt in an interview and what we settle for.

In Chapter 3, some theories of human motivation and development were discussed. You have probably been exposed to other theories as well and have become partial to some particular ones. It is important to be aware of your beliefs along this line for two reasons. First, you can evaluate various methods and philosophies of interviewing in the light of your basic beliefs. You can learn to use some of the methods that are most consistent with your fundamental philosophy. Second, you can decide whether your conduct in interviews is in harmony with your philosophy. For example, you may sincerely believe that most people have the capacity to work through their own problems if they learn the basic principles of problem identification and problem solving. If that is your belief, you will want to make sure you are providing such opportunities in your problem-solving interviews. Or you may feel that people ordinarily speak most frankly about their innermost thoughts and feelings when they are treated with positive regard and unconditional acceptance. If so, you will likely try to create such an atmosphere in interviews where awareness and understanding of the respondent's feelings is your goal.

Several investigators have conducted research involving people who are in occupations and professions that require a considerable amount of interviewing, particularly of the helping and problem-solving types. Their findings are interesting, because they point out some underlying beliefs or attitudes that seem to differentiate effective from noneffective interviewers. Effective interviewers demonstrate more genuine regard for people. They demonstrate more faith in people's capacity to function capably and to grow and change. Effective interviewers tend to have more capacity for empathy—putting themselves into another person's place. They also give evidence of more insight into—and acceptance of—their own strengths and weaknesses. They show more willingness to disclose their own thoughts and feelings when appropriate. As might well be expected, the effective interviewer also turns out to be an active listener.

An effective interviewer seems to possess another important trait: the ability to see both the similarities among people and their differences. If we view people as having many similarities to one another—for example, in the possession of a basic core of human needs which we are all driven to fulfill—we may feel more kinship or empathy with people who represent diverse segments of human society. Yet, if we do not acknowledge and appreciate the differences among people—the uniqueness of each of us, our organismic variables, and the individual ways we go about meeting our needs—we will treat people in stereotyped fashion and wonder why our interactions are so often unsatisfying.

Finally, congruence and genuineness are often mentioned as attributes of an effective interviewer. The verbal and nonverbal messages such an interviewer sends reinforce rather than contradict each other. The respondent feels that the interviewer is not only interested in him or her, but is a real person too. The effective interviewer thus provides a model of effective communication and behavior that the respondent can respect and perhaps even emulate.

GAINING INSIGHT INTO YOUR
INTERVIEWING STYLE

Another intermediate objective as you aim for the goal of maximizing your interviewing effectiveness is to develop more awareness of what you are doing in your current interviews. To this end, you have learned how to identify various types of utterances you are likely to use in interviews. You have also learned to identify some responses the other interview participant is likely to make. You will find that just having descriptive terms for some of the ways you and your respondent behave in an interview will make you more aware of those behaviors as they occur. And if you are too busy with actual verbal content during an interview to pay much attention to the types of utterances you and your respondent are making, you will be able to identify them as you play the tape recording you have made. Completing the forms contained in the Interview Analysis will also aid you in analyzing the characteristics of one or more of your interviews. Asking yourself some of the questions contained in the aids to analysis found in Chapters 1, 6, 7, and 8 may stimulate further insights.

There is no doubt that we can learn a great deal from listening to our own interviews and analyzing them in various ways. It is wise, however, also to avail ourselves of more objective sources of information regarding our interviewing characteristics and our interactions with others. For that reason, you will probably want to get feedback from other people whose opinions you value and respect. If possible, you may wish to have a co-worker or colleague sit in on or observe one or more of your interviews. Or you may ask someone to listen to a recording of one of your interviews and comment on it. As you listen to the comments of others, try to set aside defensiveness and rationalization and concentrate on getting the most benefit from their reactions and perspectives.

Enrollment in courses or workshops that provide opportunities to practice interviewing techniques in actual or simulated situations can be valuable. This is particularly true if constructive feedback is provided by the instructor or workshop leader as well as other participants. Try to encourage people to be as specific as possible in their feedback. Ask them to point out specific behaviors, types of utterances, or particular content that they thought contributed to or detracted from the effectiveness of the interview. If it is possible to reenact or role play the interview situation after you have received comments and feedback, you may find you can immediately try out some of the suggestions you have received. If reenactment or role play is not possible, you may want to jot down some of the pertinent feedback so that you can incorporate it in the near future as one of your interviewing improvement goals. Remember, you are not *obligated* to change your interviewing style as a result of feedback. But listening to the feedback seriously and trying out suggested behaviors will give you an opportunity to incorporate what seems comfortable and workable for you.

We have encouraged you to develop insight into your own style of interacting with others in the interview setting. We also strongly recommend that you increase your knowledge of various personality theories and various popular counseling and psychotherapeutic methods. This is especially important if you are in a field or profession where many of your interviews are helping interviews. You may find that certain theories or counseling methods appeal to you more than others. You may find you have a real affinity for some of them; the techniques they employ will seem to fit your particular philosophy and style. Realizing your preference for certain of these philosophies can provide you with additional insight. As a student once put it: "Six months ago I hadn't even *heard* of phenomenologists, and now I realize I *am* one!"

Finding a philosophic label that fits you is by no means a goal in itself. However, it can give you access—via the library or through classes, conferences, or workshops—to the techniques and research of numerous counselors and investigators whose basic philosophical assumptions are compatible with your own. Several surveys of psychotherapeutic methods come to mind—those of Theodore Millon (1967), Raymond Corsini (1979), Ben Ard (1975), Gerald Corey (1977), and Sol Garfield and Allen Bergin (1978) to name a few.

MAKING DESIRED CHANGES

One of the important ways we learn new behaviors is by observing them in others. We can benefit from observations of effective interviewers. We can also learn a great deal from observing ineffective interactions—particularly if we take the time to try to analyze why they were unsatisfactory to the participants. Observation can be preliminary to decision-making—deciding which of our own specific behaviors need modification. As we observe a multitude of behaviors comprising effective and ineffective interactions, we can pinpoint behaviors that we would like to emulate.

Observation can assist us in developing empathy. We can observe people of all walks of life as they express and meet their basic needs. As we observe people of different ages, we can become aware of their ways of communicating and their attention to developmental tasks. We can observe members of various cultures—becoming more familiar with their customs, beliefs, and traditional ways of interacting with others. The more we observe people, the harder it is to respond to others in a stereotyped fashion. We observe similarities but become increasingly mindful of differences. Increased empathy—viewing life from the other's perspective—is in itself a positive change.

As a result of our decisions regarding new behaviors we wish to acquire, we move to the next important step: practice. We have already mentioned the value of practicing new techniques in simulated situations as well as in our own personal everyday interactions. Not only can we hone our skill in practicing restatement of content and reflection of feeling, for example; we may find that life moves more smoothly when we make more use of these techniques. Of course, as we mentioned, practicing these techniques under supervision in more formal situations can provide helpful feedback.

If you are studying and/or observing techniques used by expert counselors in therapeutic interviews, you will be exposed to a variety of techniques more dramatic and complex than those we have discussed in this book. The successful use of these methods requires intensive study and supervision. We have limited our discussion to procedures that can increase the effectiveness of a wide variety of interviews with a minimal risk of harmful effects.

Once you have made decisions regarding desired changes and have practiced new behaviors in line with these changes, you come to the third important step in achieving effectiveness: evaluation. There are several ways of evaluating change. You may rely on your own subjective feelings of greater satisfaction as you sense that your interviews are becoming more effective. You may find it more helpful to obtain feedback or opinions from others. You may prefer to select a systematic method of evaluation. We have provided you with one method (the Molyneaux/Lane interview analysis) for taking a closer look at your interviews and interviewing style. Perhaps your use of the interview analysis prompted your decision to make some changes. In that case, you have a baseline for purposes of comparison.

An important requisite in clarifying interviewing philosophy, developing insight into interviewing style, and making desired changes is personal honesty. Honesty is important in developing insight into an acceptance of our own behavior. It is equally important in our dealings with others. The effectiveness of those interactions often depends upon our genuine efforts to view the situation realistically from the other person's perspective as well as our own. Our dealings with others can be enhanced by our willingness to share our ideas and feelings openly—keeping in mind that speech must pass through two doors: the door of truth *and* the door of love. The door of truth implies honesty; the door of love implies empathy.

Honesty, Observation, Practice, and Evaluation—all of these are important in a program of self-improvement. In summary, then, when it comes to maximizing interviewing effectiveness, there is always HOPE.

REFERENCES

Ard, Ben N., Jr., ed. *Counseling & Psychotherapy: Classics on Theories & Issues.* rev. ed. Palo Alto, Calif.: Science and Behavior Books, 1975.

Corey, Gerald. *Theory and Practice of Counseling and Psychotherapy.* Monterey, Calif.: Brooks/Cole Publishing Co., 1977.

Corsini, Raymond J., ed. *Current Psychotherapies.* 2d ed. Itasca, Ill.: F. E. Peacock Publishers, 1979.

Garfield, Sol L., and Bergin, Allen E., eds. *Handbook of Psychotherapy and Behavior Change: An Empirical Analysis.* 2d ed. New York: John Wiley & Sons, 1978.

Millon, Theodore, ed. *Theories of Psychopathology.* Philadelphia: W. B. Saunders Co., 1967.

Molyneaux/Lane Interview Analysis: Utterance Designations, Code Numbers, Definitions, and Examples

MOLYNEAUX/LANE INTERVIEW ANALYSIS
INTERVIEWER (*I*) UTTERANCES*: CODING
DESIGNATIONS, DEFINITIONS, EXAMPLES

01 *Indirect Question*—does not require question mark punctuation yet encourages discussion of a particular topic
    I: I wonder what it is like to have three children all in different schools.
    I: I'd be interested in hearing more about Jill's ballet class.
    I: This new procedure has probably affected your workload.
    I: It must be at least a three-hour drive for you to come to the physiotherapy clinic.

02 *Direct Question I*—requests specific externally verifiable statistic
    I: How old is Beth?
    I: What grade is Ryan in?
    I: What company does your husband work for?
    I: Who was the doctor who did Sean's surgery?

03 *Direct Question II*—requests information, opinion, or conclusion other than an externally verifiable statistic
    I: Does May have friends in the neighborhood?
    I: Does your husband spend much time with him?

* An utterance is everything expressed by one speaker before another person speaks.

I: How do you feel about Johnny walking to school alone?

I: What do you think was the reason for that?

04 *Leading Question*—direct question that indicates that specific answer is expected or preferred

I: You wouldn't let a child his age walk to school alone, would you?

I: That's a lot worse than wearing a hearing aid, isn't it?

I: You helped him with his homework, right?

I: Parents are responsible for their child's diet, aren't they?

05 *Double Question I*—asks two questions, the second question identical or almost identical with the first

I: When is Betty's birthday? When is her birthday?

I: Are you going to tell her? Are you going to tell her that?

I: Are you sure he is? Are you absolutely sure?

I: How can you know? Well, how could you know that?

06 *Double Question II*—asks two questions, the second question dissimilar to the first or incomplete

I: Where is the school? Is it far from here?

I: How is his penmanship—and any trouble cutting with his right hand?

I: Do you think that—have you always felt that she really has expressed herself well?

I: Does he enjoy watching television or does . . . (interrupted by respondent)

07 *Bombardment*—contains three or more questions of any type

I: Do you still read to him? Are you home at night when he's there? What hours do you work?

I: I'd like to hear more about John's speech therapist. What days does John go to the clinic—still the same as last year?

I: Does she play with the baby a lot and talk to him a lot? Does she ever sit down and pretend she is reading him a book?

I: Do you ski or paint or go to those singles bars?

08 *Mm-hm Response*—indicates that listener is tuned in and following conversation

I: Mm-hm, I see.

I: That's interesting.

I: He did?

I: Yes, I see what you mean.

09 *Approval*—expresses agreement with or favorable judgment of respondent's statement, action, and/or reported behavior when respondent has not expressed a judgment

I: I'm glad you handled it in such a mature way.

I: That's a marvelous attitude for you to take.

I: If more people felt the way you do, this world would be a better place.

I: It's really nice to meet a parent that's this concerned about his child and is doing so much to help him.

10 *Disapproval*—expresses negative evaluation of respondent's statement, action, and/or reported behavior

I: I don't think that's what you should have done.

I: If you keep nagging at him that way, he'll never read.

I: If you hadn't been absent from the meeting last night, you would understand what we're talking about now.

I: You shouldn't be saying those things, should you?

11 *Forcing Client Responsibility*—immediately redirects respondent's question back to respondent

I: Well, how do you feel he's doing? (when respondent has just asked interviewer for judgment of child's progress)

I: Yes, I could ask the doctor for that report, but do you feel that I'm the person who should do it?

I: Do you feel that that would be useful to him? (when respondent has just asked whether she should help her child with his reading at home)

12 *Information*—provides data

I: He is a slow learner, and it will take him longer than it would a normal child.

I: According to these scores, John has shown considerable improvement.

I: You can reach me at this number between nine and five.

I: I really couldn't say anything because I don't know the method. I haven't heard of their program.

13 *Reassurance*—confirms or validates respondent's stated information or supposition

I: I think you're quite right. That probably does account for his behavior.

I: Yes, that's true. There are more hearing problems in people who have been exposed to loud noise.

I: Most professionals agree that reading aloud to a young child is beneficial. (when respondent has said she thinks it's helpful that she reads to her child every night)

I: I agree with you that it's only temporary and not for the rest of his life.

14 *Restatement of Content*—repeats or summarizes actual material or data expressed verbally by respondent

I: Let me make sure I have this right. Your husband had surgery in 1965, '66, and '67?

I: You say you never thought about that?

I: Your wife's time in the hospital two years ago was a very upsetting period for you, as you mentioned.

I: You have quite a houseful then all the time.

15 *Reflection of Feeling*—attempts to verbalize current emotions expressed either verbally or nonverbally by respondent

I: So you are worried that Mary is too much on the outside, instead of playing more with the group.

I: I see that this means a very great deal to you.

I: You feel then it's almost impossible to cope with both problems at once.

I: I sense that this topic makes you very sad and is hard for you to talk about.

16 *Structuring*—orients respondent to interview situation or prescribes procedures to be followed during interview

I: The purpose of this interview is so that I can better get to know your qualifications for the job that is open.

I: We will have about a half hour to talk, so maybe we could begin with you describing the problem as you see it.

I: As I read each word on this list, just say the first thing that comes into your mind.

I: I don't think we'll be able to spend any more time talking about this now. I have a few more questions to ask you.

17 *Interpretation*—suggests possible motivation (not verbally expressed by the respondent) to account for respondent's expressed action or feeling

I: You say he's too young for skating, but are you sure it's not really because you can't bear to see him grow up?

I: You mentioned that you hate helping David with his homework. Could it be because it reminds you of problems you had in school?

I: You feel you pick on him about his speech more than his father. Well, maybe that's because you see him more and talk with him more.

I: You won't be able to keep tomorrow's appointment? Does needing professional help really bother you that much?

18 *Advice, Suggestion, or Command*—recommends or orders a course of action to be followed by respondent other than during the interview

I: If Johnny mentions anything at home tonight that he'd like to do tomorrow, please let me know.

I: Perhaps we could talk again next week.

I: The thing that you have to do is to be patient and willing to let him develop at his own speed.

I: See that that report gets out first thing in the morning.

19 *Nonpertinent Small Talk*—consists of irrelevant comments and/or social amenities

I: Did you find a parking place near the building?

I: There's coffee down the hall. I'll get some.

I: Yes, I enjoy needlepoint too, Mr. Jones. It's so relaxing.

I: Thank you for coming in today. It was very helpful talking with you.

20 *Other*—any utterance not defined above

Two basic rules:

If an *mm-hm* response or nonpertinent small talk is combined with any
other utterance, code the remainder of the utterance.
If two or more designations are appropriate, choose the one with the
higher code number.

MOLYNEAUX/LANE INTERVIEW ANALYSIS RESPONDENT (R) UTTERANCES*: CODING DESIGNATIONS, DEFINITIONS, AND EXAMPLES

Note: Interviewer (*I*) utterance in parentheses for contextual information only.

50 *Agreement*—confirms interviewer's statement or leading question
(*I:* It kind of frightens you.)
R: It frightens me; yeah, that's it.
51 *Disagreement*—denies or differs with interviewer's statement or leading
question
(*I:* You should tell Don's teacher that Don should sit up in the front
of the classroom where he can hear her better.)
R: Oh no. I don't think that's a good idea.
52 *Request for Information*—seeks data from interviewer
(*I:* We have this time today to discuss anything you'd like that you
think would be helpful to us in working with Patty.)
R: What sort of things would you like me to tell you about?
53 *Information*—provides data
(*I:* How did you hear about our clinic here?)
R: I had a neighbor who had a little boy come here to this clinic, so
she told me about it.
54 *Problem Area*—identifies or indicates situation as currently causing
stress or concern
(*I:* How are things going at home?)
R: Not good at all. I can't seem to keep up with my job and the house-
work and all the other things my husband wants me to do.
55 *Insight*—expresses awareness of motivation or consequences of behavior at time of utterance not previously understood or verbalized
(*I:* Well, we've talked quite a bit today about your relationship with
your daughter.)
R: Yes—and, you know, as we've been talking, it's occurred to me

---

* An utterance is everything expressed by one speaker before another person speaks.

that I've gotten to where I don't pay hardly any attention to what Jeanne can or can't hear anymore. It's as though I want to forget all about her hearing loss and the hearing aid.

56 *Planning*—verbalizes own planned future behavior

(I: You're not the only one. I've talked to other people who say they won't drive on the freeway because it's too dangerous.)

R: Yeah, but being stranded at home is ridiculous. The first of next month I'm going to call the driving school near where we live and start taking lessons.

57 *Mm-hm Response*—indicates listener is "tuned in" and following conversation

(I: We find that this procedure is the most efficient.)

R: I see.

58 *Advice, Suggestion, or Command*—recommends or orders course of action to be followed by the interviewer or the interviewer's agency

(I: I'd be interested in knowing your reaction after observing Lisa in therapy last week.)

R: Lisa's therapist lets her get away with too much in therapy. You better tell her to set down some rules and then see to it that Lisa obeys them.

59 *Agreement with Restatement, Reflection, Interpretation, or Leading Question, Plus Asking for Information* (Agreement Plus Asking)— confirms interviewer's statement and seeks data from interviewer

(I: You seem very concerned that the other children will make fun of Bobby.)

R: Yes, I am. Don't you think that could make matters worse?

60 *Agreement with Restatement, Reflection, Interpretation, or Leading Question, Plus Giving Information* (Agreement Plus Giving)—confirms interviewer's statement and provides data

(I: Oh, I see. You found out about the clinic from your neighbor.)

R: Yes, and I came in to see what you can do. I've been to two other places that didn't help me.

61 *Disagreement with Restatement, Reflection, Interpretation, or Leading Question, Plus Asking for Information* (Disagreement Plus Asking)— denies or differs with interviewer's statement and seeks data from interviewer

(I: You have a savings account too, don't you?)

R: No, what is the minimum deposit?

62 *Disagreement with Restatement, Reflection, Interpretation, or Leading Question, Plus Giving Information* (Disagreement Plus Giving)—denies or differs with interviewer's statement and provides data

(I: It seems from what you're saying that Carol doesn't get along too well with her co-workers.)

R: No, I wouldn't say that. She gets along O.K. with the girls in accounting and with most of the salesmen.

63 *Nonpertinent Small Talk*—consists of irrelevant comments and/or social amenities
     (I: Goodbye. Thanks for coming in.)
     R: Goodbye, and have a good time on your vacation.
64 *Other*—any utterance not defined above

Two Basic Rules:

If an *mm-hm* response or nonpertinent small talk is combined with any other utterance, code the remainder of the utterance.

If two or more designations are appropriate, choose the one with the higher code number.

Molyneaux/Lane Interview Analysis: Research Findings 150 Student-Parent Interviews

TABLE B–1   Interviewer Utterance Designation, Occurrence,
Mean Percentage, and Interquartile Range

Indicator	Utterance Designation	Total Number	Mean Percentage	Inter-quartile Range*
01	Indirect Question	750	7%	3– 9%
02	Direct Question I	956	8%	3–10%
03	Direct Question II	3087	26%	16–33%
04	Leading Question	117	1%	0– 1%
05	Double Question I	339	3%	0– 4%
06	Double Question II	283	2%	1– 3%
07	Bombardment	109	1%	0– 1%
08	*Mm-hm* Response	2105	15%	5–23%
09	Approval	232	2%	0– 3%
10	Disapproval	1	0%	0%
11	Forcing Client Responsibility	7	0%	0%
12	Information	1733	13%	5–18%
13	Reassurance	252	2%	0– 3%
14	Restatement of Content	1554	13%	8–18%
15	Reflection of Feeling	283	2%	0– 2%
16	Structuring	166	2%	1– 2%
17	Interpretation	6	0%	0%
18	Advice, Suggestion, or Command	115	1%	0– 1%
19	Nonpertinent Small Talk	281	2%	1– 3%
	Total	12376	100%	

* The interquartile range is the range that includes the middle 50 percent of the percentage scores obtained by the sample population.

TABLE B–2   Respondent Utterance Designation, Occurrence,
Mean Percentage, and Interquartile Range

Indicator	Utterance Designation	Total Number	Mean Percentage	Inter-quartile Range*
50	Agreement	1088	9%	5–12%
51	Disagreement	22	0%	0%
52	Request for Information	503	4%	1– 6%
53	Information	6855	55%	46–64%
54	Problem Area	2010	17%	9–23%
55	Insight	6	0%	0%
56	Planning	45	0%	0%
57	*Mm-hm* Response	498	4%	0– 4%
58	Advice, Suggestion, or Command	42	0%	0%
59	Agreement with Restatement, Reflection, Interpretation, or Leading Question, Plus Asking for Information	19	0%	0%
60	Agreement with Restatement, Reflection, Interpretation, or Leading Question, Plus Giving Information	956	9%	4–11%
61	Disagreement with Restatement, Reflection, Interpretation, or Leading Question, Plus Asking for Information	0	0%	0%
62	Disagreement with Restatement, Reflection, Interpretation, or Leading Question, Plus Giving Information	32	0%	0%
63	Nonpertinent Small Talk	224	2%	0– 3%
	Total	12300	100%	

* The interquartile range is the range that includes the middle 50 percent of the percentage scores obtained by the sample population.

TABLE B-3   Percentage of Feelings Expressed by Respondent Occurring in at Least 1 Percent of Utterances

Feeling Designation	Positive		Negative		Ambivalent	
	Total Number	Percent	Total Number	Percent	Total Number	Percent
Feelings toward child's (clinic enrollee) future	468	4%	137	1%	247	2%
Feelings toward child's (clinic enrollee) skills, development, personality, and interests other than speech and language	164	1%	109	1%	46	1%
Feelings toward medical agencies (including school medical services) and/or physicians and dentists	224	2%			75	1%
Feelings toward self (respondent) other than as parent	78	1%			68	1%
Feelings toward language, speech, or hearing services and/or therapists	66	1%	94	1%		
Feelings toward spouse (if other than child's natural parent)			75	1%		
Feelings toward children other than immediate family	116	1%				

TABLE B–4 Factor Loadings for Interviewer Utterances

Defining Variables	Oblique Factor Coefficients
Factor 1 (Businesslike; not orienting respondent to interview situation)	
119 Nonpertinent Small Talk	−.87866
116 Structuring	−.44470
Factor 2 (Interrogatory, using open questions; not reflecting or restating client input)	
101 Indirect Question	−.73143
115 Reflection of Feelings	−.62437
114 Restatement of Content	−.51240
103 Direct Question II	.40030
Factor 3 (Interrogatory, using open questions; not using Mm-hm Response)	
108 Mm-hm Response	−.87115
103 Direct Question II	.61525
109 Approval	−.51457
Factor 4 (Judgmental)	
117 Interpretation	.81901
104 Leading Question	.72367
109 Approval	.44056
Factor 5 (Bombarding)	
107 Bombardment	.86989
105 Double Question I	.82696
Factor 6 (Not using closed questions)	
102 Direct Question I	−.94732
Factor 7 (Self-assured)	
111 Forcing Client Responsibility	.89162
116 Structuring	.40297
113 Reassurance	.39196
Factor 8 (Critical)	
110 Disapproval	.89648
106 Double Question II	.56651
Factor 9 (Interrogatory, using open questions; not providing information)	
112 Information	−.78016
118 Advice, Suggestion, or Command	−.77640
103 Direct Question II	.46948
113 Reassurance	−.44484

TABLE B–5   Factor Loadings for Respondent Utterances

Defining Variables	Oblique Factor Coefficients
Factor 1 (Information-giving, but not personally responsive to interviewer)	
257 Mm-hm Response	−.79169
250 Agreement	−.66025
251 Disagreement	−.59500
253 Information	.51735
252 Request for Information	−.42532
Factor 2 (Judging interviewer statements and elaborating own statements)	
260 Agreement with Restatement, Reflection, Interpretation, or Leading Question, Plus Giving Information	.81415
262 Disagreement with Restatement, Reflection, Interpretation, or Leading Question, Plus Giving Information	.68669
253 Information	−.47880
259 Agreement with Restatement, Reflection, Interpretation, or Leading Question, Plus Asking for Information	.39553
Factor 3 (Agreeing; not future-oriented)	
258 Advice, Suggestion, or Command	−.78408
256 Planning	−.60691
250 Agreement	.50364
252 Request for Information	−.47583
Factor 4 (Sociable)	
263 Nonpertinent Small Talk	.78417
259 Agreement with Restatement, Reflection, Interpretation, or Leading Question, Plus Asking for Information	.64352
Factor 5 (Information-giving; no stated problem area)	
254 Problem Area	−.82291
255 Insight	−.66566
253 Information	.51122

TABLE B-6   Second Order Factor Loadings

Defining Variables	Canonical Coefficients	Canonical Correlations
Super Factor I		
Interviewer Factor 1	.50310	
Interviewer Factor 2	−.53502	
Interviewer Factor 9	.55904	
		.84
Respondent Factor 1	.35629	
Respondent Factor 2	.79699	
Respondent Factor 3	.42303	
Super Factor II		
Interviewer Factor 2	.59136	
Interviewer Factor 9	.62951	
		.72
Respondent Factor 1	.59785	
Respondent Factor 2	−.53348	
Respondent Factor 4	−.36287	
Super Factor III		
Interviewer Factor 1	.86971	
Interviewer Factor 9	−.49957	
		.55
Respondent Factor 1	−.38904	
Respondent Factor 4	−.89583	

Index